D1084980

Cambridge Opera Handbooks

Giuseppe Verdi
Otello

Giuseppe Verdi,
Otello

(James Arnold)

JAMES A. HEPOKOSKI

Professor of Music History
Oberlin College Conservatory

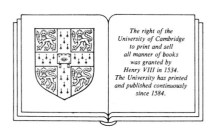

The right of the University of Cambridge to print and sell all manner of books was granted by Henry VIII in 1534. The University has printed and published continuously since 1584.

CAMBRIDGE UNIVERSITY PRESS

Cambridge
London   New York   New Rochelle
Melbourne   Sydney

Published by the Press Syndicate of the University of Cambridge
The Pitt Building, Trumpington Street, Cambridge. CB2 1RP
32 East 57th Street, New York, NY 10022, USA
10 Stamford Road, Oakleigh, Melbourne 3166, Australia

First published 1987

Printed in Great Britain at
the University Press, Cambridge

British Library cataloguing in publication data

Hepokoski, James A.
Giuseppe Verdi, Otello. – (Cambridge
opera handbooks)
1. Verdi, Giuseppe. Otello
I. Title
782.1′092′4   ML410.V4

Library of Congress cataloguing in publication data

Hepokoski, James A. (James Arnold), 1946–
Giuseppe Verdi, Otello.
(Cambridge opera handbooks)
Bibliography
'Discography by Malcolm Walker'
Includes index.
1. Verdi, Giuseppe, 1813–1901. Otello. I. Title.
II. Title: Otello. III. Series.
ML410.V4H48   1987   782.1′092′4   86–17189

ISBN 0 521 25885 5 hard covers
ISBN 0 521 27749 3 paperback

WD

CAMBRIDGE OPERA HANDBOOKS
General preface

This is a series of studies of individual operas written for the opera-goer or record-collector as well as the student or scholar. Each volume has three main concerns: historical, analytical and interpretative. There is a detailed description of the genesis of each work, the collaboration between librettist and composer, and the first performance and subsequent stage history. A full synopsis considers the opera as a structure of musical and dramatic effects, and there is also a musical analysis of a section of the score. The analysis, like the history, shades naturally into interpretation: by a careful combination of new essays and excerpts from classic statements the editors of the handbooks show how critical writing about the opera, like the production and performance, can direct or distort appreciation of its structural elements. A final section of documents gives a select bibliography, a discography, and guides to other sources. Each book is published both in hard covers and as a paperback.

Books published

Richard Wagner: *Parsifal* by Lucy Beckett
W. A. Mozart: *Don Giovanni* by Julian Rushton
C. W. von Gluck: *Orfeo* by Patricia Howard
Igor Stravinsky: *The Rake's Progress* by Paul Griffiths
Leoš Janáček: *Kát'a Kabanová* by John Tyrrell
Giuseppe Verdi: *Falstaff* by James A. Hepokoski
Benjamin Britten: *Peter Grimes* by Philip Brett
Giacomo Puccini: *Tosca* by Mosco Carner
Benjamin Britten: *The Turn of the Screw* by Patricia Howard
Richard Strauss: *Der Rosenkavalier* by Alan Jefferson
Claudio Monteverdi: *Orfeo* by John Whenham
Giacomo Puccini: *La bohème* by Arthur Groos and Roger Parker

Other volumes in preparation

For my father and mother,
Arthur and Helen Hepokoski

Contents

Illustrations

Acknowledgements

I should like to begin this study of *Otello* by acknowledging my
indebtedness to the community of Verdi scholars, now so happily
thriving, on whose work so much of what follows depends; and in
particular I am obliged to mention the splendid publications of
Julian Budden, Mario Medici and Marcello Conati, and, of course,
the late Frank Walker. The 1984–85 research for this book was
carried out largely in Italy and was made possible by the generous
assistance of a Fellowship from the American Council of Learned
Societies and two individual grants from Oberlin College. I should
like to thank G. Ricordi & C., S.P.A., for permission to reproduce
several of the original sets and photographs of the original performers (Plates 2, 7, 8, 9, and 10), for permission to translate both
the unpublished correspondence in their extensive collection and
the letters published in Franco Abbiati's *Giuseppe Verdi*, and for
permission to quote musical passages from the autograph score and
the published Ricordi scores. Other plates (nos. 1, 3, 4, 5, and 6) are
reproduced here through the assistance and permission of the
Museo Teatrale alla Scala, Milan, Giampiero Tintori, Director;
additional unpublished correspondence appears with the permission of Pierluigi Petrobelli, Director of the Istituto di Studi
Verdiani in Parma; I wish also to thank the Bibliothèque-Musée de
l'Opéra in Paris, which generously permitted me to examine the
original Verdian sketch from which Ex. 2 was transcribed. I should
like to acknowledge the kind assistance of Francesco Degrada,
Mimma Guastoni, Teresita Beretta, Luciana Pestalozza, Fausto
Broussard, Carlo Clausetti, Pierluigi Petrobelli, Marisa Casati, and
Lina Re during my work in Italy. Special thanks are also due to
Harold S. Powers, from whom I have learned much about Verdian
structures, and with whom many of the ideas in this book were first
discussed. I should also like to thank Andrew Porter for furnishing
me with a photocopy of what became Ex. 1 of this book; Roger

Parker and Warren Darcy for their helpful comments concerning an early (and somewhat expanded) draft of Chapter 7; the American Institute for Verdi Studies in New York and its director, Martin Chusid, for making available many documents crucial to the first stages of research for this book; Will Crutchfield for his information on the ever-expanding field of early operatic recordings; Ursula Günther, Philip Gossett, Joseph Kerman, David Rosen, and David Lawton for their continuing advice and encouragement; William Ashbrook for his excellent summary of the stage history of *Otello*; Malcolm Walker for the discography; and the staff of Cambridge University Press, and particularly Rosemary Dooley, Michael Black, Penny Souster, and Lucy Carolan for their helpful suggestions and support.

List of abbreviations within the text

Abbreviation	Longer citation (see the Bibliography for the full citation)
Ab.	Abbiati, *Giuseppe Verdi*, 1959
Alb.	Alberti, *Verdi intimo*, 1931
Budden	Budden, *The Operas of Verdi 3*, 1981
Cop.	Cesare and Luzio, *I copialettere di Giuseppe Verdi*, 1913
CV	Luzio, *Carteggi verdiani*, 1935–47
CVB	*Carteggio Verdi–Boito*, 1978
DS	Ricordi, *Disposizione scenica per l'opera Otello*, 1887
OG	*Otello . . . Giudizî della stampa*, 1887
VR	Cella and Petrobelli, *Giuseppe Verdi–Giulio Ricordi: Corrispondenza e immagini 1881/1890*, 1982

'Unpublished; Parma' refers to previously unpublished correspondence whose original is located in the Biblioteca Palatina, Parma.

'Unpublished; Ricordi Arch.' refers to previously unpublished correspondence whose original is located in the Archivio Storico of G. Ricordi & C., Milan.

All musical citations from *Otello*, unless otherwise specified, refer to the currently available vocal score published by G. Ricordi & C., Milan (plate number 52105, ed. Mario Parenti, 1964). Citations refer to page number / system number / bar number: thus 181/4/1–2 refers to the Ricordi vocal score, page 181, system 4, bars 1–2.

All textual citations from *Othello* refer to the edition of the play published in The New Cambridge Shakespeare, ed. Norman Sanders (Cambridge, 1984).

Otello refers to the opera; *Othello* to the play.

xi

1 *Synopsis*[1]

Act One

With the dazzling suddenness of a conjurer's gesture, the convulsive world of *Otello* appears before us in full boil. It is the most aggressive initial gesture in opera: a wild, *tutti* eleventh chord grasped, Zeus-like, and hurled forward in syncopation – the opera has begun. We are outside a castle in Cyprus, near the shore in the midst of an unleashed evening storm replete with queasy violin and horn undulations and high-woodwind lightning-flashes. The Moor Otello, general of the Venetians and ruler of Cyprus, is still perilously at sea, returning from battle with the Turks. On shore a crowd of worried citizens anxiously awaits news. As galleys are seen in the distance, a group of Cypriots cries out 'Una vela!' ('A sail!'), and Montano, the Venetian former governor of the island, exclaims with a clap of thunder that he spots the Venetian 'winged lion' – Otello's ship ('È l'alato Leon!'). With the trumpet-signals and the annunciatory cannon-shot, the Moor's galley comes into on-stage view. The chorus witnesses its pitching and tossing and, terrified, describes the storm's fury, 'Lampi! tuoni! gorghi!' ('Lightning! thunder! whirlpools!'), *Dies-irae*-like in its dimensions. Insistently mounting judgment-day trumpets, cornets, and trombones push them fearfully to the front of the stage for the brief melodic centre-piece of the storm scene, their *fortissimo* prayer for Otello's safety, 'Dio, fulgor della bufera!' ('God, You the splendour amidst the storm!'). As the music splits again into briny motivic work, they turn back towards the sea, calling for help, for they now learn that Otello's ship is damaged. On shore, Iago – Otello's ensign, and also a villain who secretly hates the Moor – grabs the hand of his foolish Venetian confidant and dupe, Roderigo, and makes his way forward through the crowd pointedly to exclaim to him as an aside his wish that Otello's ship be destroyed, 'L'alvo / Frenetico del mar sia

1

1. The opening storm-scene of *Otello*: engraving by A. Bonamore, 'La Scena della Tempesta', in *Verdi e l'Otello*, a special number of the *Illustrazione italiana* (February 1887)

la sua tomba!' ('May the frenetic ocean-bed be his tomb!'). But immediately afterwards the crowd cheers, 'È salvo!' ('He's safe!'). Off-stage voices are heard helping the Moor land as the storm begins to abate. Finally Otello himself strides forward in full glory. In heroically sculpted lines he proclaims a victory aided by heaven itself:

> Esultate! L'orgoglio musulmano
> Sepolto è in mar, nostra e del ciel è gloria!
> Dopo l'armi lo vinse l'uragano.
>
> Exult! Moslem pride
> Is buried in the sea. The glory is ours and heaven's!
> After [our] arms conquered them, so did the storm.

Followed by Cassio (his captain), Montano, and his full train, Otello enters the castle. Iago and Roderigo remain on stage to mingle with the crowd, who start up a victory chorus ('Vittoria! Vittoria!'): a static but internally energetic *tableau* that serves as a conclusion to the storm-scene.

By the time the last echoes of the storm have died away, Roderigo has moved forward, hand-on-heart and thoughtful. While people bustle in the background preparing to light a bonfire, Iago inquiringly taps Roderigo on the shoulder, and we learn that the latter loves Desdemona, Otello's wife (in the play Roderigo was her ardent but disappointed suitor). Fear not, cynically counsels Iago, she will soon grow weary of her 'thick-lipped savage'. In a cocky melodic phrase he suggests that he has a plan, 'Se un fragil voto / Di femmina' ('If a fragile, feminine vow'). Back in a simpler recitative-texture he darkly reveals the cause of his own burning hatred for Otello. Pointing to the younger Cassio (who has momentarily emerged from an inn to banter with some young women), he claims that 'quell'azzimato capitano' ('that fancy-dressed captain') usurped from him the rank that he, Iago, had more deservedly earned in battle. And now Iago remains only the Moor's ensign, as he sneers in a characteristically serpentine line punctuated with a nasty, final trill ('Ed io rimango / Di sua Moresca signoria l'alfiere!'). Brimming over with malice, he pulls Roderigo to the back of the stage, out of earshot, to continue his vituperation. In the meantime the crowd has succeeded in preparing the bonfire, and the victory-flames shoot upward to begin a second choral *tableau*, 'Fuoco di gioia!' ('Fire of joy!'). The piece is filled with Boitian wordplay and is fully developed musically in contrasting, but motivically interrelated sections. The delicate orchestral accompaniment playfully juxtaposes graceful legato sweeps with firelight-flickering *staccati*. As the chorus proceeds, benches and tables are brought out of the inn, and twelve illuminated Venetian lanterns are hung decoratively on the adjoining arbour for further festivities.

The fire spent, Iago and Roderigo return, as does Cassio. The first stage of Iago's elaborate revenge – that of discrediting Cassio by getting him drunk – now begins to take shape with the recitative, 'Roderigo, beviam!' ('Roderigo, let's drink!'). Cassio at first refuses, particularly since he is already feeling the effects of some earlier celebrating. He is persuaded, however, to join in a toast to Otello's and Desdemona's (apparently recent) wedding. With affected modesty Iago declines to sing Desdemona's praises, 'Io non sono che un critico' ('I am only a critic'), but he also quietly and swiftly manages to convince the foolish, love-struck Roderigo that Cassio, too, by reputation an 'astuto seduttor' ('clever seducer'), desires the affections of Desdemona. The plan is now to get the supposed 'rival', Cassio, drunk, for 'S'ei s'inebria è perduto!' ('if he's drunk, he's lost!'). Iago calls for wine, two taverners instantly appear with filled amphoras, and the orchestra bursts out, *forte*, with the hearty unisons – reverberating echoes from the Fire Chorus music – that form the short introduction to the *Brindisi*, the Drinking Song, 'Inaffia l'ugola' ('Wet your whistles'). Iago, Cassio, Roderigo, and the Chorus all participate in the three internally modulating strophes of the song, which swaggers with lusty *camaraderie*, although throughout there is also an unmistakable, Iago-led undercurrent of minor-mode malice and chromatic extravagance. Iago's march-like, major-key refrain, echoed by the chorus, displays the librettist Boito's taste for bizarre language and images:

Chi all'esca ha morso	Whoever has bitten at the bait
Del ditirambo	Of the arrogant and
Spavaldo e strambo	Extravagant dithyramb,
Beva con me.	Let him drink with me.

What lodges in one's mind, of course, are the momentarily minor, descending chromatics of 'Beva': two roguish sips followed by a long, and far more sinister, down-the-hatch swallow. Iago's immediately subsequent, almost barked high a^1, still on the word 'Beva' adds to the flavour of excess, whereupon the chorus and Roderigo repeat the refrain with gusto. Between stanzas Iago, refilling Cassio's glass, reminds Roderigo of the point, 'Un altro sorso / E brillo egli è' ('Another sip and he'll be tipsy'). And indeed, the drunken Cassio causes the third stanza to fall apart: he enters early, he stammers, he forgets his lines, and his legs wobble. The chorus prolongs all of this by laughing at him, while Iago urges Roderigo to pick a fight. After the last, shortened refrain, Montano enters and is shocked to find Cassio drunk. 'Ogni notte in tal guisa / Cassio preludia al sonno' ('Cassio precedes his sleep like this every night'), lies Iago. The music shoots forth in a series of excitable four-bar sequences, while Roderigo insults Cassio and tempers flare. As the towns-people whisk away the tables, chairs, and festive lanterns, Montano tries to intercede in the mounting quarrel, but Cassio wheels around and, goaded by Montano's also calling him a 'drunk' ('ebro'), draws his sword on the older man. Montano follows suit and a vigorous duel ensues, with impulsive slashes, stabs, and changes of position. At precisely this moment Iago draws Roderigo aside to instruct him, in rapid-fire patter, to rouse the sleeping populace, crying riot. The agitated duel proceeds, with Montano twice wounded, until the warning storm-bells are heard and Otello, now roused out of the castle, suddenly enters, himself holding a sword, to quell the struggle, 'Abbasso le spade!' ('Down with your swords!'). To Otello's demand for an explanation, the still-trusted Iago feigns benign ignorance, 'Non so' ('I don't know'). Otello soon learns that Montano has been wounded, and he bursts into a rage, only to dis-cover immediately thereafter that Desdemona, too, has been awakened and has entered on-stage from the castle door. 'Cassio, / Non sei più capitano', he orders ('You are no longer a captain'). Cassio lets his sword drop, and Iago picks it up, hands it to a soldier, and joyfully exclaims in an aside, 'Oh! mio trionfo!' ('O my triumph!'). The first phase of Iago's revenge-plot is now complete.

In a brief, transitional passage that – finally – melts the preceding severity, Otello dismisses everyone in order to remain alone with Desdemona in the now-serene evening. After he steps briefly to the back of the stage to make certain that they are truly alone, she moves closer to him, her eyes filled with love: a solo, muted cello swells with their emotion. As Otello embraces her, the texture splits prismatically into rich, *divisi* muted cellos, and he soon begins to sing eloquently of his immense love: 'Già nella notte densa / S'estingue ogni clamor' ('Even now in the thick night / All clamour has ceased'). She responds, 'Mio superbo guerrier!' ('My superb warrior!'), ecstatically lyrical from the beginning, and asks him to recall how their speaking intimately together was the source of their love: 'Te ne rammenti!' ('Do you remember!'), she exclaims, incandescent with the halo of an 'angelic' harp arpeggio. The string instruments remove their mutes, and a grand, measured *Largo* unfurls – the principal movement of the Love Duet – with Desdemona's moving description of her falling in love with the tales of his exploits,

> Quando narravi l'esule tua vita
> E i fieri eventi e i lunghi tuoi dolor,
> Ed io t'udia coll'anima rapita
> In quei spaventi e coll'estasi in cor.

> When you told of your exiled life,
> And its proud events and your long sorrows,
> And I listened to you, my soul stolen away
> In those fears, and with ecstasy in my heart.

Otello, too, remembers, and they exchange wonderful, lyrical memories, now military-heroic, now devotedly sympathetic. At the end of this 'reminiscence' movement Otello summarizes the effect of his tales in an *Aida*-like enrichment of the major key with modal-minor inflections: 'E tu m'amavi per le mie sventure / Ed io t'amavo per la tua pietà' ('And you loved me for my adventures, and I loved you for your pity'). Desdemona repeats the idea and a brief coda concludes this section. Increasingly overcome with feeling, Otello longs for death in this supreme moment ('Venga la morte!'), not knowing what the future might hold. He soon feels ecstatic, faint, and is compelled to sit down to recover. Now at the peak of emotion, he looks up at Desdemona, 'Un bacio . . . un bacio . . . ancora un bacio' ('A kiss . . . a kiss . . . another kiss') – the trembling, sweeping, and unforgettable music that will return in Act IV. Otello rises. Embracing Desdemona, he looks at the stars, as once again the beatific harp arpeggios begin to float upward. Then, shifting his gaze back to her: 'Vien . . . Venere splende' ('Come . . . Venus shines'). She responds, enraptured, with his name – for her a holy utterance – and they slowly move towards the castle as the gentle, *divisi* cellos from near the beginning of the duet tenderly bring down the curtain.

Act Two

The second act is launched with decisive, repeated impulses growling in the low strings and bassoons (see also pp. 143–62 below). This type of pointed three-or-four-impulse repetition had been a frequent Verdian gesture – a stylistic fingerprint – at least since *La forza del destino*. Its decoration here with a rotary spinning that sets in motion a rhythmic flow of 12/8 triplets suggests the gearing-up of some intricate action. Now in a room on the ground floor of Otello's Cypriot castle, Iago is furthering his plot by posing as Cassio's friend and consoling him after his demotion. All will be well, he insists, and Cassio will soon be basking in the love of his mistress, 'Monna Bianca'. In gently hushed, rocking phrases he counsels him to ask Desdemona, 'il Duce / Del nostro Duce' ('our general's general'), to intercede with Otello on his behalf. Indeed, he adds, she should be appearing in the nearby garden at any moment. Now all naive hope, Cassio steps outside, deep into the garden visible through a large castle window.

With Cassio gone, the rotary triplets leap forward in the strings, wrenched out of key. Iago steps to the footlights to reveal the full extent of the evil within himself. Thus begins his blasphemous Credo-soliloquy, 'Credo in un Dio crudel che m'ha creato / Simile a sè, e che nell'ira io nomo' ('I believe in a cruel God, who created me similar to himself, and whom I worship in wrath'). This is less 'sung' than declaimed, with sinister relish, in short epigrams. The whole is punctuated with the orchestral support of two 'ritornello' figures, one whose dire unisons and octaves are as close-packed and solid as marble, the other a mocking, dancing figure born out of the rotary motive. One profanation follows another: mankind is naturally wicked, having evolved from 'il fango originario' ('primal mud'); all noble concepts and sincere feelings, justice, tears, kisses, love-glances, sacrifice, honour, are worthy only of ridicule; cruel fate rules our lives. The 'Credo' ends with explicit nihilism, leeringly conveyed and rounded with monstrous, chilling scorn:

> Vien dopo tanta irrisïon la Morte
> E Poi? – La Morte è il Nulla.
> È vecchia fola il Ciel.

> After such a mockery comes Death.
> And then? Death is Nothingness.
> Heaven is an ancient fable.

Iago now spots Desdemona entering the garden with his own wife, Emilia. He quickly runs to the balcony, beckons Cassio, and pushes him out towards her. With Iago, we can observe him in the garden through the window, greeting Desdemona and beginning to ask for her help. Light, staccato strings in clipped phrases suggest Iago's nervous movements and quick reactions. He now anticipates his plan, 'Or qui si tragga Otello!' ('Now let Otello be drawn here!'), glancing all the while at each gesture that he sees in the garden and invoking Satan for help. Desdemona is seen nodding and smiling – a smile that Iago vows will drag Otello to ruin. As Desdemona, Emilia, and Cassio withdraw off-stage, Iago notices with glee that Otello is arriving. He stations himself at the balcony, his back to the entering Otello, and with an expertly contrived look of concern on his face stares out into the now-empty garden.

'Ciò m'accora' ('That grieves me'), Iago sighs – loudly enough for Otello to overhear. Their free, conversational duet begins smoothly with Iago feigning embarrassment at being overheard, while skilfully suggesting that something illicit has just been occurring in the garden. Otello has recognized the dismissed Cassio with his wife, but in ingratiatingly nuanced music Iago pretends to be holding something back. And still, Iago proffers his insinuatingly mouthed phrases to tantalize Otello with the reminder that Cassio was a go-between in his initial courting of Desdemona – a time when he was considered 'onesto' ('honest'). Otello finally erupts with exasperation. Already fearful, he demands to know the whole truth: 'Dunque senza velami / T'esprimi e senza ambagi' ('Tell me then, directly, without veilings or evasions'). And here Iago utters his fateful words, salaciously underscored by a 'forbidden-progression' orchestral swell, 'Temete, signor, la gelosia!' ('Beware, my lord, of jealousy!'). He goes on sinuously to tell of the 'idra fosca' ('dark hydra' – Boito's equivalent of the 'green-eyed monster') that poisons with its sting – a sting that Iago embeds deeply into Otello's breast with a malevolent vocal trill. Otello cries out in anguish – 'Miseria mia!!' – and, rising at the end to a howled high b^1, demands instant proof. As we hear the beginning strains of a gentle, off-stage chorus in praise of Desdemona – she is returning to the garden – Iago quickly tells Otello that while it is too early to speak of proof, he should look to his wife, scrutinize everything she does for potential clues to her behaviour: 'Vigilate . . . Vigilate' ('Be vigilant'). His venomous words merge into the contrasting Homage Chorus as Desdemona, Emilia, and some townspeople come into the garden, framed by the castle window. The Chorus, 'Dove guardi splendono raggi' ('Where you glance, rays shine'), is another static *tableau*, this one naive and pastoral, decoratively coloured with the accompanying sounds of a *cornamusa* (bagpipe), mandolins, and guitars. Children, then sailors, then women honour Desdemona with gifts of flowers, pearls, corals, and the like. Iago and Otello watch the whole scene from inside the castle. During the Chorus the former occasionally points and mimes words of suspicion to Otello, who gestures that he still cannot believe that she could be unfaithful. In the final measures of the Chorus Iago vows in a low aside to destroy this happiness.

Seeing Otello, Desdemona enters the castle and begins coyly to intercede on behalf of the discharged captain in gentle, melting phrases. She twice asks for Cassio's pardon, 'Tu gli perdona', but Otello, now truly suspicious, curtly refuses, and the gentle music suddenly bursts into agitation. When Otello claims that his head is burning, she offers him her handkerchief, but he flings it to the ground in a rage. Emilia picks it up, and Desdemona now begins a Quartet with a moving, innocent plea for her own pardon, should she have in some way offended him: 'Dammi la dolce e lieta / Parola del perdono' ('Give me the sweet and happy word of pardon'). Throughout the broad, lyrical Quartet Otello bewails the loss of her love and agonizingly searches for possible reasons for it; and Iago, spotting the handkerchief in Emilia's hands, badgers her insistently for it, and at the midpoint of the ensemble succeeds in plucking it out of her hands. At its conclusion the bewildered Desdemona exits, with Emilia; Otello laments his presumably false wife ('Desdemona rea!'); and the scheming Iago parenthetically reveals his intention to plant the handkerchief as false evidence in Cassio's dwelling. Seeing the Moor's anguish, he gloats, 'Il mio velen lavora' ('My poison is working').

Suddenly noticing Iago again, Otello reacts violently: 'Tu?! Indietro! fuggi!!' ('You?! Away! Flee!!'). But Iago only steps back to watch as Otello raves about his mounting suspicions, reflected in the driving, ascending sequences in the orchestra. He was happy before, knowing nothing, he claims, but now innocent happiness and, with it, his whole life's achievements, are gone forever. His brief, rousing 'Ora e per sempre addio sante memorie' ('Farewell now and forever, holy memories') evokes his military past only abruptly to snuff it out at its end. Iago tries to calm him, but Otello turns even more savagely on his tormentor to demand clear proof. He threatens Iago, then grabs him violently by the throat and throws him to the ground – a gesture brutally underscored in the orchestra with a convulsion of brass in octaves skidding downward in headlong chromatics.

'Divina grazia difendimi!' ('Divine grace defend me!'), exclaims

Iago. Lifting himself up, he begins to feign resentment over an angrily mounting accompaniment. As he threatens to resign from Otello's service, the Moor suddenly relents, unknowingly sealing his own fate, as the piercing woodwind chord reminds us: 'No . . . rimani. / Forse onesto tu sei' ('No . . . stay here. Perhaps you are honest'). Iago is again in complete control, and the agitated Otello renews his pleas for certainty, for proof. With a demonic leer captured perfectly in a breathy flute tremolo, Iago comes closer to him and asks darkly, 'Avvinti / Vederli forse?' ('Would you see them coupled?'). That would indeed be difficult, admits Iago. But there is still more 'circumstantial' evidence to reveal. Confidentially addressing the frozen Otello, who occasionally covers his eyes with his hands, Iago now begins his *racconto*, his fabricated narration of Cassio's talking in his sleep: 'Era la notte, Cassio dormìa, gli stavo accanto' ('It was night; Cassio was sleeping; and I was beside him'). Iago's 'secrets' float like phantasms on the muted strings, while the pretended words of Cassio are spotlighted with perfectly placed, contrasting wind-chords: 'Desdemona soave! Il nostro amor s'asconda. / Cauti vegliamo!' ('Sweet Desdemona! Let our love be hidden. Let's be very careful'). The entire *racconto* is a masterpiece of carefully declaimed, whispered monstrosities – and Otello is brought very nearly to the breaking point by it. But again Iago, always prepared, has one more piece of 'evidence' for him – and this one will be decisive. Coming closer and looking him squarely in the eye, he tells Otello that he has seen Desdemona's handkerchief – the very handkerchief that Otello admits was a 'pegno / Primo d'amor' ('first pledge of love') – in the hands of . . . 'Cassio'.

This detonates Otello's full explosion: 'Ah! mille vite gli donasse Iddio! / Una à povera preda al furor mio!' ('Ah! that God would give him a thousand lives! One is but poor prey for my fury!'). Now out of control, he swears bloody revenge and seals the sanctity of his resolve on his knees with a solemn *cabaletta*-oath: 'Sì, pel ciel marmoreo giuro! Per le attorte folgori!' ('Yes, by the marble heaven I swear it! By the twisted lightning!', etc.). When Otello comes to the end of his mighty words, Iago bids him to remain down and kneels alongside him to swear allegiance in whatever cruel deeds might be found necessary. Finally both rise and lift their right arms towards heaven. At full voice, underscored by potent lightning-bolts in the orchestra, they join their voices in an elemental repetition of their oaths. As they exit, the *fortissimo* orchestra reels brutally in heavily accented, 'forbidden-parallel' revulsion: for a horrible instant the ground seems to sink beneath our feet before the tonic is regained at the curtain-fall.

Act Three

A brief, closed-curtain prelude illustrates the working of Iago's poison. Based on the opening measures of the 'idra fosca' melody from the preceding act (the 'dark hydra' of jealousy), it is first heard in the low strings, then invades the upper register, multiplies into imitative entrances, and builds in *crescendo* into a powerful, *tutti* statement cut off at curtain-rise with an accented diminished-seventh chord. In the great hall of the castle a herald announces the imminent arrival in Cyprus of Venetian ambassadors. Otello dismisses the herald and turns back to Iago, who suggests that he will bring Cassio to the castle so that Otello, unobserved, can hear him and watch his gestures for signs of his supposedly illicit behaviour. As Desdemona approaches, Iago exits with the sinister reminder, 'Finger conviene . . . io vado. Il fazzoletto' ('It's best to pretend . . . I'm going. The handkerchief').

Gracefully terraced, descending strings escort Desdemona into the hall. Not suspecting any difficulty, she begins their free, extended Duet with a lyrically arched greeting, 'Dio ti giocondi, o sposo dell'alma mia sovrano' ('May God gladden you, husband, ruler of my soul'). He initially responds with complementary – but forced – elegance, then takes her hand in his and passes to an exchange of clever, double-edged words about the supposed 'dèmone gentil' ('gentle demon') that he believes lies concealed within it. After the string terracing rounds off this polished beginning, Desdemona brings up the issue of Cassio again. Otello starts, and the music lurches at once into a minor-mode *allegro agitato*. Quickly responding to his apparent 'illness' ('morbo'), she offers him a handkerchief to bind his forehead. He seizes her hand and demands a different handkerchief: the one, of course, which Iago has now planted in Cassio's dwelling. To lose it would be a great woe, he threatens, ominously, 'Guai se lo perdi! guai!' (This melodic contour will return as a poignant oboe-phrase at the end of the opera, within Otello's suicide soliloquy: see p. 19 below.) In two solemn, mysterious swells, Otello tells her that it was a charmed handkerchief, a talisman. To misplace it – or, he adds pointedly, his voice leaping up an angry octave – to *give* it away ('oppur donarlo') would be a grave misfortune. 'Mi fai paura!' ('You frighten me!'), exclaims Desdemona. She anxiously (and falsely) denies that she has lost the handkerchief. All at once her features change, and a smile breaks out: surely this must all be a joke, she thinks, to distract her from interceding for Cassio. When she suggests this in an amused, playful singsong, the Moor's fury only mounts higher, and he calls ever more urgently for 'il fazzoletto' ('the handkerchief'). Desdemona's words turn into terror as she realizes that he is deadly serious. He grabs her by the chin, stares at her, and forces her to swear that she is chaste. After doing so, deeply shaken and confused, she staggers towards a nearby column for support, while soft but violent shivers echo in the low instruments. She cannot understand the fury of his words, she cries out in a wrenching leap upward of a ninth: 'In te parla una Furia' ('A Fury is speaking in you'). Now in tears, she approaches Otello and pleads for mercy in the *cantabile* centre of the Duet, 'Io prego il cielo per te con questo pianto' ('I am praying to heaven for you with this weeping') – a more affecting plea of innocence cannot be imagined. But Otello is unmoved. He claims to see Hell in her face, and once again the music erupts violently. As he, too, begins to weep, Desdemona, desperate, exclaims in an unmistakably Verdian theatrical *coup* – a summary 'behold!' line fashioned as an extraordinarily more forceful recall of her 'Io prego il cielo' melody – 'E son io l'innocente cagion di tanto pianto!' ('And I am the innocent cause of such weeping!'). She asks what she has done wrong and denies Otello's charge of adultery. Then, with supreme irony, the opening music of the Duet returns: Otello's cynical 'apology'. Now breaking off the reprise in a cruel shout that rises to a high c^2 – his highest note in the opera – he sneers that he mistook her for 'Quella vil cortigiana che è la sposa d'Otello' ('that vile strumpet who is Otello's wife'). The full orchestra convulses into despair, and the stunned Desdemona, pushed out by her husband, leaves the hall.

Otello now slumps weakly into a chair. Over a groaning, bone-weary accompaniment that juxtaposes a fatal, chromatic descent for strings in octaves – like the slow passing of a hand that wipes away all happiness – with a poignant rotary twist above, clearly recalling Iago's motives from Act II, he begins to stammer out a soliloquy, 'Dio! mi potevi scagliar tutti i mali' ('God! You could have hurled all the evils at me'). He could have borne calmly any anguish, he maintains, except this one. Rising nobly – for the last time – he stands up and delivers lyrically, in three grand arches, the lines that are the key to his soul:

Ma, o pianto, o duol! m'han rapito il miraggio
Dov'io, giulivo, – l'anima acqueto.
Spento è quel sol, quel sorriso, quel raggio
Che mi fa vivo, – Che mi fa lieto!
But, o weeping, o sorrow! They have stolen my mirage
Where I, happy, becalm my soul.
That sun, that smile, that ray is extinguished
Which gives me life, which gladdens me!

But from this peak his world now falls rapidly into disorder. His wrath overtakes him, he loses control, and once again he shouts for proof. At just this moment Iago enters and points, 'Cassio è là!' ('Cassio is there!'). 'Cielo! Oh gioia!!' ('Heaven! Oh, joy!!'), shouts Otello. His monologue now concluded, he quickly hides himself towards the back of the stage, on a terrace, to spy on Cassio.

The hammered violence soon gives way to a rich, deep string figure: Cassio's entrance. Iago greets him, and he begins to ask about Desdemona's suit on his behalf. Seeing all – he has now moved forward, crouched behind a pillar – the concealed Otello notes 'Ei la nomò' ('He named her'). Iago tells Cassio to be patient. And in the meantime, as the music begins to wink roguishly, he cajoles him to tell about the woman who loves him: Iago whispers her name – Bianca – so that Otello will not hear it. Always proud of his 'conquests', Cassio responds, and a scherzo-like, playful Terzetto ensues, 'Essa t'avvince / Coi vaghi rai' ('She charms you with her beautiful rays'). Otello overhears their laughter, and concluding that they are speaking of Desdemona, bursts out twice with sorrowful exclamations: 'L'empio trionfa, il suo scherno m'ucc ide; / Dio frena l'ansia che in core mi sta!' ('The wicked man triumphs; his scorn slays me; God, restrain the anxiety in my heart!'). Cassio admits, more secretively, that not Bianca, but someone else must be in love with him. His words become lost, but he is clearly speaking of his surprise in finding a woman's handkerchief in his lodging – the token, he assumes, of a secret admirer. He even produces the handkerchief and shows it to Iago. Otello, of course, has been following all of this – or at least those portions that he could overhear – with intense horror. And Iago goes so far as to take the handkerchief and, while 'congratulating' Cassio, to wave it behind his back for Otello's benefit. 'È quello! è quello!' ('That's it! That's it!'), exclaims Otello. Shifting to a rapid-patter, *stretta* conclusion to the Terzetto, Iago teases Cassio that the handkerchief is a web in which his heart will be caught, 'Questa è una ragna'.

Cassio, for his part, can only marvel at the beautiful item in conceited wonder, 'Miracolo vago': Verdi even has him conclude his short melodic section with a fleeting, lecherous allusion to the Duke's 'La donna è mobile' from *Rigoletto* (surely as a kind of 'inside-joke' from the composer). And Otello, still hidden, joins his voices with theirs in his own private cries of betrayal, 'Tradimento, tradimento!'

Sudden off-stage trumpet-calls are heard: the arrival of the Venetian ships and the ambassadors on 'official business'. Cassio exits hastily and, even as the trumpet-signals continue and the crowd approaches, Otello rushes out from hiding with murder on his lips, 'Come la ucciderò?' ('How shall I kill her?'). He first requests a poison, but Iago suggests instead murdering Desdemona in her adulterous bed. Delighted with the idea, Otello immediately promotes Iago to the rank of captain (Cassio's old position – thus satisfying his initial grievance in Act I), and Iago leaves to bring Desdemona to the public scene to keep up appearances. At this point everyone enters in a grand processional chorus of Venetian praise, 'Evviva! Evviva!': Lodovico (the Venetian ambassador), Roderigo, Iago, Desdemona, Emilia, dignitaries, soldiers, townsfolk, and the like. Holding a parchment in his hand, Lodovico proclaims official greetings from Venice and delivers a written message to Otello. As the latter reads it, Lodovico greets the sad Desdemona, then inquires why Cassio is not present. Iago explains that Otello is angry with him. Desdemona, still pressing her case for him with blinding naiveté, adds in a descending phrase 'Credo / Che in grazia tornerà' ('I think that he will be restored to grace soon'). Otello gestures in rage at this, and when Iago perfidiously repeats Desdemona's idea she innocently continues to speak of Cassio. Nearly beside himself, Otello threatens to strike her, 'Demonio taci!!' ('Silence, demon!!'). Lodovico and the crowd react with astonishment and horror, and Otello now demands that Cassio be brought forth. Upon Cassio's entrance the Moor reports the contents of the official letter – and interrupts his report with side-insults hurled at the weeping Desdemona. According to the official decree, Otello is to be called back to Venice and the rule of Cyprus is to be placed in the hands of Cassio (much to the ambitious Iago's disgust). Now at the height of rage, Otello seizes Desdemona and throws her violently to the ground, 'A terra! e piangi!' ('To the ground! and weep!').

A massive, architectural ensemble follows, texturally the most interwoven and complex in all of Verdi. The humiliated Desdemona begins the *concertato* with three contrasting musical ideas. The first, like the onset of Otello's earlier soliloquy, is stammered out, 'A terra! sì, nel livido / Fango' ('On the ground! yes, in the livid mud'). She rises for the second idea, which begins with grand expansion, 'E un dì sul mio sorriso / Fiorìa la speme e il bacio' ('And once hope and kisses adorned my smile'), but soon shrivels back into the sorrow of the present. In the third portion, also lyrical but somewhat 'exotic' in character, she laments that 'Quel Sol sereno e vivido' ('that serene and vivid sun') can no longer dry her tears. There follow several sections of shocked reactions from the onlookers, interleaved with Desdemona's own music. And throughout Otello says virtually nothing. He has returned to his chair and, in a daze, stares numbly at the floor. Within this 'static' *tableau* of grief Iago overlays two critical streams of 'action'. He first moves over to Otello and urges him to act quickly in the uxoricide. He, Iago, will 'take care' of Cassio that very evening. Otello's few words of response, largely buried within the complexities of the *concertato*, are his only words in the ensemble. In a parallel 'active' passage Iago approaches Roderigo – who is still in love with Desdemona, as in Act I – and convinces him to slay Cassio that evening: the point, often difficult to extract from this ensemble, is to prevent Otello's (and hence Desdemona's) departure the next day. The ensemble swells in force and energy in a climactic, varied reprise in markedly faster tempo. Suddenly Otello rises from his chair to put a terrifying stop to it all by shouting 'Fuggite! Tutti fuggite Otello!' ('Begone! Let everyone flee from Otello!').

There is much motion on the stage as the exiting begins. In the midst of the swirl Desdemona makes one last appeal to Otello, but he wildly grabs her arm and curses her – the final humiliation, 'Anima mia / Ti maledico!' Within moments the stage is cleared, leaving only Otello and Iago. The Moor becomes more and more incoherent as nightmarish images of the past scenes fly before his eyes. He faints directly in front of his own throne, while Iago watches gleefully, again relishing his line, 'Il mio velen lavora' ('My poison is working'; cf. Act II, after the Quartet). An off-stage crowd is still hailing Otello as Iago moves towards the unconscious Moor to utter, 'Chi può vietar che questa fronte io prema / Col mio tallone?' ('Who can stop me from pressing my heel on this forehead?'). The distant populace continues to hail Otello as the 'Lion of Venice'. With a terrible gesture of triumph, Iago points at the prostrate Otello and declaims – again with his insidious vocal trill – 'Ecco il Leone!' ('Here is the Lion!'), and the curtain falls rapidly.

Act Four

Before the curtain rises to reveal Desdemona's bedchamber – claustrophobic and tomblike after the open-air first act and relatively spacious middle acts – a mournful English horn initiates a prelude that anticipates the motives of the ensuing scene. Its minor-mode principal idea sweeps upward only to fall back at once in a resigned sigh. Like what follows it gives the impression of a sadness beyond tears, of a resignation incapable of unbroken lyricism: it proceeds in isolated, disconnected phrases and varied phrase repetitions. Seated at a dressing-table and attended by Emilia, Desdemona is preparing for bed. Full of foreboding, she asks Emilia to lay her white wedding dress on the bed. She adds that if she were to die she would want to be buried with one of its veils. While Emilia unpins her hair, she begins to recall a sad song, the 'Willow Song', that she had heard long ago from her mother's maid, Barbara – who had been abandoned by the man she loved. All of these simple, evening preparations have a numbed quality to them, one of deeply repressed, injured emotion producing now only mechanical or ritualistic gestures: one recognizes the unmistakable ceremony of the self-preparation of the sacrificial victim. The Willow Song itself, 'Piangea cantando', participates significantly in this, and the 1887 production book requests the singer to produce 'that vague, sad, almost magnetic impression that arises from the anticipation of an unknown but great misfortune' (*DS*, pp. 88–9). The song, continually interrupted by distractions and interpolations, is that of a weeping, abandoned lover. It is punctuated by the haunting 'O Salce! Salce! Salce!' ('O willow! willow! willow!') – 'an expression of ineffable sadness', says the production book (p. 89) – and the meltingly beautiful refrain, 'Cantiamo! il Salce funebre / Sarà la mia ghirlanda' ('Let's sing! the funereal willow shall be my garland'). Towards its end, ever more in disintegration, we hear its fateful, deathly-still summary lines, which apply equally well to Otello and Desdemona: 'Egli era nato per la sua gloria, / Io per amarlo e per morir' ('He was born for his glory, I to love him and to die'). The repressed feeling, heightened by the faceting of the interruptions, is scarcely endurable: as Emilia turns to leave ('Buona notte'),

Desdemona finally releases the flood of emotion within her in a single, electrifying phrase: 'Ah! Emilia, Emilia, addio, Emilia, addio!' The tremolo, descending bass-line lament that immediately follows has the effect of sealing her doom, rendering her terribly alone – the sacrificial victim.

Now isolated and vulnerable, but regaining her resigned composure, she kneels at her prie-dieu before an image of the Madonna and begins the quiet, final glow of her 'Ave Maria'. The opening, muted string line gently, but pointedly, seems to touch on a passing re-evocation of the string terracings that began the Act III Desdemona–Otello Duet, before drifting off into the absorption of the 'spiritual', chromatic harmony. Her initial recitation soon gives way to the gentle, personal prayer that penetrates to the essence of her character and of the dramatic situation: 'Prega per chi adorando a te si prostra, / Prega pel peccator, per l'innocente' ('Pray for the one who, adoring you, prostrates herself. Pray for the sinner, for the innocent'). She concludes her prayer with mostly silent but increasingly fervent recitation, leaning her forehead on the prie-dieu ('Ave Maria . . . nell'ora della morte. Ave! Amen!'). She rises and lies down on the bed immediately. The 'Ave Maria' rays still glow in the high strings – and she falls asleep.

From the dark abyss five octaves below, double-basses alone, muted, begin isolated, ominous upward swells. Otello enters from a secret door at the back of the room, scimitar in hand. With chillingly skilled, soft steps, he lays down the weapon, closes off a separate exit behind a tapestry, looks at Desdemona, moves to a side-table and blows out the candle, and begins to move towards the bed – all of this to a held-breath single line in the double-basses, with occasional nervous punctuations from low, staccato violas (a motive that will dominate the ensuing action) and a soft bass drum. He raises the bed-curtains and gazes at the sleeping Desdemona; emotion begins to well up within him. Bending over her (the reverse image of that found in the Act I Love Duet) he kisses her three times – we hear again the 'Bacio' music from the Love Duet. With Otello's third kiss she awakens, 'Chi è là? / Otello?' ('Who is there? Otello?'). The Murder Scene consists of a crescendo of emotion beginning with Desdemona's initial, naive calm and mounting to uncontrolled terror. Its music is very free – a kind of enhanced and powerfully sculpted recitative – and consists largely of dramatic declamation underpinned by musical transformations of a single, previously heard orchestral motive, an agitated, short group of semiquavers heard several times, for instance, in staccato octaves, around Otello's first question, 'Diceste questa sera / Le vostre preci?' ('Have you said your prayers this evening?'). In many ways the scene is Verdi's most 'experimental': a striving for the immediacy of pure 'drama' unmediated by obvious, conventional structures (but see Chapter 7 below; Parker and Brown 1985–86). Desdemona soon learns that she is to be killed. Terror-filled, she gets up from her bed and begs to know the reason. 'Ami Cassio' ('You love Cassio'), shouts Otello, over a fierce, orchestral 'Amen'. Desdemona denies everything – denies the evidence of the handkerchief – and pleads that Cassio be summoned to confirm her story. But Otello responds darkly (and erroneously), 'Muto è per sempre . . . Morto' ('He is mute forever . . . dead'). Desdemona now realizes that there is no escape. Otello grabs her violently by the arm as she pleads for mercy. In an agitated crescendo that explodes into savage diminished-seventh triplets and syncopations, he throws her on the bed and strangles her with his bare hands – even as loud knocking is heard at the door. The music ebbs in diminuendo with her life. Otello steps back, looks at her motionless body, and says – over another orchestral 'Amen' – 'Calma come la tomba' ('Calm as the tomb').

Suddenly – more knocking at the door – Emilia's voice is heard asking for entrance. Otello closes the bed-curtains on the side facing the door and lets her in to learn (over still more 'Amens' in the orchestra) that Cassio, still alive, has killed Roderigo. From the bed, however, Desdemona's dying voice is heard once more. Emilia rushes to her bedside to ask who has killed her. Lying motionless, she breathes her last words, protecting Otello, 'Nessuno . . . io stessa . . . al mio / Signor mi raccomanda . . . Muoio innocente . . . Addio' ('Nobody . . . I myself . . . Commend me to my Lord . . . I die innocent . . . Farewell'). Otello now admits that it was he who killed her, for Iago had told him that she had been unfaithful to him with Cassio. Emilia responds with fury and runs to the door to cry loudly for help. Lodovico, Cassio, and Iago rush in and discover the murder, 'Orrore! Orror!' Emilia at once moves resolutely towards her husband and insists that he deny Otello's charges against him – did he say that Desdemona had been unfaithful? He responds coldly, 'Tal la credea' ('I believed her to be such'). Otello anxiously mentions the handkerchief-proof, and Emilia, suddenly understanding everything, reveals that Iago took the handkerchief from her. Cassio confirms the innocence of the handkerchief, and

Montano suddenly rushes in (with two guards) to report that the dying Roderigo has incriminated Iago in the whole plot. Otello begs Iago for a refutation. Iago at first pretends that he is about to speak, and then, with a resolute 'No!', he suddenly unsheathes his sword and dashes out through the door, pursued by the guards.

Now fully aware of his deed, Otello rushes to grab his scimitar, while Lodovico vainly tries to stop him and Emilia, weeping, moves towards Desdemona's bed. Over stunned, initially static chords – first major, then chilled to minor – Otello begins his final soliloquy. 'Niun mi tema / S'anco armato mi vede' ('Let no one fear me, even though you see me armed'). It is, again, very free, a dramatic heightening of recitative, an 'experiment' in pure musical declamation. He has now reached his journey's end, all is over, and a last burst of *forte* orchestral radiance gives way to bleak dejection: 'Oh! Gloria! Otello fu!' ('Oh! Glory! Otello was!'). As a solo oboe movingly recalls one of his fatal warnings to Desdemona in the Act III Duet ('Guai se lo perdi! guai!' – see p. 11 above), he drops the scimitar. Emilia moves away, and he climbs the steps of the bed and gazes with deep love on the slain Desdemona. His last farewell begins and ends with solo voice alone and is underpinned in the centre with a brief triple-time death-march:

> E tu . . . come sei pallida! e stanca, e muta, e bella,
> Pia creatura nata sotto maligna stella.
> Fredda come la casta tua vita, e in cielo assorta.
> Desdemona! Desdemona! . . . Ah! . . . morta! . . . morta! . . .
> morta! . . .
>
> And you . . . how pale you are! and tired, and mute, and
> beautiful,
> A pious creature born under an evil star.
> Cold as your chaste life, and taken up into heaven.
> Desdemona! Desdemona! Ah! Dead! Dead! Dead!

With decisive swiftness he pulls out a concealed dagger from his doublet and, stabbing himself, falls to the ground. Mortally wounded, he drags himself again to the bed and agonizingly climbs the two or three bed-steps to kneel beside Desdemona. He addresses her movingly in two lines, then, for his final words – as the 'Bacio' music from the Love Duet again returns – he tries with a supreme effort to rise and kiss her. Each time, pathetically, his strength gives out. Twice he manages only to kiss her hand, dangling from the bed. With the third effort he dies, rolling down the bed-steps onto the floor below.

Pria d'ucciderti . . . sposa . . . ti baciai.
Or morendo . . . nell'ombra . . . in cui mi giacio . . .
Un bacio . . . un bacio ancora . . . un altro bacio . . .

Before killing you . . . my wife . . . I kissed you.
Now, dying . . . in the shadow . . . in which I lie . . .
A kiss . . . a kiss again . . . another kiss.

2 Creating the libretto: Verdi and Boito in collaboration

For several years after the first Milanese production of *Aida* (8 February 1872) Verdi considered his operatic career to be over. His lean strength and vision had matured in the *Risorgimento*, where his name had become a byword for Italian unity, but now the Italian musical world was changing rapidly. Younger composers and prominent critics were aggressively reaching out to non-Italian traditions, verbal 'philosophies', and instrumental music for guidance. The older, simpler world was passing away. Youthfully strident cries for operatic reform in the 1860s had been followed by an invasion of the early Wagnerian operas and an increasing internationalization of the repertory of the major theatres. The Italian premiere of *Lohengrin* on 1 November 1871 in Bologna – a centre for the new aesthetic – led to several more Wagnerian performances in the 1870s: *Lohengrin* in Florence (1871), Milan (1873, a notable fiasco), Trieste (1876), Turin (1877), and Rome (1878); *Tannhäuser* in Bologna (1872) and Trieste (1878); *Rienzi* in Venice (1874), Bologna (1876) and Rome (1880); *Der Fliegende Holländer* in Bologna (1877) (Jung 1974: 183–6). Other signs of the new interest in things Germanic were the Milanese presentation of Weber's *Der Freischütz* in 1872 (in Boito's translation, with the recitatives set by Faccio) and the successful 1879 production in Turin of Goldmark's *Die Königin von Saba* – but the crisis was not exclusively of German origin. Meyerbeer was now a staple of the Italian repertory – as seen, for instance, in the frequent La Scala performances of his *L'Africaine* (1866, 1867, 1870–1, 1877–8) and other works. Gounod's *Faust* had been introduced at La Scala in 1862 and was revived in 1863, 1865, 1871, 1874, and 1877; *Roméo et Juliette* appeared in 1867–8 and 1874–5 and was followed in early 1879 by the much-discussed La Scala premiere of Massenet's *Le roi de Lahore* (Gatti, 1964).

To Verdi, although himself a cautious but determined reformer –

while never admitting it – much of this seemed a too-eager capitulation to foreign tastes. To make matters worse, he himself had been directly accused of betrayal and capitulation. He carried with him not the tumultuous public success of *Aida*, but the heated controversies born from the inevitable journalistic comparisons between his new opera and *Lohengrin*. Especially wounding were the responses of some of the minor critics, who inflamed the issues of nationalism and Verdi's supposed loss of 'individuality' – i.e., vocal directness – in his striving for the effects of Meyerbeer, Gounod, and Wagner: formal subtlety and a refined orchestral complexity. To L. Perelli in the *Gazzetta di Milano* (10 February 1872) *Aida* displayed little more than artificial borrowings from this 'Franco-Germanic School': 'It is no longer *creation*; it is *combination*, *composition*, *manipulation*.' Worst of all was Pietro Cominazzi's sneering diatribe in *La fama* (20 February). Cominazzi charged that Verdi, obviously with the 1871 *Lohengrin* applause still ringing in his ears, had become an 'obsequious imitator of Wagner', a 'follower and perhaps servile imitator of the new German art'. Even an enthusiastic, 'progressive' admirer (Leone Fortis?) in the prestigious *Il pungolo* (9 February) expanded at length on this new *Aida* as 'Il *Lohengrin* Italiano'. Hence Verdi's celebrated, and characteristic, outburst to Giulio Ricordi on 4 April 1875, 'A fine result, after a career of thirty-five years, to end up as an *imitator*!!!' (Ab., III, 749). Throughout the 1870s Verdi remained pessimistic about the future of Italian opera, and he nourished his bad temper in a number of letters to close friends. His frequent complaints about the new Italian musical atmosphere often betray an unmistakably personal tone: that is, many of them seem not easily separable from his own exaggerated sense of having been ill-treated by the critics, as in his late March 1879 letter to Opprandino Arrivabene, speaking of his negative reaction to a recent performance of Boito's *Mefistofele*: 'You see what it is not to be any longer *dans le mouvement*!!' (20 or 30 March; cf. Ab., IV, 62; *Cop.*, 627; Alberti 1931: 226).

The delicate diplomatic task of stirring this musical Achilles back to operatic battle fell to the young editor Giulio Ricordi, whose business interests in doing so were perfectly clear, but who also, it must be added, felt a sincere dedication to the cause of Italian art. Ricordi's hope was to lure Verdi back to the theatre with the prospect of setting an irresistible libretto: one written by Ricordi's close friend, the highly gifted Arrigo Boito, some twenty-nine years

Verdi's junior. This was no easy task. In the 1860s the young fire-brand Boito, a prominent figure in the iconoclastic, anti-bourgeois circle known as the Milanese *scapigliatura*, had not only been caught up in the whole movement of the *musica dell'avvenire* (music of the future) as its chief spokesman but had also appeared directly to insult Verdi in print (Walker 1962: 449). Before any collaboration could occur, the composer's deep-seated suspicions would have to be allayed.

Indeed, long after Verdi had made his peace in the late 1860s with two of Boito's closest friends, Franco Faccio (who would be selected as the future conductor of *Otello*) and Giulio Ricordi, he remained aloof from the icily brilliant poet–musician, who in fact was now nourishing an ever more profound admiration for Verdi's mature works. In the meantime Boito had redeemed himself from a failed Milanese *Mefistofele* premiere in 1868 through a marked success with the revised, somewhat more conservative version produced in 'Wagnerian' Bologna in 1875 (Nicolaisen 1977–8). And all the while he was turning more and more to highly polished libretto-writing (Catalani's *La falce*, Ponchielli's *La Gioconda*, and so on), beginning work on his own *Nerone*, and, surely, becoming increasingly interested in writing a libretto for Verdi himself. (Walker 1962: 447–72 furnishes a convenient discussion of Boito's pre-*Otello* years.)

Throughout these years Ricordi and Faccio continued to hope to reconcile the 'difficult' Verdi with Boito. And surely by the late 1870s the three plotters had devised the idea of an enticing *Otello* project. It was now a matter of finding and seizing the opportune moment. An error of timing or tone could be fatal. After a few cautious preliminaries and missed opportunities (Ab., IV, 91–2), the subject of *Otello* was finally broached in Milan in the last week of June 1879, when Verdi was in Milan to conduct a benefit performance of the *Messa da Requiem*. Ricordi's managing of the critical moments includes some of the happiest and most famous events of the composer's life. After the 30 June performance the *maestro* had been deeply touched by cheering crowds and an open-air, surprise *serenata* outside the Hotel Milan by the Faccio-led La Scala orchestra (Ab., IV, 84; Walker 1962: 473). The editor's later account to his biographer, Giuseppe Adami, of what ensued during the rest of Verdi's visit is celebrated:

The idea of the opera arose during a dinner among friends, when by chance [!] I brought the conversation around to Shakespeare and Boito. When *Otello* was mentioned, I saw Verdi look at me mistrustfully, but with interest. He had certainly understood; he had certainly reacted (*vibrato*). I believed that the time was ripe. My accomplice was the capable Franco Faccio. But I hoped for too much. The next day when, on my advice, Faccio brought Boito to see Verdi with the plan (*progetto*) of the libretto already drafted, the maestro, after having examined it and found it excellent, did not wish to compromise himself. He said, 'Now write the poetry for it. It will always be good, for me . . . for you . . . for someone else.'

    (Adami 1933: 64; see also Walker 1962: 473; Budden, III, 300–1)

In a much later letter, from 18 December 1879, Giuseppina Verdi remembered that the group had also discussed Rossini's *Otello* (1816), an opera that would remain psychologically present throughout Verdi's *Otello* project. All at the dinner had denounced its libretto (by Francesco Berio di Salsa) as an 'odious caricature' of the Shakespearean original (Luzio 1935: II, 95). Even Rossini's music had been criticized, with the exception of the 'stupendous' Gondolier's Song on lines of Dante in the final act. Whether Boito was present during this discussion is unclear, but his 'rapid' production of the scenario could have been planned in advance to be a response to the Rossini–Shakespeare conversation.

    Reluctant to commit himself, Verdi at first reacted cautiously. But Ricordi and Boito plunged onwards with what they now termed the 'chocolate project', in honour of the black Moor. Boito, who in June had assured Ricordi that he was working on his own *Nerone* – '*Est ante oculos Nero*' (Nardi 1942: 461) – turned at once to the task of preparing an *Otello* libretto. This meant turning seriously to translations of Shakespeare as source material. He was not, however, limited to translations alone. Boito could struggle through English – indeed, he eventually came to possess and mark three copies of Shakespeare in English (a one-volume, 1854 Leipzig edition of the *Complete Works*, a multivolume set of the pocket-size 'Handy-Volume Shakspeare' (*sic*), and the 1883 'Chandos Classics' printing of *The Works*), all of which may be consulted at the Biblioteca Palatina in Parma. Despite his close attention to certain textual details in these *Othello* editions, it is clear that the English original was not his principal, most comfortable source for the libretto. Blanche Roosevelt, for instance, reported that Boito told her in an 1887 interview that he had learned *Otello* by heart in 'François Hugo's magnificent translation and that of the Italian author [Andrea] Maffei [1869]' (Roosevelt 1887: 240). To these two translations one could certainly add what was surely Verdi's main source, Carlo Rusconi's problematic, occasionally inaccurate prose translation, stemming from 1838 (this – in eleven successive, often differing editions up to 1884 – was the standard mid-century Italian Shakespeare (Busi 1973: 71–8; Weaver 1984)), and perhaps Giulio Carcano's well-known 1852 poetic translation as well (first published in 1857; see Busi 1973: 79).

But clearly, Boito's most important primary source was François-Victor Hugo's French translation. He owned, underlined, and annotated at least three editions of Hugo's Shakespeare: two are now available in the Biblioteca Palatina in Parma; the third, in the Museo Teatrale alla Scala in Milan. From its copious marginal markings and underlinings in red, blue, and black pencil, it is clear that the La Scala copy was Boito's principal working source: *La tragédie d'Othello, Le More de Venise*, in the fifth volume of the *Oeuvres complètes de W. Shakespeare* (1860 edition). This was a careful translation accompanied by a thirty-five-page introduction, twenty-two pages of well-researched notes and commentary, and Gabriel Chappuys' translation of the seventh novella in the third decade of Giraldi Cinthio's *Hecatommithi* (Venice, 1566), the main source of the story of Shakespeare's *Othello*. A large number of the passages that Boito marked, many of them the work of summer 1879, correspond with the eventual *Otello* libretto. It is particularly moving to trace his growing excitement in reading and working with this play: his calm, careful annotations in the earlier scenes eventually give way to blue-pencil stars in the margins – emotional explosions – during the murder scene, beginning shortly after the entrance of Othello (Hugo, pp. 367–73; *Oth.*, V.ii).

Carving a compact libretto out of the play was essentially a task of creative condensation (Dean 1968; Aycock 1972; Filoni 1979–80; Budden, III, 305–22, 412–13; see also Chapter 8 below). For the opera Boito suppressed most of Shakespeare's first (Venetian) act and began with the storm scene (*Oth.*, II.1), but he inserted portions from at least three major sections of Act I into his own first act. Significantly, one finds the relevant lines underscored in his copy of Hugo: Iago's grievances from *Oth.*, I.i, 19–67[1] (Hugo, pp. 233–5; cf. *Otello* 32/2/2 ('gonfie labbra') and the 26 bars beginning 33/3/3); Roderigo's intention to drown himself and Iago's subsequent plotting in *Oth.*, I.iii, 301–3, 327–8 ('I have professed me thy friend'), 332–3 ('It cannot be'), 342–5 ('If sanctimony'), 350 ('I hate the Moor'; cf. Hugo, pp. 257–9; and the 27 bars beginning 31/1/2); and Othello's recounting to the Venetian Council of how Desdemona fell in love with him through hearing tales of his exploits, in *Oth.*,

I.iii, 127–69, which Boito fused with I.iii, 248 ('I saw Othello's visage in his mind') and lines from Othello's victorious entrance into Cyprus in *Oth.*, II.i, 174–93 ('O my fair warrior!', etc.) to form the text of the Love Duet, 'Già nella notte densa', at the end of the opera's first act.

In addition to its selective underlining and marginal flagging, Boito's copy of Hugo contains a few words written in the margin that further link this translation with the libretto-making process. Boito, for instance, occasionally wrote 'lir' or 'liric' in the margins to indicate, one supposes, his consideration of *versi lirici*, rhymed, regular verse (often solo pieces or passages of *arioso*) for that passage of the libretto: for example, those corresponding with Iago's first mention of jealousy in the opera, Act II (Hugo, 301; *Oth.*, III.iii, 167–9), Otello's stanza in the Act II Quartet (Hugo, p. 305; *Oth.*, III.iii, 265–70), and so on. Moreover, to the left of his underlining of the eavesdropping scene, *Oth.*, IV.i, 115–16, directly opposite Cassio's laughter and Othello's response, 'Tu triomphes, Romain! tu triomphes!', Boito wrote 'due volte' ('two times'): this clearly refers to his formation of two initial stanzas of text, with Otello's refrain, in the Act III Terzetto (Hugo, 330; cf. *Otello*, 237/1/3–237/4/3, 238/4/2–239/3/1). And, similarly, at the point when Othello kisses the sleeping Desdemona in *Oth.*, V.ii, 15, he wrote in very light red pencil 'reminisc[en]za del 1° atto' ('reminiscence from Act I'); later, at Othello's death, V.ii, 355, 'qu'à mourir en me tuant sur un baiser' ('Killing myself, to die upon a kiss'), he drew a horizontal line across the page and wrote 'Fine' ('End') (Hugo, 365, 383). Also noteworthy are two 'metrical' notes in the margins. The first occurs alongside Iago's narration of Cassio's dream (Hugo, 312; *Oth.*, III.iii, 414–27), where Boito wrote 'mart. lir.' at the point of the first direct (and italicized) quotation, '*Suave Desdémona, – soyons prudents! cachons nos amours*', and 'lir' beside the immediately succeeding lines. Boito was here proposing a metrical shift in the middle of the *versi lirici* of Iago's 'Era la notte' in Act II. In fact, one does find that for the fictitious Cassio-quotations (also italicized) in the libretto, but not in the Shakespearean original) Boito breaks from the established metre (unusual, 15-syllable lines, 3 × 5) to introduce the Italian Alexandrine metre, or *martelliano* (also called *doppio settenario*, 2 × 7): '*Desdemona soave! Il nostro amor s'asconda / Cauti vegliamo! l'estasi del ciel tutto m'innonda*', etc. (187/1/2). The second metrical note occurs a few lines later, at Othello's oath of vengeance, 'Oui, par le ciel' (Hugo, 313; *Oth.*,

III.iii, 461–3): here the librettist wrote '14 sdrucciolo'. This indicates his adopting of a novel, '14-syllable' metre (by the Italian
methods of counting) with its final accent on the antepenultimate
syllable (thus producing the 'sdrucciolo' ending, ‾ ˄ ˄). This results
in radically lengthy lines with 16 'actual' syllables, an Italian
evocation of the classical trochaic catalectic tetrameter, doubtless
employed here for its archetypal, elemental effect: 'Sì, pel ciel
marmoreo giuro! Per le attorte folgori!', etc. (193/3/3; see p. 184
below).

Such were Boito's concerns in the summer of 1879. 'Tell Giulio',
he wrote in July to Eugenio Tornaghi, Ricordi's secretary, 'that I am
manufacturing chocolate' (*CVB*, I, xxvii). A double set of letters in
July, from Ricordi's wife to Giuseppina and from Ricordi to Verdi,
playfully informed the composer of Boito's work. On 18 July Verdi
warned Ricordi again: 'But be careful . . . I have not pledged myself
in the slightest' (Ab., IV, 86). Assailed by bouts of painful facial
neuralgia, Boito drafted the first three acts of *Otello* in July and
August. He reported his progress to Ricordi from Venice, where he
had gone for his health:

Fear not, I have tried to take up work again these days, profiting from the
morning hours, in which the neuralgia gives me some rest. Even without
working too hard the job will be finished in August. The hardest part of the
work is managing to condense the boundless sublimity of the text into rapid
dialogues (*dialoghi spicci*). Rereading what I wrote in Milan, I found a way
of cutting it, and there was much to reduce into leaner forms (*forme più
snelle*). I know for whom I am writing and I want to do the best that I can.
(Ab., IV, 92)

On 24 August he wrote again to Tornaghi: 'Tell Giulio that
tomorrow or the day after tomorrow I shall begin the first lines of
the last act. *Everything will be done in time*' (*CVB*, I, xxvii; Ab., IV,
87). Ricordi was counting on rapid progress and had already
concocted a plan to bring the completed libretto to Verdi at
Sant'Agata, accompanied by Boito and Faccio, in the first half of
September 1879. His hopes were momentarily dampened by a side
issue. On 26 August the composer reacted angrily to the reprinting
in Ricordi's *Gazzetta musicale di Milano* of Rossini's 1847 opinion
that his temperament could never produce a successful comic opera
(Ab., IV, 88–90). It was a minor incident, and even as the editor was
pacifying Verdi he continued to press the *Otello* matter. But on
4 September Verdi ruled out any visit of Boito to Sant'Agata, at
least for the moment. A personal meeting over the libretto, he

reasoned, would be awkward and could lead to the impression of a commitment:

> In my opinion the best procedure (if you agree and if it suits Boito) is to send me the finished poem so that I can read it and offer my opinion calmly, without its committing either of the two parties. Once these rather thorny difficulties have been removed, I shall be very happy to see you here with Boito. (*CVB*, I, xxvii)

On the same day, 4 September 1879, Ricordi received a progress report (with ominous hints of delays and revisions) from Boito in Venice. Most significantly, this letter reveals one of his central concerns in drawing up the libretto, the employment of provocative, often innovative poetic metres both as a challenge and a stimulus to Verdi (see pp. 183–6 below).

> I am applying to this work a particular rhythmic (*ritmica*) construction throughout (in the lyric part), and I believe that this will greatly interest our *Maestro* and will also astonish you quite a bit. It will be a powerful incentive for the carrying out of that project so dear to our hearts. But this idea came to me late, and now it is best that I redo all of the lyric part of the second and third act. My health is perfectly restored, and I will be able to have reconstructed and finished the entire work by the 9th or 10th of this month. I think that I have found a form that will admirably serve both the Shakespearean text and its musical illustrator! (Ab., IV, 92)

As usual, these remarks were passed on to the composer.

Much to Ricordi's distress, more delays followed. On 17 September he wrote to Verdi with the hope that he could send off the libretto in a week: Boito had written that he had finished the text but was recopying it 'with such trepidation that he would like to do it all over again from the beginning' (Ab., IV, 94). Boito was well aware of the editor's pressure. On 21 September he wrote to Tornaghi, 'If I don't give Giulio the strangled Desdemona this week, I fear that he will strangle me' (*CVB*, xxvii). Boito returned to Milan on 28 September but still insisted on recopying the libretto and, as an anguished Ricordi informed Verdi on the following day, 'redoing two scenes that don't satisfy him fully' (Ab., IV, 94). Now assailed not only by the neuralgia but also by a painful abscess in his mouth, Boito slowed down the pace of his work, while on 7 October Ricordi wrote an apologetic letter to Verdi and enclosed a letter that Boito had sent him declaring (once again) his devotion and sincerity amidst intense physical pain (Ab., IV, 95–6). Finally, by the first week of November 1879 Ricordi was able to send Verdi a portion of the libretto, probably at least the first two acts. On 7 November

Giuseppina wrote the editor (clearly an oblique Verdian response) that she and Verdi would come to Milan around the 20th and that the composer and librettist could speak at that time:

Inter nos, what he [Boito] has written so far of the African seems to suit his [Verdi's] taste and is very well done. And it is certain that the remainder will be done equally well. Let him finish the poem calmly, then, abandoning himself to his fantasy (without torturing it). As soon as it is finished, let him send it to Verdi without delays or hesitations, before he comes to Milan, so that he can read it tranquilly and – in case – make his own observations in advance. I repeat, the impression is good: modifications and refinishing (*la lima*) will come later. (*CVB*, I, xxix)

On approximately the same day (Ricordi passed the note on to Verdi on 8 November) Boito informed the editor:

Yesterday I worked on the Fourth Act, and I am pleased. There is still the *terzetto* of Act III, an important piece, which makes me despair! Occasionally I abandon it to advance some other scene; then I return to the *terzetto*, and I find it more sour (*arcigno*) than ever! Yet I'm not despairing. Rather, I am certain that I shall call on you shortly with the chocolate hot and ready. And how happy we shall be! (*CVB*, I, xxix)

Verdi received the remaining portions of the libretto on 18 November: 'Just now I have received the chocolate', he wrote to Ricordi. 'I'll read it this evening' (*CVB*, I, xxix). Doubtless composer and librettist talked at length a few days later in Milan.

Work on the *Otello* libretto – initial production and subsequent revisions – took place in seven different phases, or distinct periods of time, over a period of seven years, until mid-1886. With a completed draft now in Verdi's hands, the first phase was over. The revision process would be lengthy and complex. But what do we know about this initial draft? It is no longer available as a complete, separate document, although portions of it undoubtedly constitute some of the collection of Boito's autograph libretto manuscripts (several scenes exist in more than one draft), still preserved by Verdi's heirs at Sant'Agata. In addition to interpreting the material in these revised libretto documents[2] one may infer much about the original *Otello* from comments and revisions made by Verdi and Boito over the next few years.

Act I was probably the act most similar to its final version. Its initial storm scene, however, might have been somewhat shorter (Boito's ms. libretto bears his folio number '2' on the seventh actual folio, which, in addition to other evidence, suggests some expansion). And the moment of Otello's entrance was more prolonged:

TUTTI: Evviva Otello.
IAGO (*a Rodrigo* [*sic*]):   (Sia dannato Otello!)
OTELLO (*a Iago*):
          E Desdemona?
IAGO: Attende nel castello.
OT (*a Iago, famigliarmente*):
          Onesto Iago, Cassio, buon Montano
          E voi tutti esultate, e suoni a festa
          Tutta Cipro. L'orgoglio musulmano
          Sepolto è in mar, nostra e del cielo è gloria
          Dopo l'armi lo vinse la tempesta.
ALL: Long Live Othello!
IAGO (*to Roderigo*):   (Othello be damned!)
OTELLO (*to Iago*):
          And Desdemona?
IAGO: She is waiting in the castle.
OT. (familiarly, to Iago):
          Honest Iago, Cassio, good Montano
          And all of you, exult, and let all Cyprus resound
          With festivities. Moslem pride
          Is buried in the sea. The glory is ours and heaven's.
          After [our] arms conquered them, so did the storm.

In his dialogue with Roderigo Iago originally lacked the three –
somewhat puzzling – lines based on Shakespeare's 'Were I the
Moor, I would not be Iago' (*Oth.*, I.i, 58; *Otello*, 35/3/1). And,
following Shakespeare in the parallel passage, *Oth.*, II.i, 191–3,
Iago, having observed from the shadows the kiss of the Love Duet,
maliciously observed, just before Otello mentions the Pleiades:

          (Soave accordo ove l'amor si stempra
          Con blando accento
          E vago!
          Infrangerò l'armoniosa tempra
          Di quel concento.
          Fede d'onesto Iago!)

          (Sweet sound where love melts
          With mild and beautiful
          Tone!
          I shall shatter the harmonious quality
          Of that joined union.
          Faith of honest Iago!)

In Act II Iago's solo piece after the dismissal of Cassio ('Vanne! Ti guida il tuo dimone!') was not yet the familiar 'Credo', but four egoistic quatrains of *doppio quinario*, celebrating his power and beginning, 'Tesa è l'insidia; – ho in man le frodi, / Ti gonfia Invidia – che mi corrodi!' ('The trap is set; I have the deceptions in hand, / Swell up, Envy, you who corrode me!'; complete text in Luzio 1935: 110; Boito 1942: 1537). The third quatrain contained a line that would (in 1884) be embedded into the 'Credo':

> D'Otello il fato – io guido, io nomo.
> Son scellerato – perchè son uomo,
> Perchè ho la scoria – dell'odio in cor,
> Mentr'ei di gloria – vive e d'amor.

> I guide, I worship Otello's fate.
> I am wicked because I am a man,
> Because I have the dross of my hatred in my heart,
> While he lives on glory and love.

Otello's and Iago's subsequent conversation – the first step in Otello's undoing – originally led immediately, without the Homage Chorus, to Desdemona's entrance and the Otello–Desdemona dialogue, 'D'un uom che geme'. (And Iago, of course, lacked his two parenthetical lines, now beginning 151/1/1, a modified variant of his comment excised from the Love Duet. Otello's line at this point, 'Quel canto mi conquide', was originally 'Quel volto mi conquide', 'That face conquers me'; Luzio 1935: II, 107.)

In Act III the autograph libretto shows that Boito originally planned Otello's fainting and Iago's gloating over him (based on *Oth.* IV.i, 35–46) to occur at the conclusion of his 'Dio! mi potevi scagliar tutti i mali' monologue (derived from *Oth.* IV.ii, 46–63). Here tormenting echoes of past lines goad Otello's mounting frenzy:

> Ah! Dannazione!
> Pria confessi il Delitto e poscia mora! [*sic*]
> Confession! . . . Confessione!
> Vederli insieme avvinti . . . Ah maledetto
> Pensiero . . . Confessione . . . ciò m'accora . . .
> Sangue . . . la prova . . . l'idra . . . il fazzoletto . . .
> Satana!! Oh . . . [*sviene*]

> Oh, damnation!
> First confess the Sin and then die!
> Confession! Confession!
> See them coupled . . . Oh, cursed

Thought . . . Confession . . . I like not that . . .
Blood . . . proof . . . the hydra . . . the handkerchief . . .
Satan!! Oh! . . . [*faints*]

The earliest version of Iago's next lines is unavailable in the autograph libretto, but pasted over it is an early, fifteen-line revision –
a critically important passage for Verdi – that begins: 'Svenuto? / Il
mio velen lavora' ('Fainted? / My poison is working!'; complete text
in Luzio 1935: II, 111; Nardi 1942: 1538). Verdi asked his friend the
Neapolitan artist Domenico Morelli for a sketch of this scene in
early January 1880 (Budden, III, 302).

We know little for certain about Boito's original conclusion for
Act III – the portion after the Terzetto – except that it was the single
portion of the libretto that Verdi wanted largely recast, probably,
feeling the demands of operatic convention, to provide the opportunity for a more theatrical *concertato* ensemble. It may be – as
Luzio 1935: 111–12 seems to suggest – that the earliest reading in the
autograph libretto manuscripts preserves this original ending; or,
on the other hand, this reading could conceivably be that of Boito's
first revision, early August 1880 (see below, p. 36).[3] In any event,
this earliest available reading is remarkably concise, and, except for
its final quatrain, is reasonably close to *Oth.*, IV.i, 162–234. After
the Terzetto and the sounding of the signal announcing the arrival
of the Venetians, Iago persuades Otello to murder Desdemona by
suffocation, not by poisoning, and vows that he will take care of
Cassio himself. Otello promotes Iago to the rank of his captain. At
this point Lodovico, the ambassadors, and everyone else enter.
Otello begins to read the official letter given to him (it is never made
clear that the letter calls him back to Venice and replaces him in
Cyprus with Cassio; rather, it is based only on *Oth.*, IV.i, 217, 'This
fail you not to do, as you will – '). As Desdemona continues to intercede for Cassio, Otello explodes with rage, 'Demonio, taci!', and
brutally grabs Desdemona's arm. The remainder of the act contains
only five, and perhaps six, formal quatrains in rhymed *endecasillabi*
(11 syllables). The first five, for Iago, Otello, Desdemona,
Roderigo, and (together) Lodovico, Emilia, the Herald, and the
Chorus, furnish the standard operatic reactions. A sixth quatrain,
for Otello – on a different, but perhaps originally contiguous folio –
provides a sudden change of mood and a vigorous, but artificial,
conclusion for the ensemble:[4]

Che? nel dì che consacra la vittoria
Su Cipro un velo di squallore incombe?
Voglio il suon della gioja e della gloria!
Or sù! tuoni il cannon! squillin le trombe.

What? On the day that consecrates our victory
Shall a mist of gloom fall over Cyprus?
I want the sound of joy and glory!
Up, now! Fire the cannon! Sound the trumpets.

This leads at once to fanfares, the rapid movements of troops and flags, and the fall of the curtain.

Whatever the actual shape of Boito's original ending to Act III, we first hear of its need for alteration – and, it seems, expansion – in Ricordi's 24 July 1880 reminder to Boito, which unfortunately provides few of the details: 'You will recall that on your orders I wrote to him to say that . . . you would get busy with that famous [Act III] finale for which you had already planned the dramatic events, lacking only the versification' (Ab., IV, 169). Determining the proper contents of the eventual *concertato* finale, the most explicitly non-Shakespearean aspect of the opera (Budden, III, 306), would be difficult: no fewer than three complete versions and six additional fragments may be found in the autograph libretto manuscripts.

The original Act IV was less immediately troubling but still quite different from its final version. Desdemona's Willow Song was disposed in two ten-line stanzas each composed of two quatrain blocks of *doppio quinario* verse (5 + 5 syllables) divided by two lines of *ottonario* (8 syllables). The first stanza began thus:

Sotto ad un salice – sedea la mesta
E senza speme – languìa d'amor.
Lenta chinava sul sen la testa,
Lenta la mano premea sul cor.
　　E in quell'alma gemebonda
　　Salìa l'onda del dolor.

Under a willow – the sad woman sat
And without hope – she languished for love.
She slowly bowed her head on her breast,
Slowly pressed her hand on her heart.
　　And in that moaning soul
　　Welled up the wave of sorrow.

The two concluding lines of the song's final quatrain would eventually be included in the final version of the song:

Ei m'abbandona – la mia memoria[5]
Più non lo scuote – nè i miei sospir.
Egli era nato – per la sua gloria,
Io per amarlo – e per morir.

He abandons me – My memory
No longer stirs him – nor my sighs.
He was born – for his own glory,
I, to love him – and to die.

Following the song Boito originally included Desdemona's questions to Emilia (following *Oth.*, IV.iii, 55–62):

DES.   Emilia, addio. Come m'ardon le ciglia;
        E presagio di pianto. O buona Emilia
        Pensi che esistan spose sì corrotte
        Da tradir la lor fede?
EM.   V'è chi lo crede.
DES.   Io non lo credo. – E tardi. Buona notte.

DES.   Emilia, farewell. How my eyes are burning;
        It is a premonition of weeping. O good Emilia
        Do you think there exist wives so corrupt
        As to betray their faith?
EM.   Some believe it so.
DES.   I don't believe it. It's late. Good night.

And, finally, Boito's original ending, preserved in the autograph manuscript of the libretto, is longer than the final version and includes several of the details from *Oth.*, V. ii, that were later omitted. here Otello stabbed Desdemona after smothering her ('S'agita ancor ... Quest'agonia non si prolunghi', 'She still stirs ... / This agony must not be prolonged'), following some actors' (probably inaccurate) interpretations of *Oth.*, V.ii, 88–90, and despite an explicit note condemning this tradition in the Hugo translation, p. 412 (cf. pp. 166–8 below). Otello's and Emilia's dialogue was more extended and included Otello's curse at Desdemona's actual death, 'L'inferno afferri quella mentratrice!' ('Let Hell seize that lying woman', from *Oth.*, V.ii, 130). As in Shakespeare, Emilia's and Iago's confrontation was more violent: before revealing her knowledge of the handkerchief, she curses him as 'Maledetto del cielo!' ('Cursed by heaven'), and Iago responds, 'Taci', drawing his sword and lunging at her. Unlike the model, *Oth.*, V.ii, 221–49, she is saved by soldiers, who seize Iago, whereupon she tells her tale. At the moment that Lodovico (not Montano, as in the final version) recounts the dying Roderigo's indictment of Iago, Otello rushes at

Iago and wounds him: 'Non morto? e sia per tuo supplizio vivo. / Dolce cosa è il morir' ('Not dead? So remain alive for your execution. / Dying is a sweet thing'). Lodovico picks up Otello's sword, which had fallen to the ground, hands it to the guards, and orders Iago to be taken off to prison. In the meantime Otello, unnoticed, grasps another sword, brandishes it, and is given a twenty-one-line (!) solo piece, 'Mirate, ho un arma ancora' (Luzio 1935: 119–20), the first eight and last four lines in rhymed, regular *doppio settenario* verse (7 + 7), the freer, internal lines in *endecasillabi sciolti* (11s). The first eight lines (the last four of which were retained in the final version); were derived from *Oth.*, V.ii, 257–63 ('Behold, I have a weapon'), 270–4 ('O ill-starred wench!'), and 279 ('O Desdemon! Dead Desdemon! Dead! O! O!'); the last thirteen lines, 'Una parola ancor', were based on 334–52 ('Soft you; a word or two before you go'). Its final quatrain, the moment of Otello's self-stabbing, closely follows *Oth.*, V.ii, 347–52:

> Che una volta in Aleppo – vedendo un tricotato
> Turco in turbante offendere – l'alto onor dello Stato
> A vendicar l'ingiuria – sozza ch'ei profferì
> Lo afferai per la strozza – e lo colpii . . . così.

> That once in Aleppo, seeing a malignant
> Turk in a turban offend the high honour of the State,
> To avenge the foul injury that he gave,
> I grasped him by the throat and killed him . . . thus.

As the onlookers cry out, Otello moves towards Desdemona's bed: 'Ah, ch'io disciolga . . . l'anima affannata' ('Ah, let me release . . . my weary soul'). The concluding three lines of the opera are as in the final version, 'Pria d'ucciderti', etc.

This much established, it is a relatively simple matter to chronicle the libretto modifications over the following years. After Verdi received the libretto and met with Boito in Milan in November 1879, nothing further was accomplished for eight months. And Verdi had still made no commitment to set it. As Giuseppina wrote to the Countess Negroni Prati Morosini on 18 December 1879, 'It seems that Verdi must have liked it, since after reading it he bought it, but he put it beside Somma's [libretto for] *Re Lear*, which for thirty years has slept a profound, undisturbed sleep in its portfolio. What will happen with this *Otello*? No one knows' (*CVB*, I, xxix–xxx). Verdi's musical thoughts turned instead to completing two brief sacred works: a *Pater noster* and an *Ave Maria*, both of which were premiered in Milan on 18 April 1880. And he spent from 12 February to early April 1880 in Paris for the French premiere of *Aida* (22 March, a great success). Boito was similarly occupied, with the London premiere of *Mefistofele* (6 July 1880).

The second phase of activity on the libretto occurred between late July and November 1880 and concerned only the most pressing problem: that of finding a suitable ending for Act III. Urgèd onwards by Ricordi, Boito sent Verdi a revised draft of the scene with the Venetian ambassadors in late July or early August (Nardi 1942: 466). This draft, it seems, is lost, although, as mentioned above (p. 32), it is possible that it is identical with the earliest of the versions of the Act III ending still preserved in the *Otello* libretto manuscripts. The composer responded directly to Boito (his first letter to him since 1862) and maintained that the conclusion was not sufficiently dramatic. He proposed either a quicker curtain (very shortly after 'Demonio, taci!', which could be followed only by a brief reproach – and hence no ensemble) or 'inventing' for dramatic reasons a non-Shakespearean ending. Following a slow *concertato* in which everyone, led by Lodovico, reacts to Otello's insulting of Desdemona, Verdi suggested a sudden Turkish invasion of Cyprus, replete with drums, trumpets, and cannons – ideas perhaps suggested by Boito's earlier 'militaristic' conclusion (if, indeed, that had been the proposed conclusion). At this point Otello would suddenly return to his status as hero, brandish his sword and lead the Venetian troops off to victory. As battle-sounds are heard off-stage, Desdemona was to bring down the curtain, Aida-like, with a prayer for Otello. But Verdi, reasonably enough, had doubts about this ending, particularly about the sudden reversal of Otello's mood. 'Are these needless scruples', he asked Boito, 'or are they serious objections?' (15 August 1880, complete letter in *CVB*, I, 1–2; trans. Walker 1962: 477–8).

Boito was now in a difficult position. He was reluctant to reject the suggestion of the touchy *maestro*, and yet saw that Verdi's proposal would weaken the intensity of the drama. After hesitating – 'I am delaying responding to him until I can give him the fruit of the seeds that he has planted in my thought', he wrote to Giuseppina (on Ricordi's advice) from Monaco on 4 September (*CVB*, I, 3) – Boito produced the verses for the ending that Verdi had requested. The composer received them, without any commentary from Boito, on 14 October: 'I've read it. Divinely well done! And now what do you think of the scruples that I manifested in my last letter?' (*CVB*, I, 3). Boito was obliged to respond and did so on 18 October. His letter is both a masterpiece of tact and a minor treatise on operatic form (see Budden, III, 309). The ending was indeed a bad idea from the dramatic point of view, he argued, for it momentarily released Otello from his nightmarish torments, destroyed everything created thus far, and would oblige them to recreate the atmosphere all over again for the murder: 'That attack by the Turks gives me the same impression as a fist breaking the window of a room where two persons were about to die of asphyxiation' (*CVB*, I, 4). Boito went on graciously to insist that, whatever the dramatic problem might be in the abstract, Verdi's musical genius must be allowed to prevail: 'You, Maestro, could with one pen-stroke reduce the most compelling arguments of the critics to silence' (*CVB*, I, 5).

By 24 November Boito, ever more concerned, had received no response from Verdi (Ab., IV, 136), who had now moved to Genoa for the winter. In the next few days, perhaps even after a meeting with Verdi in Genoa – the documents are unclear on this point – Boito was charged with writing still another version of the Act III ending. Evidently acting on an idea given him by Verdi (as an unpublished letter of Ricordi's suggests), he immediately jotted down the elements of a new, theatrical conclusion. Still acting through the buffer of Ricordi, he had the editor mail this 'fragment', 'a few lines on paper-slips' (*CVB*, II, 291), to Verdi on 30 November 1880. Verdi's response to Boito on 2 December tells us something about this fourth version:

Well done, the third finale! I like Otello's fainting in this Finale [at the end of the scene] better than where it was before [i.e., following Otello's 'Dio! mi potevi scagliar']. Only I neither find nor feel the ensemble piece! But we can also do without this. We'll discuss it later. (*CVB*, I, 6)

This version, apparently not one of those in the libretto manuscripts (could it have been a scenario or partial draft?), may thus have solved the problem of finding a dramatic coup for the curtain, but it seems to have lacked a clear, extended set of effective *concertato* stanzas – and, of course, the transferring of Otello's fainting to the end of the act left the conclusion of Otello's Act III Monologue to be revised. This new, still unsatisfactory Act III ending marks the end of the second phase of libretto-shaping. At this point Verdi and Boito turned to the full-time task of revising *Simon Boccanegra*, which was premiered at La Scala on 24 March 1881.

Phase three began on 25 May 1881, with Boito's letter to Verdi, 'Don't think that I have forgotten the Moor of Venice . . . Within a couple of days I will busy myself efficaciously with the Moor' (*CVB*, I, 50). Surprisingly, his initial task was not to be a further polishing of the new Act III ending, but the addition of an Homage Chorus to Desdemona in Act II, something that he and Verdi had apparently spoken about previously. Boito sent the new text, 'Dove guardi splendono', etc., which mixed and contrasted internal stanzas in a standard *quinario* metre (5 syllables) with exterior stanzas and refrain lines in an 'unusual' trochaic *senario* (6 syllables), to Verdi with a full dramatic (if somewhat unsatisfactory metrical) explanation on 17 June. In the same letter he added that 'if this Chorus seems all right to you, the most difficult part of the *Otello* retouching is done; I will now get to work on the [Act III] ensemble. Then I will still try to make a few cuts in Otello's part' (*CVB*, I, 51–7; see the trans. and discussion in Budden, III, 311–12; see also p. 184 below). Verdi acknowledged receipt of the Homage Chorus in a letter of 23 June and added some advice that demonstrates that their conception of the Act III finale had changed again since the prior December: 'Get busy then on the finale, and make it a well-developed piece, a piece *on a big scale*, I should say . . . The colossal power of the drama demands it.' Somewhat cryptically (to us, given the existence of choral *tableaux* in Act I), he added, 'The idea (which I still like) of setting *Otello* to music without a chorus was and is, perhaps, a crazy one!' (*CVB*, I, 57; trans. Walker 1962: 485).

A few days later, during the first weeks of July, Boito, Faccio, and Ricordi visited Verdi. Boito had finally breached the walls of Sant'Agata. As he wrote to Tornaghi on 10 July, 'We have settled with the Maestro the last dubious point of the work [undoubtedly the expansion of the scene, including especially the conception of the formal *concertato* stanzas, along with the mending of the 'Dio! mi potevi scagliar' ending], and I am now occupied in giving form to the result of that exchange of ideas' (*CVB*, II, 308; trans. Walker 1962: 485). The largest problem in creating this new, 'big finale' was to produce a Desdemona-led 'lyrical', or static, piece (in the *concertato* tradition) that simultaneously permitted the unfolding of essential 'dramatic' action. This action would have to unfold in two conversations, both led by Iago: the double-murder plot with Otello and the convincing of Roderigo, still enamoured of Desdemona, to ambush and kill Cassio. Boito's solution, probably improved after a second visit to Sant'Agata in mid-August (*CVB*,

II, 308) was to write formal *settenario* (7-syllable) quatrains or octaves for all of the participants in the 'lyrical' portion (Verdi was given the option of expanding Desdemona's verse to twelve lines) but to set off the 'active' portions, including the crowd reactions, in rhymed *endecasillabi*, usually broken up into rapid dialogue. Moreover, the *endecasillabi* permitted Verdi a great deal of freedom, for Boito had written lines that could also be split up into 'lighter' *quinari*. He proudly demonstrated this by subdividing the 11-syllable lines in some of the copies of the text now preserved in the libretto manuscripts. For example, from the Iago–Otello dialogue (and notice in particular the cleverly embedded rhyme, abcbadceda . . .):

IAGO:	(Una parola) [/]
OT:	E che?
IAGO:	T'affretta – / Rapido
	Slancia / la tua vendetta! / Il tempo vola! /
OT:	Ben parli.
IAGO:	E l'ira / inutil ciancia. / Scuotiti!
	All'opra / ergi tua mira! / All'opra sola! [etc.]
	(Cf. the embedded submetres or double scansions in *Falstaff*, Hepokoski 1983: 32–3)

Boito finally sent off the text to Verdi, along with a now-famous, lengthy explanatory letter on 24 August: 'Just as we had planned it, the ensemble has its lyrical and dramatic parts fused together' (*CVB*, I, 58–61; see also Budden, III, 312–13). The composer responded gratefully on 27 August: 'The finale is very well done indeed. What a difference between this one and the first!' (*CVB*, I, 61–2; trans. Budden, III, 313). He added a few suggestions for the dialogue after the *concertato* proper, that is, after Otello disperses the crowd, and also proposed that earlier in the ensemble the chorus react negatively to Cassio's election as Otello's successor. (This last idea, of course, was never adopted.) With Boito's immediately ensuing modifications the Act III ending was now in place, and the third phase of libretto-creation came to an end. Indeed, to the best of our knowledge, except for a brief question about a line in the Love Duet from Boito on 10 August 1882 – basically a substitution for the word 'arce', which Verdi had found 'too studied' in the original 'L'arce ascesa alla breccia fatal' (*CVB*, I, 63–4) – *Otello* remained untouched for the next twenty-nine months. Verdi was still not committing himself to the project. In the interval he set to work (primarily from September 1882 to March 1883) revising *Don Carlos*.

The fourth phase began in late January and early February 1884. Boito was spending the winter in Nervi, that is, close to Verdi's Genoese winter home. The two saw each other frequently, and it is clear that Boito began again to retouch portions of the libretto, particularly in the first act (perhaps the opening storm?), as he informed Tornaghi in mid-February (*CVB*, II, 318). Whatever the revisions had been, Verdi was delighted: 'How quickly you've done it!' he wrote to Boito on 7 February. 'If only I could do likewise' (*CVB*, I, 69). Shortly thereafter, probably in mid-March, Verdi began to compose the first act. But his progress was brought to an immediate halt by a notorious and most unfortunate incident. Boito, in Naples for a performance of *Mefistofele*, was misquoted in the 24 March issue of the Neapolitan journal *Roma* as having said at a banquet in his honour that he regretted not having been able to set *Iago* (*Otello*) to music himself. The librettist, of course, had said nothing of the sort, but the story was picked up by other journals and spread throughout Italy. At first believing the story to be true, Verdi was deeply offended. Through Faccio, he offered Boito his libretto back. Ricordi, Faccio, and Boito were thunderstruck. The inevitable series of personal explanations, apologies, and assurances followed, in which Boito again skilfully used all of the tact that he could muster (19 April 1884, *CVB*, I, 69–73; Budden, III, 315–16; Walker 1962: 488–90). On 26 April the barely appeased Verdi wrote Boito a note of absolution but noted that he had stopped composing: 'All this has cast a chill over this *Otello*, and stiffened the hand that had begun to trace out a few bars! What will happen in the future? I don't know!' (*CVB*, I, 73–4; trans. Walker 1962: 490).

Shortly thereafter – the exact date is uncertain – Boito sent Verdi a peace-offering: a new *Credo* for Iago in Act II. Verdi, he recalled, had wished for something freer than the *doppio quinario* solo in the original libretto, and this new 'evil Credo' displayed a less regular verse: twenty-three rhymed lines mixing lines of 11, 7, and 5 syllables – a 'broken, non-symmetrical metre (*metro rotto e non simetrico*)', as Boito put it (*CVB*, I, 74–6). (Strictly speaking, the Credo is not based on any specific, extended passage in *Othello*: for its conceptual sources, see pp. 181–2 below.) Verdi may not have realized that Boito had first offered its concluding lines, 'La Morte è il Nulla. / È vecchia fola il Ciel' ('Death is Nothingness. Heaven is [merely] an ancient fable'), to Ponchielli as part of a short-lived, new bass aria for Alvise in the revision of *La Gioconda* for Venice (21 October 1876), that is, for the second of the four versions of that opera. Although Ponchielli eventually removed the aria for the fourth and final *La Gioconda* (Milan, 12 February 1880; see also Budden, III, 283, 318), its music had been printed in an early vocal score. The relevant lines had occurred as a refrain in Alvise's 'new' aria ('Muori e distrugga l'orrido / Sepolcro il tuo bel viso') at the close of Act III Scene i, following his confirmation of the supposed poisoning of Laura and the beginning of the next scene, the arrival of the guests. In the first of the two stanzas the refrain substitutes 'vieta' ('old-fashioned') for 'vecchia': see Example 1. Verdi welcomed the new Credo as 'very powerful and completely Shake-spearean' on 3 May 1884 (*CVB*, I, 76). But, at least for the moment, he had put aside work on *Otello*.

The fifth phase of libretto construction began seven months later, in December 1884, as Verdi – now decisively – once again took up its composition. While drafting the Act II Quartet he determined that he needed more lines for Iago and Emilia. On 9 December he requested more text from Boito (*CVB*, I, 78–9), who responded with quatrains that Verdi wished to be placed in the second half of the Quartet, immediately after Iago obtains the handkerchief from Desdemona (*CVB*, I, 78–81; see also pp. 53–5 below). Through-out much of this winter Boito was once again close at hand in Nervi, and as Verdi composed his way through the opera we may presume that several alterations were made in the text. One minor revision, a plot-clarifying insertion of three lines before the Act III Trio, beginning with Cassio's 'Io qui credea di ritrovar Desdemona' (234/2/1) is mentioned in Boito's letter to Verdi of 7 February 1885 (*CVB*, I, 82). This phase of libretto-work, about which we know little, ends with Verdi's move back to Sant'Agata in early May.

Phase six, September and October 1885, involves some changes in Act IV – the last major modifications in the libretto – requested by Verdi as he was composing that act. This stage began with Boito's arrival at Sant'Agata on 13 September. During this visit Verdi and Boito agreed upon the text of a new Willow Song for Desdemona, 'Piangea cantando', and refashioned the conclusion to the opera. The new Willow Song, probably requested by Verdi (see p. 58 below), was not based directly on the parallel passage in Shake-speare, Desdemona's 'The poor soul sat sighing by a sycamore tree' (*Oth.*, IV.iii, 38–54) but rather on what Boito knew of Shakespeare's

Ex. 1

own source, an anonymous English ballad, the song of a man, curiously, not a woman.[6] A twenty-three-stanza form of this 'early' song had been reprinted, with the title 'Willow, Willow, Willow', in Thomas Percy's 1765 collection, *Reliques of Ancient English Poetry* (see Percy (1765); rept. 1961, 199–203; another version was printed in W. Chappell's 1888 *The Roxburghe Ballads*). François-Victor Hugo had translated into French Percy's stanzas 1, 5, 6, and 7 – the stanzas closest to the Shakespeare song – and included them in his commentary to his *Othello* translation (1860: p. 411, n. 51). Here it was that Boito found them, along with the implication that the four translated stanzas constituted a complete poem, described as 'the original' of Desdemona's 'romance'. The four stanzas determined the ordering and content of Boito's new Willow Song. In both Boito and the Hugo translation one finds material either treated quite differently by Shakespeare or not in the play at all: the crucial, repeated refrain, for instance, 'Chantez: Oh! le saule vert sera ma guirlande' ('Sing, O the greene willow shall be my garlànd' – not a repeated refrain in the play, although a version of the line does appear there, *Oth.*, IV.iii, 48), preceded immediately by 'O saule! saule! saule!' ('O willow, willow, willow!' – this, too, occurs in Shakespeare, but not characteristically as a trigger for a refrain); and the initial image of Hugo's 'third' stanza, totally lacking in Shakespeare, 'les oiseaux muets se juchaient près de lui, apprivoisés par ses plaintes' ('The mute birds sate by him, made tame by his mones'), carried over into Boito's own third stanza ('Scendean gli augelli a vol dai rami cupi / Verso quel dolce canto'). Boito noted this poem in his copy of Hugo with a blue-pencil caret in the left margin, and he underlined a single phrase in the third stanza, 'attendrissaient les pierres' ('[The salt tears fell from him, which] softened the stones'), clearly an image that had impressed him. (Shakespeare had also used it in *Oth.*, IV.iii, 44, but it had not appeared in Boito's earlier Willow Song.)

A radically shortened ending for the act, which either also dates from this September 1885 collaboration or had been prepared at some earlier time undocumented by correspondence, is preserved in the libretto manuscripts. As specifically requested by Verdi, Desdemona pleads for mercy with a lyrical quatrain, in rhymed *endecasillabi*, before her murder, 'Signor, pietà! Chiedo la vita in dono', etc. (Luzio 1935: II, 120; trans. in Budden, III, 319), but gone are the stabbing of Desdemona, Iago's warnings to and ultimate attack upon Emilia, Otello's wounding of Iago (here he lunges at him but is held back by Lodovico and the soldiers), and Otello's lengthy concluding speech. Instead, immediately after Desdemona's death (and only seven lines after Emilia's entrance), crowd noises are heard off-stage and Lodovico, Cassio, and the soldiers lead in the now-arrested Iago in chains. Roderigo's charge is briefly repeated and the handkerchief deception exposed; throughout, Iago remains silent, and responds only with a curt 'No', to Otello's demand for an explanation (cf. *Oth.*, V.ii, 301, 'From this time forth I never will speak a word'). As in the play, Iago is led off to torture, whereupon Otello immediately stabs himself – no extended pre-suicide speech – and concludes with the three familiar lines of the final version, ending with the kiss.

In all probability Boito and Verdi also discussed – and perhaps agreed upon – the outlines of still another ending, of medium length, which ultimately became the model for the definitive ending: one in which neither Emilia nor Iago are wounded, but one in which Desdemona retains her lyrical quatrain before being murdered, and Iago flees (and hence is not brought to justice – at least on-stage, although Lodovico explicitly calls for his eventual imprisonment). Otello, however, was still denied a concluding monologue. Verdi began setting this 'medium-length' ending in late September. On 5 October he wrote Boito that he had finished (*CVB*, I, 85–9) and enclosed a transcription of the text as he had set it. He had excised Desdemona's lyrical quatrain, but, most significantly, had included a speech of moderate length for Otello before his suicide – not yet 'Niun mi tema', but a shorter, six-line monologue largely extracted from Boito's earlier – and longer – soliloquy. This now began with the lines, 'Tutto è finito! / La gloria è un lampo, un sogno menzogner!' ('All is finished! / Glory is a mere flash, a lying dream'), and concluded with a quatrain that Verdi and Boito had decided to abandon, but that Verdi had reinstated in the act of composition: 'E tu . . . come sei pallida!', etc. (*CVB*, I, 85–9). Verdi was now requesting a few additional connecting lines and polishings. Replying on 9 October that he could not provide these without hearing the music that Verdi had composed thus far, Boito suggested another meeting at Sant'Agata. He arrived on 16 October, with (at least) the Hugo translation of Shakespeare in hand (he would inadvertently leave it behind and ask Verdi for it after his departure). Presumably at this time most of the final details for the Act IV conclusion, particularly the substitution of the three 'Niun mi tema' lines (from *Oth.*, V.ii, 264–6, 'Be not afraid, though you do see me weaponed') into the beginning of Otello's final soliloquy, were decided upon. Verdi set to work at once with the orchestration of Act IV (*CVB*, I, 92).

The seventh and final phase of libretto-work comprises several small, late changes that Verdi requested while orchestrating (and revising and rechecking) the remainder of the opera, from January until September 1886. In all probability, Boito was once again close at hand in Nervi for the first few days of 1886 (*CVB*, II, 336), and it also seems that he met with Verdi in Milan between 20 and 22 February (*CVB*, II, 343) and again in Genoa in early March (with Muzio, who reported that the music for the Act I Love Duet had just been revised; Ab., IV, 279) and late April (*CVB*, II, 345). Doubtless some minor alterations were made during these encounters. On 11 January Verdi wrote Boito asking whether Montano ought not to appear in the Act III finale and whether he could reduce four lines before the *concertato* to two (surrounding the moment of Cassio's entrance and concluding 'Nell'animo lo scruta'; *CVB*, I, 93–4). With regard to the former issue Boito charmingly (and instantly) replied that, having been wounded in Act I, Montano was confined to bed; with regard to the latter he revised the verses that were troubling Verdi (*CVB*, I, 95). Shortly thereafter, the composer determined once and for all that the title of the opera should be identical with that of Rossini's, *Otello*, and not *Iago* – hardly a surprise, since in most of his correspondence he had referred to his work by that title. He was now concerned that the general public be aware of this. To Boito, on 21 January:

People are talking and writing to me constantly about *Iago*!!! . . . For my part it would seem a hypocrisy not to call it *Otello*. I would prefer them to say, 'He wanted to fight with a giant [i.e., Rossini] and was crushed', rather than 'He wanted to hide behind the title of *Iago*'. If you are of my opinion, let's begin then to baptize it *Otello*, and tell Giulio this at once.

(*CVB*, I, 99–100)

On 8 May Verdi questioned Boito about the fidelity to the Shakespearean original of some 'recently made' lines in Act I, Iago's 'Se il Moro io fossi / Vedermi non vorrei d'attorno un Jago' ('If I were the Moor / I would not like to see an Iago around me'). Boito had taken these words almost without change from Carlo Rusconi's translation of *Oth.*, I.i, 58: 'che se io fossi il Moro, non vorrei vedermi intorno un Jago'. But now Verdi, doubtless forewarned by other translations that he had consulted – he mentions Hugo and Maffei – noticed that the English original (here he may have been helped by Giuseppina) said something rather different. The problem, he explained, was that he preferred Rusconi's mistranslation (*CVB*, I, 103). Verdi's letter is of more than casual interest, for here we find him seeking a librettist's approval for the retention of a line – something not often encountered in Verdian letters, and an indication of the respect that Boito had earned. Boito answered two days later with the justification that Verdi clearly desired, and he even buttressed it with an elaborate 'literary' explanation: 'What I am about to write seems a curse. I prefer the [mistranslated] phrase in the Rusconi. It expresses more things than does the [original] text. It reveals the evil soul of Iago, the good faith of Otello, and proclaims to all spectators the essential tragedy of deceit', etc. (*CVB*, I, 104). Verdi responded approvingly on 14 May and announced that he had also cut several lines from Otello's entrance after the storm. Apparently, to judge from Boito's reply two days later, both men had agreed that the originally planned entrance (see p. 30 above) was insufficiently dramatic. This 'condensation' of mid-May 1886 crystallized the precise form of one of the most powerful – and powerfully concise – entrances in all opera, 'Esultate! L'orgoglio musulmano', etc. (*CVB*, I, 105–7).

By July 1886 Ricordi had transcribed the libretto and was preparing it for printing (the proofs would eventually be printed in October). Verdi was particularly concerned that all of the texts after Desdemona's initial stanza in the Act III *concertato* be printed in three columns on a single opening in the centre of the libretto, 'because I would like the public to be able to see and understand everything at a glance' (17 July; *CVB*, I, 108–10). For his part, Boito – clearly remembering the *indiscrezione* following the March 1884 Neapolitan banquet – was particularly concerned about keeping the libretto private. On 28 July he instructed Tornaghi to plug his ears when he read it, and to show it to no one else besides Alfredo Edel, who had been selected as the costume and prop designer (*CVB*, II, 35). In the meantime, on 21 July, Boito, responding to the composer's concern that Desdemona's presence in the *concertato* was not sufficiently explained, had sent Verdi two brief additions to the text surrounding the entrance of the Venetian ambassadors. Thus he had Iago suggest that Desdemona welcome the ambassadors 'to avoid suspicions' (on 25 July Boito sent Verdi an even more concise form of these lines, the form actually used: 'Ma ad evitar sospetti' etc., *Otello* 255/4/2ff); and he added Emilia's and Desdemona's

two-line conversation beginning 'Come sei mesta' (7 bars beginning
261/3/3).

At the end of August Verdi sent a 'pro memoria' slip to Boito
(probably via Ricordi, who had brought Romilda Pantaleoni, the
future Desdemona, to meet the *maestro* on 29–30 August) asking
whether the women should be included in the Act I *Brindisi* and
informing him that he had reinstated and set to music a previously
cut quatrain in the Otello–Desdemona Act III Duet: the four lines
beginning 'Pur già qui annida il dèmone gentil del mal consiglio',
Otello 207/3/2ff (*CVB*, I, 113). (Boito later changed the 'Pur già' to
'Eppur': see *CVB*, II, 355.) With regard to the matter of the women,
Boito advised that Verdi should include the women if he wished to
do so for 'musical reasons' (*CVB*, I, 114–15; see trans. in Budden,
III, 321). The composer seems first to have decided to do without
the women's voices (9 September), but, in fact, they are present in
the final version of the score. In a separate, libretto-proofreading
issue, on 19 October, Ricordi noted that Verdi had not adjusted the
text of the Homage Chorus in his autograph score to incorporate the
latest textual changes (*CVB*, II, 352). As it turned out, Verdi, probably inadvertently, would never enter these changes into the autograph score, with the result that its text still contains a number of
(presumably) rejected variants (e.g., 'Come a un sacro altar /
Madri, bimbi, spose', fol. 147ᵛ–8 (134/2/2–135/1/1); 'Dalla
voragine', fol. 153 (141/2/3); 'Coi voti nostri', fol. 153ᵛ (142/2/3);
'Per te la florida', fol. 155 (144/1/4–144/2/2), etc.).

The last pre-premiere addition to the libretto sprang from Verdi's
desire in mid-December 1886 to include at the end of the Homage
Chorus a reshaping of Iago's malicious lines (from *Oth.*, II.i, 191–3)
that had been cut from the end of the Love Duet (see *Otello*, 151ff).
The idea came to Verdi while rehearsing Victor Maurel, the first
Iago, who was famous for his powers of declamation. The composer
wrote to Ricordi about the matter (and about the exact placement
of Iago's 'Eccola; vigilate') on 15 December 1886 (*CVB*, II, 356). So
far as is known, this is the only textual change in the opera suggested
by the abilities of a specific singer.

3 The composition of the opera

There can be little doubt that from the beginning Verdi regarded the *Otello* project as a potentially unwise intrusion into the 'modern' Italian musical crisis. Despite the critical controversy that had swirled around the 1871–72 *Aida*, that opera would have provided a fitting conclusion to a long and distinguished operatic career. To be sure, there was also a risk in composing no more operas: Verdi was laying himself open to the charge that operatic progress had passed him by, that he would not – or could not – keep up with the pace of musical events in the new Italy. Throughout the later 1870s he seemed willing to have risked this charge – even to have accepted it – and his bitter denunciations of Italian modernism may in part reflect this attitude. But the undertaking of a new opera would immediately place him in a difficult position. He would once again be obliged to defend his stance with regard to the vastly over-simplified dialectic raging in the press: Italian melody and lyricism versus Ultramontane complexity and 'profundity'. 'National' integrity and Italian 'individuality' had become central issues. But now the stakes were higher, and the game was being played in intensified social and musical circumstances. Any new Verdian opera to appear after a decade or more of operatic silence would be scrutinized from beginning to end. Especially with a libretto by Boito, it would inevitably be taken as a manifesto by example.

Verdi's dilemma in arriving at an appropriate style for *Otello* is clear. On the one hand, merely to maintain unaltered the style of *Don Carlos* and *Aida* – even if Boito's text had permitted it – might seem an explicit admission of age and historical irrelevance. The composer refused to produce a work that, however 'melodic' and successful with the public, could be viewed critically, and con-descendingly, as evidence that he was now indeed an old man alien-ated from musical 'progress'. Compositional silence, permitting oblique critical inference, was one thing; the production of a concrete work inviting direct critical proof was quite another. It was clear, then, that the best defence was, if not an attack, at least an aggressive, decisive stylistic advance. On the other hand, to compose an opera in a more modern style – the only reasonable solution given the innovative structure of the libretto – would be to risk being misconstrued and to expose himself even more directly to the hated (and largely misguided) charges of Wagnerism and the denial of his Italian past. Put another way, Verdi might well have been prepared to write his own concise, melodic, and theatrical version of a 'symphonic' or 'motivic' opera – one developed directly out of his own concern for the forceful projection of dramatically expressive words and images – but he was unwilling to be obliged to defend the procedure against simplistic charges of Germanic influence. All of this touches on the central paradox of Verdi's later years, the gap between his written opinions and his own musical practice. Above all, Verdi needed to consider himself eminently 'Italian', which seems to have meant to him a natural striving for a luminous, sharp-edged clarity of musical thought coupled with a close attention to the sonorous possibilities of the human voice. It could be that Verdi's private and public polemics against the rise of Germanism in Italy, the insistence on the Italian traditions of melody, and so forth, were essential tactics in his own – seemingly contradictory – move towards a more complex opera. By emphatically rejecting Germanism in print, that is, he may have been working both to construct an acceptable self-image and to blunt the arguments of those who were suggesting that he was now sacrificing to foreign gods.

It is not surprising, then, that Verdi was reluctant to commit himself at once to the composing of *Otello*. Still, he found the proposal attractive, and Boito's libretto was probably very much on his mind in the months immediately following his receipt of the initial draft in November 1879. Thus in early January 1880, a time between the December 1879 completion of the brief *Pater noster* and the immediately subsequent completion of the *Ave Maria* for Soprano and Strings, he wrote to the Neapolitan painter Domenico Morelli proposing a demonic sketch of Iago gloating over the fainted Otello (Ab., IV, 111; Morelli pleased Verdi with his suggestion that Iago should instead have 'the face of an honest man (*uomo giusto*)'). It appears that the new libretto was still occupying his thoughts over the next few months, during his visit to Paris to prepare and conduct the French premiere of *Aida* (with Victor Maurel – the future Iago – as Amonasro). From Paris his colleague and former pupil

Emanuele Muzio wrote to Ricordi on 25 February and 4 March: 'Speaking of *Otello*, [Verdi] told me that he had already begun to set it to music . . . But, by God, *Iago* is begun – and having begun it, he will finish it, and once it's completed it will have to be given' (Ab., IV, 176). Muzio's report is probably exaggerated and overly optimistic, but it does suggest that some musical ideas for the opera had already occurred to Verdi. Whether he had actually noted anything down on paper is uncertain. Almost a year later, however, in January 1881, Muzio mentioned to Ricordi that he remembered that the *Otello* music 'is completely alive in [Verdi's] mind' (Ab., IV, 177). In any event, except for a third passing comment from Muzio in late 1882 (see below), we hear no more about *Otello* composition for the four years after the period of the 1880 *Aida* rehearsals.

Verdi's work in the intervening years – two sets of extensive and important opera revisions, for *Simon Boccanegra* (in 1881, with Boito) and for *Don Carlos* (in 1882–83, with Camille Du Locle) – may be understood as the composer's grapplings with the advanced style that he planned to use in *Otello*. The revisions were moderately risk-free experiments for the new style as well as opportunities to judge the critical response to it: a gearing-up for the *Otello* project. And yet, even during the revision of *Don Carlos* the initial stages of the composition of *Otello* may have been taking shape. Following his suggestion to Verdi that he compose *Otello* to help defray expenses for the projected hospital at Villanova d'Arda, Emanuele Muzio wrote from Genoa to Giulio Ricordi on 29 December 1882 that 'this morning . . . I saw some pages of music on the piano along with others containing *Otello* poetry that were not there last year. Those are thoughts that he does not let escape when they are good' (Ab., IV, 206). But shortly thereafter, on 15 March 1883, Verdi wrote to Arrivabene, 'I haven't thought about [*Otello*], I'm not thinking about it, and I don't know whether I'll think about it in the future. By now theatrical conditions are so bad that it's useless writing operas!' (Alberti 1931: 300).

The new *Don Carlo* was premiered at La Scala on 10 January 1884 (with Francesco Tamagno, the future Otello, in the title role). Immediately thereafter, Verdi and Boito resumed discussions in Genoa about the *Otello* libretto. By mid-March 1884 Verdi had finally begun to draft the opera. Because of its deliberate, four-year gestation thus far – and given the (often unreliable) Muzio's insistence on hearing and seeing some *Otello* materials – it is reasonable to assume that he had already determined many of its principal musical ideas and effects. 'The Maestro is writing', wrote Boito to Ricordi on 20 March 1884, 'in fact he has already written a good part of the beginning of the first act and it seems to me that he is enthusiastic' (Ab., IV, 234; Nardi 1942: 490). But within a week this buoyant optimism was cut short, chilled by the incident of the widely reprinted misquotation of Boito's words spoken at a Neapolitan banquet (see p. 40 above). It is unclear how much of *Otello* had been drafted – surely at least a substantial portion of the first act – but Verdi, seemingly appeased by late April with numerous apologies and even the newly conceived Credo-text for Iago, would not resume his compositional drafting again until the end of the year.

This does not mean that the opera did not continue to occupy his mind. Boito and Giuseppe Giacosa arrived at Sant'Agata on 29 September 1884 for a few days' visit: by this time all misunderstandings had been cleared away, and it was a happy encounter for all parties. Giacosa's report of the visit, published some seven months later in the *Corriere della sera* and reprinted in the 17 May 1885 issue of Ricordi's *Gazzetta musicale di Milano* (and again, with variants, in the 12 February 1893 *Verdi e il Falstaff*, a special number of *Vita moderna*), provides a rare – if idealized – glimpse into the earliest stages of Verdi's compositional process: the point at which the first musical ideas are born out of the text:

I remember having felt one of the most rarefied spiritual pleasures in hearing Giuseppe Verdi read the verses of the play that he is now setting to music. In company with Arrigo Boito, I had the highest honour of being [Verdi's] guest at the Villa of S. Agata. It was last October [1884]. In my presence the great *maestro* discussed with Boito several parts of the libretto that the latter wrote for him, following step by step the adaptation (*sceneggiatura*) of the Shakespearean *Othello*. And commenting with profound dramatic wisdom, he read aloud entire scenes of the drama. With our eyes Boito and I expressed to each other the religious sentiment of admiration that filled our souls. In that reading we felt outlined the harmonies that will course around the world. The voice, the accent, the cadences, the impulses, the rages were such, so much did they show a troubled kindling of the soul, so much did they enlarge the sense of the words beyond measure, that it seemed clear to us that the source of the musical idea was in them. We saw with our own eyes, so to speak, the flowers of melodies germinating, words brought to their ultimate and highest phonic power, transforming themselves into waves of sound sweeping with them the infinite anguishes of which the human soul is capable.   (*CVB*, II, 326)

Giulio Ricordi, in a similarly exaggerated (but probably generally accurate) piece from February 1893, 'How Giuseppe Verdi Writes and Rehearses', also stressed the origin of Verdi's musical ideas in the verbal text:

> Verdi writes very few sketches during the period of composition: [only] simple reminders, indications of musical impulses, and nothing more [*sic*: Ricordi may be referring to the period prior to the drafting of larger sections of the opera]. Verdi conceives the opera while reading the libretto. The composer plans the first general outlines of his own work by reciting the lines. In so doing, he studies the inflections of his voice, the various colors that the words assume in the sentiments of wrath, pity, and love. The great maestro has always done it in this way . . .
> (Ricordi's entire article is translated in Hepokoski, 'Under the Eye', 1985.)

Shortly after his customary winter move to Genoa, on 30 November, Verdi resumed work on *Otello* – this time decisively. He composed most of the opera's central core – probably in chronological order from where he had broken off work (perhaps near the end of Act I) up to at least the end of Act III – in Genoa from early December 1884 to late April 1885, when he began to prepare for his move back to Sant'Agata. (By 7 February Boito – near at hand in Nervi for most of this period – was supplying additional lines just before the Act III Trio: see p. 41 above.) This was remarkably efficient work by any standard. Still, the sudden outpouring of the opera had been preceded by years of careful consideration. We may be certain that by late 1884 the composer had already formulated clear ideas about the music, or at least about the general musical effects of several sections. He may well have jotted some of them down in the form of isolated sketches.[1] To Verdi, however, 'composing' a work meant producing a relatively continuous draft, or possibly a set of smaller, contiguous drafts, that carried most of the fundamental vocal-melodic and bass lines of the entire work: a continuity draft (similar to that reproduced in full for *Rigoletto* by Gatti, i.e., typically only with notated vocal parts, an indication of the principal instrumental bass or treble, and only occasionally filled-in harmonies), establishing the basic shape of the opera without close attention to inner detail. From what we can determine from the handful of available late-period sketch and draft pages (*Otello* and *Falstaff*), Verdi created his operatic shapes – including some progressive, intricate formal designs – rapidly and securely. He then returned to them at later points, sometimes repeatedly, for inner-voice, orchestral expansion (orchestration) and, quite often, a much more deliberate reshaping, enhancing, and polishing of local detail. The few initial drafts that are accessible impress us with the firmness and clarity of their already advanced thought; but, of course, historians concerned with chronicling Verdi's compositional process are inevitably drawn to those passages that he ultimately altered.

At present we are permitted only three tantalizing glimpses into this early period of composition: a single sketch-page from the end of the Act II Quartet, currently located in the Bibliothèque de l'Opéra in Paris (an 1887 gift to Charles Nuitter); a photograph of a page from, presumably, the longer (but currently inaccessible) draft of Act III, Desdemona's 'Io prego il cielo per te con questo pianto', in Carlo Gatti's *Verdi nelle immagini*, p. 187; and a single folio, written on both sides, from a draft of the Act III Trio, located in the Pierpont Morgan Library in New York.

Only the Act II Quartet sketch, fifteen and a quarter bars beginning with Desdemona's descending solo, '['t'allie-]ti il core, / Ch'io ti lenisca il duol' (164/2/1), is datable with any precision. Verdi wrote this music on a single page – separately from a more continuous draft of Act II – after receiving additional lines for the Quartet that he had requested from Boito on 9 December 1884. While composing the first half of Act II in early December, that is, he had found himself short of lines for the Quartet. The essential problem was that the existing text had brought Emilia's and Iago's lines up to the point of the latter's seizing of the handkerchief ('A me quel vel!') and no further. But Verdi's conception of the piece was now to place the theft of the handkerchief, the pivotal dramatic act of both this ensemble and the opera as a whole, at the mid-point of the Quartet, dividing it into two contrasting halves (see the analysis in Chapter 7). 'In the Act II Quartet the dialogue between Iago and Emilia finishes too quickly', he explained. 'I would need four lines, asides, for each' (9 December; *CVB*, I, 78–9). Thus he was requesting two additional 'concluding' quatrains for Emilia and Iago – the one fearful, the other demonically triumphant. While waiting for the new lines Verdi doubtless continued his compositional draft, leaving a gap for the second portion of the Quartet. Boito sent alternatives for the new text shortly after 9 December (his undated letter is reprinted in *CVB*, I, 79–81), and Verdi must at this time (mid-December 1884) have written the single page –

Ex. 2

now the Paris sketch – to join up with what he had already composed.

The sketch differs from the final version in two principal ways. First, it is written in B major, not B♭ major, revealing that the Quartet was conceived a half-step higher; the transposition would not occur until very late in the compositional process, October 1886 (see pp. 66–8 below). Second, it lacks the three bars before the final cadence (167/2/1–168/1/1) that Verdi inserted into the final version well over a year later, during the process of orchestration. The original approach to the cadence, bars 7–11 of the Paris Sketch – notice also the differing text for Emilia – is shown in Example 2. (For a more extensive discussion and transcription of the sketch – certain small variants are omitted here – see Hepokoski 1987.)

We know much less about the compositional contexts of the two remaining draft-fragments, the Gatti photograph of 'Io prego il cielo per te con questo pianto' and the Pierpont Morgan Act III Trio

Ex. 3

Guar - da le pri - me   la - gri -me   guar - da le pri - me   la - - -

- - gri - me che   da me spre - me il duol le pri - me la - gri - me

document. Always assuming a generally chronological sequence of drafting, we may suppose that both documents were written in the early months of 1885, the former perhaps before 7 February (the date of Boito's Act III textual revisions before the Trio) and the latter shortly after this date. In the twenty-six bars of the 'Io prego' draft it is clear that the two climactic measures, the descent from the high b♭^{2}, 'lagrime che da me spreme il duol, le prime' (220/1/1–2), were originally planned as four, proceeding in doubled note-values (Example 3), thus continuing the broad, striding crotchets of the beginning of the sketch. The revision, an intensifying compression (mostly of crotchets into quavers, resulting in a dramatic rush to the stressed cadence formula that follows), is also visible on the sketch, but in the vocal parts only: the original bass-line is untouched. On the sketch itself, then, a broader asymmetrical period, 8 + 9, was telescoped into a more concise one, 8 + 7.

The Act III Trio Sketch, widely reproduced in facsimile (both *recto* and *verso* of the single folio in Chusid 1974: 136–7; the *recto* only in Porter 1980: XIX, 656 (*The New Grove Dictionary*) and Turner 1983: 90), is considerably more complex than those mentioned above and can be only touched upon here. It consists of fifty-three bars, beginning with the onset of the second strophe of text and music, four bars before Cassio's 'Son già di baci sazio e lai' (237/4/4). Among the several details in the draft-fragment differing from the final version, three seem particularly worthy of mention here. Verdi first composed the final line of Otello's refrain-response in the second strophe, 'Dio, frena l'ansia che in core mi stà!', as an emphatic howl of pain, rising up to a sustained, high a♭^{1} (Example 4), his highest note in the Trio. The final version, while still turbulent, is nowhere as explosive: perhaps Verdi, attending to the parentheses around Otello's lines (they are, after all, asides),

Ex. 4

l'em-pio m'ir - ri - - de   il suo scher-no m'uc- ci - de   Dio - -

- - fre - na l'an -sia   che in co - re mi sta

decided it was best to suppress these outbursts in favour of a more accumulative tension.

A second difference lies in its multiple realizations of the six-bar transition, 'Nel segno hai colto' (239/3/3), from the A♭ major of the first two strophes to the B major (C♭ major in the final version) in which the expanded third strophe begins: clearly, this is a passage that Verdi found troublesome to compose. Curiously, the fact of the six-bar unit remains constant, but there are no fewer than three versions of it in the sketch, and a fourth early version is erased in the (later) autograph score.

Finally, Otello's later words, 'Or gli racconta', etc., were at one point on the draft given four separate bars – Example 5 – instead of being overlaid on the orchestral melody proper, as in the final version. Curiously, his similar response eight bars later, 'Le parole non odo', etc. (241/3/2ff), retains the bass-figuration of the Example 5 reading even though its music is no longer included in the final

Ex. 5

or gli rac - con-ta   il mo-do il lo- co [sic]   l'o-ra

score. (It is a curious characteristic of late Verdian revisions to eliminate the models or patterns for later repetitions. Given two nearly identical statements of an idea, one of which is to be modified or excised, Verdi's preference seems to lie with altering the first statement.)

The composition of the *Otello* draft was suspended for nearly five months, when Verdi returned to Sant'Agata from Genoa in early May 1885 (stopping in Milan on the way back, 1–3 May, to have five teeth and one root pulled by an American specialist – all this in preparation for the dentures that would come a few months later). In the leisurely summer that followed Verdi visited Montecatini and the baths at Tabiano; we know little of his precise activity at this time. On 10 September he wrote from Sant'Agata to Boito, who was planning a visit beginning on the 13th: 'Alas! Since I've been here (I blush to say it) I've done nothing! The country, to some extent, the baths, the excessive heat and, let us add, my unimaginable laziness have prevented it' (*CVB*, I, 84; trans. Walker 1962: 492). All of this changed with Boito's visit.

Because Verdi's next letter to the librettist (5 October) deals exclusively with major Act IV revisions, one may presume that the two of them had concentrated on that act in mid-September. It is possible that by the time that Boito arrived on 13 September Verdi had already drafted the music for the early textual version of Desdemona's Willow Song (see pp. 33–4 above). In any event, it seems that he requested a different Willow Song text at this time, the one first alluded to in Verdi's 5 October letter (*CVB*, I, 85–9; see pp. 41–3 above). The result, 'Piangea cantando', is the most metrically complex text in the opera, mixing in surprising ways – and certainly in ways that disturb the underlying strophic structure – *quinario*, *setennario*, *endecasillabo* and *doppio quinario* metres. Since the precise Boito would be unlikely to produce such a metrically confused text on his own (but see p. 185 below), one concludes that he and Verdi produced a 'compromise' text to retain some of the features from the earlier setting that the composer did not wish to discard. Some of the old Willow Song music is probably embedded into the new setting, most likely in those spots where the old text was preserved, particularly in the lines: 'Egli era nato – per la sua gloria / Io per amarlo – e per morir'.

Boito's visit also saw some major reshaping of the conclusion of Act IV (see pp. 43–5 above). On 5 October Verdi wrote to Boito:

I have finished the fourth act, and I breathe again. I was having some difficulty avoiding too many recitatives (*i troppi recitativi*) and to find some rhythms [and] some phrases for so many broken-up (*spezzati*) and unrhymed lines (*versi sciolti*) . . . [But after my textual alterations] there are a few disconnected lines for which you will have to supply the connection . . . I'm transcribing the whole scene as I have now put it to music.

(*CVB*, I, 85; trans. partially from Budden 1981: III, 319; for Verdi's textual changes, see p. 44 above.)

Verdi retouched the draft of Act IV – improved the 'disconnected lines' and probably also added three lines at the beginning of Otello's final monologue, which now began 'Niun mi tema' – during or shortly after another visit from Boito on 16 October. The opera was now completely drafted. Boito had been close at hand, readily available for consultation, during each of the three periods of composition: March 1884, December 1884–April 1885, September–October 1885.

Verdi began orchestrating Act IV at once. This entailed the initial entering of a 'skeleton score' onto the orchestral paper (typically the voice and bass-line: a copying – and simultaneous revising – of the earlier draft) and a later filling-in of the inner parts. (It is unknown whether any previously drafted portion of the opera had yet been copied out in skeleton score.) On 27 October 1885, to Boito: 'I am still working with the fourth act, which I want to finish completely, including the instrumentation, in order to seal it shut and not speak of it any more until . . . until . . . ' (*CVB*, I, 92). Thus the bulk of Act IV was composed in late September and early October and probably orchestrated by the first weeks of November, before his move to Genoa later in that month. He may have done little or no work on the opera in December, although he was beginning to be bombarded with letters from singers, impresarios, and businessmen about the new opera. Boito seems to have been nearby at the beginning of the new year, and we soon hear of Verdi's activity once again. With Act IV now 'finished', he turned at various points during the first five months of 1886 to the task of orchestrating – and revising and polishing where necessary – two portions of the score: the Act III *concertato* with its surrounding music; and most of Act I, which he had already determined to revise as early as 14 January, although the actual revision was carried out two months later (*CVB*, I, 95). During this January–May 1886 period we hear nothing of Act

II and the first portion of Act III. These sections were apparently not to proceed much further than the skeleton-score stage, if indeed they had even come that far.

On 11 January 1886, for instance, Verdi wrote to Boito about some lines in Act III, before the *concertato* (*CVB*, I, 93–4; see p. 45 above). Further evidence of creative work comes from Emanuele Muzio, who visited Verdi in Genoa in early 1886. The composer played much of *Otello* for him, and the delighted Muzio wrote to Ricordi on 28 January:

> The Maestro is very absorbed right now and is putting into score the quintet with chorus that comes after the insult that Otello makes to Desdemona in the presence of everybody [*sic*: obviously the *concertato*, although for the majority of its most developed sections the ensemble is a sextet with chorus]. Along with the internal choir that Boito heard [the Act II Homage Chorus?] and the Jealousy Duet between Otello and Iago ['Sì, pel ciel' at the end of Act II], it is one of the most beautiful pieces. You will hear how much novelty there is, how much passion, vigour, and tears there are. *Salce! Salce! Salce!* in the fourth act [Willow Song] gives one shivers and makes one cry.   (Ab., IV, 277)

Verdi, now also occupied with the selection of singers for his new opera (see Chapter 5), pressed onwards with the orchestration. By early March 1886 he was working on the troublesome Act I. Once again – as so often during periods of composition or revision – Boito paid a visit to Verdi, as did Muzio, who wrote to Ricordi on 14 March, 'Boito entered the Maestro's room when he was at the pianoforte and was letting me hear for the second time the duet-finale of the first act – the only piece that I [or 'he', i.e. Boito] hadn't yet heard because he just finished it in these last few days' (Ab., IV, 279). Thus it was the Love Duet that had been bothering the composer in Act I, and he subjected it to a major revision in early March 1886. (His fears about the proposed singer for Otello, Francesco Tamagno – see pp. 97–8 below – seem not to have been an issue in the revision.) It may be that only at this time did Verdi decide to excise the gloating lines for the eavesdropping Iago near the end (see p. 30 above; significantly, in the manuscript libretto the lines are not crossed out, which would suggest that their removal was not the result of an early decision). But we know nothing specific about the first version, save that its text, apart from the Iago passage, must have been virtually identical with that of the final version: the few Love Duet textual changes in the manuscript libretto are probably precompositional and are small and non-structural – the alteration

Ex. 6a

of a word or line here and there. It would appear, then, that substantial portions of the first draft of the duet are embedded in the revised version. These would include the crucial 'Bacio' idea, which must have been similar since it recurs in Act IV, and since the autograph score at that later point shows no signs of significant revision.

Curiously, the version of the March 1886, revised Love Duet that Verdi first wrote into his autograph score – perhaps as late as May or June 1886 – still differed in several details from the final version. Otello's passage, 'Pingea dell'armi il fremito' (98/1/1), for example, was originally set to different music. Only its first two measures are recoverable on the original fol. 100ᵛ (Example 6a), over which Verdi later pasted his revised version; the remaining pages of the original passage were removed and replaced.[2] And in this early, spring 1886 stage, the duet – and hence the act – did not yet end with the reprise of the *divisi* cellos playing the 'Già nella notte densa' phrase. The earlier ending, still clearly visible in the autograph score, fols. 112ᵛ–13, featured a gentle harp descent, echoed with woodwind responses, all under softly trilling violins (Example 6b). A somewhat similar effect, with a slightly accelerated tempo, would be used several years later to end Act III Part I of *Falstaff*. (For another, later change in the duet, see pp. 71–2 below.)

Ex. 6b

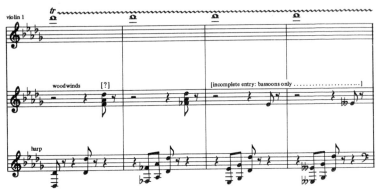

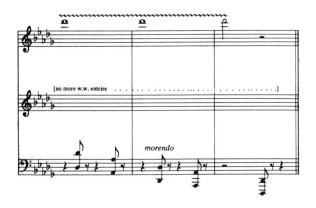

In early May 1886 (and back at Sant'Agata), we find Verdi worrying over two portions of Act I, clearly an act that was progressing
very slowly: a brief phrase for Iago (8 May) and the final form of
Otello's 'Esultate!' entrance in the same act, finally determined at
this time (14 May; see pp. 45–6 above). Verdi was still orchestrating
the first act during his customary summer trip to Montecatini, from
24 June to 13 July, and nearly completed his work there. As he later
(7 August) wrote to Ricordi: '[At Montecatini] I *did* work – certainly not to the point of killing myself, but enough. If only I had
stayed there another three days I would have finished the
instrumentation of the first act! And there are certainly plenty of

notes in that wretched Act I!' (unpublished; Parma). Back at Sant'Agata Verdi wrote to Boito (17 July) that he planned to check much of his work: 'Tomorrow I hope to have the drive to leaf through and review what has been done' (*CVB*, I, 108). Boito himself had two brief additions for Act III to propose on 21 and 25 July (see pp. 46–7 above). As the autograph score reveals, Verdi responded to the first by expanding from nine to twenty the number of bars between Otello's 'Questa giustizia tua mi piace' (255/1/1) and the choral 'Viva!' (257/1/1). Originally, a briefer Otello–Iago dialogue was held over off-stage trumpets, and the seven bars before 'Viva!' (256/2/3ff) were texted, 'Iago, fin d'ora mio capitan t'eleggo', etc. Thus the preceding parallel six-three chords, 'Ma ad evitar sospetti' (255/4/2) and the eight bars leading into them, 'A Cassio / Jago provvederà' (255/1/2) are late musical interpolations. For the second addition, the passage beginning 'Come sei mesta' (261/3/3), Verdi composed seven new bars for Emilia and Desdemona as Otello reads the ambassadors' letter, and he slightly revised the music into and out of the interpolation, most notably Iago's 'Messere, son lieto di vedervi' (262/1/4).

Notwithstanding these tinkerings, work on the opera had slowed down. In the last week of July 1886 Franco Faccio visited Sant'Agata to hear the new opera and, especially, to determine whether the part of Desdemona was suitable for the soprano he had been urging, Romilda Pantaleoni – with whom he was in love. On 7 August Verdi informed Ricordi: 'Faccio was here – but we are still at the *status quo* . . . The worst thing is that I've done nothing since I returned from Montecatini! It's almost been a month!!!' (unpublished; Parma). Faccio's 14 August letter to Ricordi confirms the state of the opera's completion at the beginning of the month:

It's not possible to tell you here about the music for *Otello*, which I now know almost entirely, and which I heard with the emotion that you can easily imagine. The elevated idea must not be contained within the brief limits of a letter . . . [In late July–early August] he still had things to do . . . But it is the task of instrumentation, not composition. At the time that I had the misfortune of leaving the Maestro, there remained very little for him to complete in the orchestration of the first act, but almost all of the instrumentation of the second and third remained to be done. The last, the marvellous last act, is completely finished, and one could say that it emerged from Verdi's mind completely orchestrated, so genial and spontaneous is the compositon.   (unpublished; Ricordi Arch.)

Thus in August 1886 Verdi still had a great deal of work before him, even if – and this is uncertain – he had already laid out the skeleton scores of Acts II and III. Urged onwards by Ricordi, Verdi probably returned briefly to the orchestration of the end of Act I (including the 'new' Love Duet retouchings?) and passed on to the much more extensive work with the second and third acts in the ensuing weeks, although there is no mention of this activity in the existing documents.

An important collection of newly available, still largely unpublished letters from Verdi to Ricordi, now housed in the Biblioteca Palatina in Parma,[3] permits us to chronicle both Verdi's completion of the opera over the next months and the stages of Ricordi's production of the first vocal score. (The letters also furnish a wealth of new details about the selection of singers: see Chapter 5 below.) The essential facts are these. On 29–30 August Ricordi visited Sant'Agata with Romilda Pantaleoni, and it seems likely that at this time, in addition to some Act I and III libretto-questions to be passed on to Boito (see p. 47 above), Verdi gave the editor the autograph score of Act IV (only). The fourth act was thus the first portion of the score to be deemed finished. Back in Milan Ricordi had a complete copy made (now lost) of the score, began to have some of the parts extracted, and assigned the task of reducing the opera to a vocal score to Michele Saladino, who was also a well-established professor of composition (since 1870) at the Milan Conservatory. Saladino began work on Act IV on 8 September.

In the meantime Verdi had not been idle. On 7 September he announced to Ricordi that he was virtually finished with Act I and the concluding part (only) of Act III (the large scene after the Trio, including the *concertato*). Tongue in cheek, he proposed a dramatic delivery:

Saturday morning [11 September 1886] at 9.05 either I or someone sent by me will be in Piacenza with the package, etc. Let's understand each other: when the person you send sees someone with a large package he can ask him: 'Are you from the Maestro?' And he, 'Are you from Casa Ricordi?', etc. In this package you will find all of the first act, and [*e*, not *a*, as printed] all of scene vi of the third act! Eternal God! So many notes!!! thus your copyist will have much to work on. And I shall rest for four or five days, because one's eyesight tires looking at those damned scores with 32 staves – and mine is really tired. Wire me if everything is all right for Saturday.

(*VR*, 49)

By this point *Otello*-work at Casa Ricordi was in full swing. Still with only Act IV in hand, the editor wrote to Verdi on 9 September:

'Everybody is in good spirits: some remember having made the first copy of *Aida*, some of the *Mass*, others of *Un ballo in maschera*, etc.

In short, in four days they have made a copy of the [Act IV] score, the singers' parts for the reducer, Desdemona's part, and they have extracted the string parts!' (*VR*, 49). On 11 September Ricordi sent his chief copyist, 'Garegnani' (Carlo Carignani, the future reducer of *Falstaff*?), to Piacenza to receive Act I and what Verdi on the same day (in an unpublished letter to Ricordi) called a 'large part' of Act III (perhaps more than Scene vi?). Garegnani also returned to Verdi his now-copied manuscript of Act IV. The composer apparently glanced through the final act again: the next day he instructed Ricordi to make a few corrections in the copied score at the point where Otello kisses the sleeping Desdemona (*VR*, 49). On 15 September the editor sent him Saladino's Act IV reduction for approval and correction. Verdi made the necessary corrections immediately, and by 20 September Ricordi was able to give the reduction to the engravers (*VR*, 50). (Saladino's Act IV reduction, with corrections in Verdi's hand, still exists in the Ricordi Archives. As will be seen, it is the only complete source of one early version of the Willow Song.) In late September Giulio Ricordi and his wife, Giuditta, visited the *maestro*, who took a much-needed pause in his work at this time. Throughout all of this activity, Verdi had still retained – and, one presumes, had continued to orchestrate – the unfinished Act II and the first part of Act III.

During his visit to Sant'Agata the editor had apparently convinced Verdi to make a mid-October trip to Milan, in order to help plan the scenic and musical details of the *Otello* premiere during the next La Scala Carnevale season. On 10 October, one day after his seventy-third birthday and two days after acknowledging receipt of the Act III finale reduction, Verdi announced to Ricordi: 'I have finished the third act, and I will bring it to Milan with me. I was also hoping to bring the second with me, but I have not worked very much in these last few days, and I won't work either today or tomorrow' (unpublished; Parma). Verdi arrived in Milan for a three-day visit on the evening of 14 October. From information in subsequent letters, we may conclude that in this 'third instalment' the composer was able to deliver not only the first part of Act III but also a substantial part, at least the first half, of Act II: Ricordi, for instance, queried Verdi on 19 October about a small point in the Act II Homage Chorus (see p. 47 above).

While learning the role of Desdemona, Romilda Pantaleoni was the *maestro*'s guest for two weeks, from 17 to 28 October (see p. 93 below). During this time Verdi continued to correct *Otello* material sent by Ricordi: for example, the printed proofs of the fourth act, from 18 to 21 October. And, hearing the role sung daily, he altered a few of Desdemona's phrases to suit Pantaleoni. On the 18th he wrote Ricordi that 'I haven't [yet] decided with Pantaleoni what would be best in the two *refrains* [of the Willow Song]' (*VR*, 51). On the 21st: 'I'm returning the printed [proofs of the] fourth act and a little separate slip of the [Willow] Song, where the *refrain* has been changed. I have gone ahead and changed the colours and accents on the notes of the *Salce, salce, salce*, and they will be more effective' (*VR*, 51). As Saladino's manuscript reduction shows (fols. 21–2), Verdi was modifying the originally varied refrain of the second strophe, shown in Example 7, to make it identical with that of the first. Thus he decided to make the first two varied strophes largely congruent before embarking on a radically disintegrative third strophe (see p. 142 below). His 'Salce!' changes concerned the first strophe, in which the first set of the three exclamations (329/1/5–329/2/3) originally began triple-*pianissimo* and swelled to a *forte* with diminuendo on the third 'Salce!' (fols. 17ᵛ–18; see p. 73, Ex. 11b below). Additional significant changes in the Willow Song would follow in January 1887.

Moreover, it was while rehearsing Pantaleoni that Verdi decided to transpose the Act II Quartet down a half-step, from B major to B♭ major (see p. 55 above). The newly available correspondence makes it clear that by 23 October Ricordi had returned to him the section of the autograph manuscript that contained the Act II Quartet. On that date Verdi, requesting the preceding, sixth fascicle of the manuscript as well, wrote that 'the seventh fascicle of Act II is not enough, because I want to make the transposition of a step [begin] earlier . . . ' (unpublished; Parma). Tornaghi sent off the requested material on 25 October. From corrections and erasures in the autograph score one may determine exactly which portion of the opera was affected: Verdi transposed a half-step lower a sixty-one-bar block of music that begins twenty-five bars before the Quartet (at the *Allegro agitato*, Desdemona's 'Perchè torbida suona', 156/1/1, which was originally underscored by an F-major, not an E-major, six-four chord) and ends a few measures after the Quartet proper, at Iago's '[Ciò s'a-]sconda' (170/3/1: Verdi also recomposed the last three bars). It seems clear that the transposition was made not for any overriding theoretical or structural

Ex. 7

reason, but to suit Pantaleoni, perhaps to turn a number of her high $c\flat^3$s into $b\flat^2$s (it may also be worth pointing out that the part of Otello in the Quartet also contained two high $c\flat^3$s), or, more likely, to produce that magnificent low $b\flat$ – the lowest note in her part – at the beginning of the Quartet (158/1/4; Hepokoski 1987).

Also of interest in Verdi's letter of 23 October is the confession that he has not yet completed the opera: 'I have not yet done any of the instrumentation that remains for me to do' (unpublished; Parma) – probably the last portions of Act II. On 24 October: 'Today the whole day [was] lost orchestrating *Otello*' (Ab., IV, 293). And on the 26th, also sending back the printed proofs of Act I and Saladino's manuscript reduction of the Act III Trio, 'I hope to be able to orchestrate a little bit today – but who knows?' (unpublished; Parma). Pantaleoni left Sant'Agata on the 28th, and four days later, the last orchestral touches on Act II having been completed, Verdi made the now-famous announcement to Boito: 'It's finished! All honour to us! (and to *Him*!! [Shakespeare? or Otello?]). Farewell' (*CVB*, I, 117; trans. Budden, III, 322). On the same day, 1 November, he sent a more extended, practical letter to Ricordi:

I'm writing to tell you that *Otello* is completely finished!! Really finished!!! Finally!!!!!!!!! I don't dare send it [i.e., the final portions of Act II] to you by mail because there are too many new fascicles, and it would be a terrible misfortune if they were lost! Let's do as we did before. Send Garigagni [sic] to Fiorenzuola. Let's establish it for Wednesday, the 3rd. I myself will be in Fiorenzuola at 2 and we would have had a good half-hour to chat together (*confabulare*) if necessary.   (Ab., IV, 294–5)

To recapitulate, Verdi accomplished the *Otello* orchestration at different periods from late October 1885 (beginning with Acv IV) to 1 November 1886 and relinquished it in four instalments: Act IV (29–30 August 1886, to Ricordi at Sant'Agata); Act I and the last portion of Act III (11 September, to 'Garegnani' in Piacenza); the remaining (first) portion of Act III and the first part of Act II (14–16 October, to Ricordi in Milan); and the remaining portion of Act II (3 November, to 'Garegnani' in Fiorenzuola).

In the next two months Verdi and Ricordi kept up a lively correspondence (again, most of which has only recently come to light) concerning both the composer's continued revision of passages in the vocal-score proofs and the preparations for the La Scala premiere. (For his rehearsing of Tamagno and Maurel during this period, see Chapter 5.) Although the proofs that Verdi altered during this November–December 1886 period have been lost – unlike, say, the similar proofs for *Falstaff* six years later (Hepokoski 1983: 45–52) – the available correspondence reveals a composer concerned with maximizing the effects of the smallest details of the score. Equally important, the letters testify to Ricordi's patient willingness to delay, modify or entirely redo the engraving of the plates. The vocal score that emerged in early 1887, although not flawless, was carefully considered, produced as lovingly and carefully as possible, and checked and double-checked by Verdi and Ricordi. Some of the most provocative of the proof-changes mentioned in the correspondence are:

4 November: the alteration of Iago's Act II 'Ardua impresa sarebbe' (184/1/2) into its present arch-like contour (omitted from Verdi's 4 November 1886 letter in Ab., IV, 298).

11 November: Verdi's uncertainty about the climactic line, 'Quella vil cortigiana che è la sposa d'Otello' at the conclusion of the Act III Desdemona–Otello duet (225/1/1–4). 'I have set that line twenty times and I can't find the right notes – and maybe I won't find them. But who knows? Maybe I'll need Boito's help. We'll see in Milan [during the Tamagno rehearsals]' (Ab., IV, 299). Portions of an early vocal setting, partially restorable from the autograph score, fols. 241ᵛ–2, are shown in Example 8.[4]

15–16 November: the rewriting of a significant portion of the concluding Otello–Iago duet, 'Sì, pel ciel', in Act II. On 13 November Ricordi mentioned that he would refrain from having the corresponding pages of Act II engraved until the revision was made: clearly the modification was a substantial one. He sent off the relevant portion of the Act II autograph score on 15 November and Verdi returned it, corrected, on the 16th (Ab., IV, 299). The original version is unknown. (The composer would return to this troublesome duet in early May 1887 for a major post-premiere revision: see pp. 77–8 below.)

2 December (back at Sant'Agata after rehearsing Tamagno in Milan): the rewriting of the 'Tu alfin, Clemenza' passage (probably six or seven bars, beginning 230/2/2) in Otello's Act III solo, 'Dio! mi potevi scagliar tutti i mali'. 'I don't think the gain is dramatic, but something musical – *more continuity* (*fila di più*). It doesn't change the tempo. And it's good that the violins take up the phrase with which Otello's Song ends ['che

Ex. 8

mi fa lieto']: then it becomes faster. So tell Faccio to have this passage given to Tamagno, and if it is satisfactory (it couldn't be unsatisfactory), send me back the fascicle [of the autograph score] and I'll orchestrate it' (*VR*, 54). A portion of the earlier version is restorable from the autograph score, fol. 249^v (Example 9).[5]

2 December: the insertion of an additional 'è quello', Otello's fearful recognition of the handkerchief in the Act III Trio (244/2/3) (*VR*, 54); and the cutting of two bars immediately preceding the entrance of the off-stage trumpets after the Act III Trio (just after 250/4/3), along with the addition of a 'Bada' or two for Iago, the last of which now dovetails with the trumpet entrance, fol. 278 (251/1/1). Although Verdi's description of the latter change is unclear (*VR*, 54), the autograph score seems clearly to reveal the actual correction.

Ex. 9

8 December: a revision of the harmony near the beginning of the
Act I Love Duet, under the words 's'estingue ogni clamor'
(95/1/ 3–4), in order to make it 'more correct' (unpublished;
Parma). The probable original harmony, inferable from
erasures on fol. 96 of the autograph score, is shown in Example
10.

15 December (immediately after auditioning Maurel): the addition
of Iago's malevolent lines at the end of the Act II Homage
Chorus (see p. 47 above; undated in Ab., IV, 303; dating in
CVB, II, 356).

The most provocative and audible modifications that Verdi made in
the *Otello* score just before the premiere, however, seem to have
been accomplished during the January rehearsals in Milan: more
significant alterations in the Willow Song.[6] The composer might

Ex. 10

have had these changes in mind when he informed Ricordi from Sant'Agata, where he was making a brief, post-Christmas trip on 29 December: 'I would like to arrive [in Milan] a day or two before my rehearsals begin, because I would like to give (for my part) some things (*passare alcune cose*) to Pantaleoni without anyone knowing about it – not even Faccio' (unpublished; Parma). The alterations – strokes of genius – principally involved: the replacement of an earlier, simple three-note upbeat at the beginning of the Willow Song melody (and at many – but not all – of its recurrences) with the far more expressive, florid anacrusis that we know today; a rewriting of some of the accompaniment, most notably to the first strophe; and a small but telling change in the orchestral postlude. Ricordi must have been surprised to learn that the revisions would require no fewer than five plates of the vocal score (which he had considered finished on 30 December 1886) to be re-engraved: pp. 324, 325, 328, 329, and 330, all of which do indeed display evidence of re-engraving in the first edition (anomalous engraver's letters at the bottom of the pages). The earlier version is preserved in Saladino's Act IV manuscript reduction and is confirmed by still-visible erasures in the autograph score.

Example 11a shows the earlier beginning of the act in Saladino's reduction. (Verdi also extended the introduction by adding two bars at its end, the minim descent from C♯ to the same pitch an octave lower. Originally, the introduction ended with the first C♯ at 325/5/1, and the curtain was to rise five bars earlier, with the second appearance of the open-fifth minims, at 325/3/4.) Example 11b shows the earlier opening of the first strophe, with its more conven-

Ex. 11a

Ex. 11b

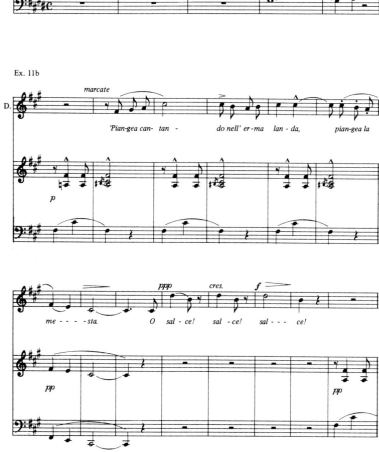

Ex. 11c

tional, syncopated accompaniment (for the 'Salce!' dynamics, see p. 66 above). Example 11c shows the beginning of the second strophe, whose second bar had to be expanded into two bars to accommodate the longer upbeat. The accompaniment later in the strophe was also revised. The revisions of the three-note upbeats cease abruptly midway through this strophe: the line beginning 'e dalle ciglie' (331/1/1) retains the 'original' anacrusis. Thus the florid upbeats seek and revert to their elemental shape. And Example 11d shows the relevant portion of the original postlude. In his correction Verdi lifted the a♮ in the English-horn–clarinet–horn inner voice in the fifth bar up a major third, thus eliminating the A♯–a♮ clash and producing that unforgettable, hollow open fifth–open fourth between the upper voices (337/3/1). He also altered the parallel passage eight bars later: the present flute g♯[1] (337/5/1) was originally a third lower, e[1].

Verdi seems to have taken a special interest in this Willow Song

Ex. 11d

throughout the composition of *Otello*, perhaps because of the inevitable parallels that would be drawn with the corresponding song in Rossini's opera, one of its most successful moments. It was here, and in the subsequent 'Ave Maria', that Verdi must have felt most acutely the shadow of the past master. We know of no evidence to prove that he conceived his Willow Song either 'in competition' with or as an act of homage to Rossini. But given his own sense of being the last great master of the Italian lyrical-vocal tradition – now dying, along with 'povera Barbara' – it seems reasonable to suppose that this moment of the opera was a particularly sensitized passage that he wished to handle as carefully as possible. The retouchings of the refrain and 'Salce' in October 1886 and the masterly final January 1887 revisions impress us as valedictory labours of the highest love.

4 Compositional afterthoughts and revisions: Milan, Venice and Paris

With the new Willow Song pages re-engraved, as seems likely, in January 1887, the now-completed first vocal score was bound and prepared for publication (plate number 51023, 364 pp.). The earliest copies bear the blind stamp 1/1887 (see, e.g., Hopkinson 1978: II, 156–7), although the score was not released for sale, or even deposited in the required national libraries, until 6 and 7 February, the days immediately following the 5 February premiere. Ricordi followed this in October with the important four-volume printed orchestral score, for rental only (pl. no. 52214, 365 pp., 'stampato in luogo di manoscritto', a new, 'modern' format reflecting the growth and sophistication of the firm). The actual printing of the orchestral score was accomplished not in Milan, but in Leipzig, by G. Röder – of course, with the Ricordi imprint. Plans for having it printed, *alla moderna*, were well under way by March 1887, and by 18 May Ricordi wrote Verdi (unpublished) that he would soon be able to send him some orchestral proofs from the first act. The *libroni* records in the Ricordi Archives provide a 9 July 1887 date for the orchestral score: this would normally be the date on which engraving work was begun, but here the date seems clearly later. In any event, Ricordi sent Verdi an early copy of the printed orchestral score on 12 October (unpublished letter), and, most significantly, Verdi praised it on 16 October: 'The printed orchestral score is beautiful! It only lacks a few errors to be perfect' (unpublished; Parma). The first orchestral score, in fact, is not flawless, but because it differs in so many small details from the autograph score – individual words of text, phrasings, articulations, and so on, all of which can give rise to fierce editorial and performance dilemmas – it is important to realize that Verdi was consulted during its proof-stages and ultimately gave it his blessing.

In the period immediately surrounding the first performances in February Verdi made two additional, definitive changes. Both are traceable primarily through modifications made in subsequent issues of the vocal score. The first, which probably reflects a decision made during the January rehearsals, and hence one sung at the premiere, involves a single bar early in the Act I Love Duet, Desdemona's '[In quei spa-]venti e coll'estasi in cor' (97/4/2). Verdi had mistakenly set slightly differing words, 'In quei spaventi e coll'estasi nel cor', and this line had been printed in the first edition of the vocal score. As Boito might have pointed out, the problem was one of text. The first setting, Example 12a, implied an unorthodox 12-syllable line with *tronco* ending, out of place in a quatrain of *endecasillabi*. (Notice also the false accent produced by the *tenuto* e^2 on the 'improper' second syllable of 'estasi'.) The new version, Example 12b, which returns to the correct text, drops a syllable by the principle of elision (*sinalèfe*), joining the final vowel of 'estasi' with the first of 'in'. The precise date of the change is unclear. Verdi's autograph score, however, contains the revision in the 'January 1887' violet ink (see p. 191 above) over the erased original version on fol. 100^v. The earliest printed edition of which I am aware that contains the new reading is a vocal score in the Santa Cecilia Conservatory Library, Rome, with blind stamp 5/1887, but Casa Ricordi failed to reproduce it consistently in all of its other, later editions. The revision does appear, for instance, in the first French edition (7/1887) and all of the subsequent Italian scores (such as the 'Edizione unica', 8/1897), but the Italian–German and Italian–English editions (both 7/1887) remained unchanged. To make matters worse, the original reading was mistakenly retained in the first printed orchestral score – an error that neither Ricordi nor Verdi discovered. The rejected, early reading was thence transferred into the first orchestral score published for sale (1913, pl. no. 113955). The result, of course, has been further confusion in the later editions. Example 12b is doubtless Verdi's last word on the matter.[1]

The second, more substantial, alteration occurred nearly three months after the premiere: the recomposition of eighteen bars of accompaniment (only) in the final portion of the Act II Otello–Iago

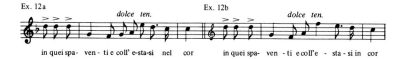

Ex. 12a   Ex. 12b

in quei spa- ven - ti e coll' e-sta-si nel cor   in quei spa- ven - ti e coll'e - sta - si in cor

duet. The passage affected begins on the downbeat of the reprise, where the two first join their voices, '[Sì, pel] ciel' (197/3/2), and ends mid-phrase, after Otello's '[questa] man ch'io' (200/3/1). The final fourteen bars of the act are identical in both versions. Although Verdi's motivation for the revision is unknown, two letters show that he rewrote this passage in the first days of May 1887 for the forthcoming 17 May Venetian premiere. (In the interim *Otello* had also been performed in Rome.) Having already received at some earlier date the relevant portion of the autograph manuscript, he wrote on 29 April to Ricordi, 'I had forgotten about the fascicle of Act II of *Otello*! I'll do it, I'll do it – although unwillingly!' (*VR*, 60). And on 2 May:

Today I send you the *stretta* of the Finale of the second [act]. Of course (*ben inteso*) now the first will become better (*ora diventerà migliore il primo*). Mind that it is performed in Venice. And tell Faccio not to say anything to anyone, so that maybe nobody will realize it. Unless this is done, *they will howl* that I have redone *Otello*!!   (*VR*, 60)

Verdi's claim that he was making the revision 'unwillingly (*a malincuore*)' may refer to a preference for the version that he was about to discard (perhaps because of some difficulties that he had perceived in its execution or vocal–orchestral balance), or, more likely, it may be no more than one of his habitual complaints about taking up work again. The second letter reveals a touchy composer fearing that public knowledge of a revision could lead to a charge of compositional weakness or indecision. Ricordi's effectiveness in suppressing the rejected version was far from complete. The early version remained unaltered in the Italian and Italian–English vocal scores for decades (perhaps until the 'Ripristino 1944' edition), although the currently available vocal scores do print the revision. All printed orchestral scores, of course, carried the revision. The brilliant effect of the early version may be sampled from its opening bars, Example 13 (bars 2ff). In the 'Venice' revision Verdi replaced the blocklike hammering figure with a more rhythmically complex accompaniment (in many ways an intensification of the orchestration found at the beginning of the duet) featuring brutal accents on the second beat and a forward-driving syncopated figure in the horns.

During the last stages of its composition, Ricordi and Verdi had assumed that *Otello* would soon be performed in French at the Opéra. The translation had been worked on by Boito (and

Solanges) and Du Locle from ca. November 1886 to mid-April 1887. In mid-March 1887, shortly after the *Otello* premiere at La Scala, Ricordi pressed the composer on the point of the obligatory ballet for Paris (which Boito and Verdi had earlier decided to place in the Act II Homage Chorus) for inclusion into the French score, and, if possible, into the printed (Italian) orchestral score. Ricordi had even given him some authentic seventeenth-century (!) dances as a spur to his imagination. On 25 March Verdi reacted negatively, sensing the absurdity of a mere entertainment in this tightly-packed score:

> With regard to the ballet, or better, the *divertissement*, why print it? It's a concession (a *lâcheté*) that the authors wrongly make to the Opéra. But artistically speaking, it's a monstrosity. To interrupt the furious action with a ballet?!!! The opera must stand as it is; therefore it's useless to print the ballet. (Ab., IV, 329)

Nevertheless, he agreed to think about it and asked Ricordi to find more dances, preferably from a later period. At about the same time he learned from Muzio in Paris that the Opéra, having had doubts about the most likely candidate, Rose Caron, was hard put to find an acceptable Desdemona. This was the last straw. On 2 April, to Muzio: 'I ask you formally, in my name, to notify the sainted (*SS.*) Directors of the Opera that from this moment all the *Otello* negotiations are broken off' (Ab., IV, 330). The ballet project now seemed more abstract and unnecessary than ever. After a few half-hearted attempts to examine more early dances sent to him on 15 April 1887 by the Italian musicologist Oscar Chilesotti, Verdi abandoned the task. Ricordi published the first French vocal score in July 1887 without ballet – it was simply the Italian score translated into French (pl. no. 51635, with 365 pages, one more than in the Italian score: two bars in the Act III *concertato*, those originally appearing on p. 296, were re-engraved on two separate pages).

The matter of an *Otello* performance at the Opéra lay dormant for over six years. Interest in a Parisian *Otello* revived when the Opéra broached the subject with a message to Ricordi in early September 1893. Despite Verdi's initial refusals, Ricordi visited Paris from 20 to 30 October 1893 and probably conferred cautiously with Pierre (Pedro) Gailhard, the principal Director of the Opéra, at this time. Even in these tentative, early stages, however, Gailhard had made it clear that he wanted some modifications made

Ex. 13

in the French libretto. By the beginning of 1894 a French performance, probably still planned for the relatively distant future, spring
1895, was a concrete possibility. On 13 January Verdi received a
letter from Gailhard again expressing dissatisfaction with the existing French libretto (*CVB*, II, 443) and now proposing a new translation that he had had made for the recitative and Willow Song at

the opening of Act IV. Sensing a potential scandal, Verdi referred the matter at once to Boito, who saved the situation by agreeing with Gailhard (18 January 1894; *CVB*, I, 222–3). At this point Boito and Du Locle began to revise other portions of the libretto as well. Thus the new, 1894 French vocal score would contain many textual alterations from the version published in 1887.

Wishing to capitalize on the excitement of the triumphant French *Falstaff* at the rival Opéra-Comique (Verdi himself had been in Paris from 4 to 25 April 1894 to supervise the rehearsals and attend the 18 April premiere), Gailhard and his co-Director, Eugène Bertrand, began to push for a production of *Otello* in October of that year. This would require rapid, efficient preparation. Boito informed Verdi of the new plans (always subject to his approval) on 11 May (*CVB*, I, 227–8): the new translation, he said, was virtually completed. After receiving the composer's sanction, it would be sent off to Du Locle for minor additions. And Mme Caron, mentioned Boito, now seemed in good voice. Boito came to Sant'Agata on 17 May to discuss the 'new' libretto, which by this time also included some important changes in the text of the Act III *concertato* (see below). Further negotiations followed in the subsequent weeks, and after his requisite grumbling Verdi seems to have agreed to the entire project – and, of course, to the necessity of composing a ballet, which he and Boito, probably during one of their several meetings in early 1894, had now decided should be inserted into Act III, as an adjunct to the arrival of the ambassadors. Thus on 6 June, immediately upon his return from a trip to Milan to discuss *Otello* with Gailhard, Ricordi, and Boito, the composer wrote to Ricordi: 'Don't forget to find some songs, some Cypriot dances, etc.' (*CVB*, II, 452, 454). Chilesotti was to be consulted again, as would be Giovanni Tebaldini and several others, but the scholars, as will emerge, found nothing to satisfy him.

In the meantime he had decided upon a more significant revision for the French *Otello*: a radical shortening, orchestral thinning, and nearly total recomposition of the lengthy Act III *concertato* – the ensemble that had given him and Boito so much trouble in the initial formulation of its text. The problem with the earlier version of the ensemble, as Julian Budden points out (III, 406), was one of ensuring that the audience would understand Iago's two embedded dialogues, both essential to the plot, but both overwhelmed by the complexity and sheer size of the surrounding ensemble. The 1887 production book (*DS*, pp. 79–82) had addressed the problem by counselling explicit stage action to draw the audience's attention to Iago and by demanding a clearly enunciated *mezza voce* delivery of the dialogues. But it is evident that the early performances must have failed to satisfy Verdi. On 3 February 1889, in preparation for a La Scala revival of *Otello*, Verdi had proposed to Ricordi that the orchestra be softened in bar 38 as Iago's dialogue begins and that the chorus be regrouped: 'And it is just here where one needs to put a void into the orchestra – a void that would be dramatic' (Ab., IV, 371). Six days later, on 9 February, Verdi had again stressed that dramatic values – clarity and comprehensibility – were to supersede purely musical values:

About the Third Act Finale again. Also here there can be neither dramatic truth nor effect if one doesn't manage to isolate Iago completely; in such a way that the public's eyes are turned only towards him, that his words, not his voice, reign over everything – while underneath is heard a murmur that is indistinct and also, if you like, imprecise! Imprecise! This word would make a musician's hair stand on end, but it doesn't matter.   (Ab., IV, 372)

The rewriting of the ensemble for Paris was no mere sop to Parisian custom or inadequate performers; it was an aesthetic decision. We first hear of the revision in a note to Boito from 16 May 1894, in which Verdi mentions having left behind in Genoa the manuscript version of 'the changed lines in the third-act finale' (*CVB*, I, 229). The subject probably also surfaced during his eight-day visit to Milan in late May and early June 1894, and at this time Ricordi probably gave him a copy of the printed orchestral score of Act III as a guide. Verdi returned to Sant'Agata on 6 June and composed the revision in the next few days. As the separate autograph score of this ensemble shows (it is still preserved in the Ricordi Archives in Milan), Verdi wrote the revision to Boito's Italian text, not to French words. He sent it off to Ricordi on 13 June: 'For your information (*per norma*) I am sending with this [letter] the Finale of the Third Act completely orchestrated along with the printed orchestral score' (unpublished; Ricordi Archives). Ricordi had a manuscript reduction made at once for the composer's approval. On 22 June (a letter that he misdated the 23rd) Verdi replied: 'I received the Finale reduction and I hope to be able to return it to you today. There are still some errors in the original score. Meanwhile, I shall fix the reduction [and then] the reduction [*sic*: Verdi clearly means 'the original'] when I come to Milan' (unpublished; Ricordi Archives). On 24 June 1894 Verdi and Giuseppina went to Milan for a week's visit. He probably retouched or corrected the autograph of the new *concertato* at this time. From Milan they travelled directly to their traditional summer cure at Montecatini, where they stayed for two and a half weeks, until 17 July. It was here that Verdi continued to receive fruitless models for the ballet along with the proofs, it seems, of the new ensemble. On 10 July to Ricordi: 'I'm sending back the Act III Finale. It's fine, unless there are a few wrong notes that I am incapable of correcting' (*CVB*, II, 455).

A comparison of the two versions of the A♭ *concertato*, 'A terra! . . . sì . . . nel livido / Fango', raises a number of provocative structural and aesthetic issues. The 1887 version – retained in all modern scores – is one of the most architecturally structured big blocks in the opera. In brief, it divided into three major sections:
(1) Desdemona's solo exposition in three contrasting, lyrical subsections (beginning 271/1/1 and rounded in A♭, although each subsection begins in a different key, A♭, E♭, and F).
(2) The solo quartet passage (274/1/1, moving from an initial A♭ to a momentary tonicization of C♭ at its end – functioning, of course, as an immediate ♭VI of E♭) leading to an interpolation of part of Desdemona's exposition (E♭, 277/1/1) and the ensuing, 'active' plotting of Iago (279/1/1, 'Una parola', largely in E♭ minor). This is followed by a freely varied, expanded repetition of all of the second-section material (285/1/1, now

starting in B♭), in which Iago eventually plots with Roderigo (beginning 290/1/1, 'I sogni tuoi', modulatory).

(3) A *più mosso, forte* ensemble reprise of the initial section
• (301/1/1, a varied full-ensemble *da capo*, whose accelerated tempo suggests the urgency of a traditional *stretta*). It includes the interpolation of material varied from the second section (308/1/1) to 'synthesize' or 'unify' the first and second sections. The entire ensemble, of course, is broken off at the moment of Otello's violent 'Fuggite', 315/1/2: his outburst deflects it from final, tonal closure in A♭. The thematic material of this monumental structure, with its explicit, *in extenso* rounding, may be schematized as: A B C / D B' E – D' C' E' / A' B'', E'' C. (Budden, in 'Time Stands Still', 1981, omits C' from his scheme, considering it a portion of the preceding D'.)[2]

Largely still unknown today (it has received a few recent performances: see Budden, 'Time Stands Still', 1981: 893), the June 1894 revision is considerably shorter, reduced from ninety-six to seventy-five bars: the first two sections were made more concise; the third (the varied *da capo*) remained the same length. The final sixty-five bars of Act III – after the ensemble – were unaffected by the revision. Discounting for the moment the numerous variants of orchestral and vocal detail from the first version, the Paris version may be schematized as: A B / F G B' – H E' / A' B' E'' C. Perhaps the most radical alteration was the removal of the C subsection. 'Quel sol sereno e vivido', from Desdemona's exposition, the first two subsections of which had also been compositionally retouched. (The reader may recall that the C quatrain was an 'extra' quatrain of text that Verdi had at first not planned to use, but included only at the moment of composition itself: see p. 39 above.) But he did not remove it from the reprise, where, somewhat inexplicably from a structural point of view, it still forms the climax at the end of the ensemble – but now with B's text. Even though the C idea is linked by intervallic motives to other ideas, its sudden appearance here at the end seems a structural weakness. On the other hand, one must admit that its retention did have some clear advantages: not only the immediate effect of the melody itself, but also the preservation in the orchestral bass-line (312/1/1, 313/1/1) of an easily recognizable restatement of a similar motive – a *forte* ascent and descent through a fourth – from the Act II conclusion, 'Sì, pel ciel', as a reminder of that fearful oath, the source of the present calamity. Julian Budden defends it still further with the ingenious observation that it 'makes a further breach in the [problematic] sense of stasis by bringing the musical argument forward to a new stage' ('Time Stands Still', 1981: 892). Moreover, as Frits Noske has suggested in a discussion unconcerned with this revision (1977: 141–2), the intervals of this C idea anticipate those of the anacrusis to Desdemona's Willow Song, which will open the next act.

In the 1894 version Iago starts to plot with Otello at the very beginning of the second section (in the early version twelve bars precede the onset of the dialogue). The initial portions of this section were correspondingly recomposed. The original solo quartet melody, for instance, is reduced to mere *piano* motivic work (accompanied lightly by the orchestra) – the musical equivalent of the 'murmur that is indistinct . . . imprecise' that Verdi had longed for in 1889 – while Iago's lines below stand out in higher relief. Throughout, the experience of the *concertato* in *Falstaff*, II.ii, is evident. And similarly, the orchestral and ensemble texture of much of the subsequent Iago–Roderigo dialogue (an extract of which has been published in Budden, III, 407–11) is correspondingly thinned out, lighter, more 'Falstaffian'.

The 1894 version of the *più mosso* reprise begins not with the earlier, overlapped entrances for the chorus, but with a newly added quatrain for Iago, who is now instructed to deliver it 'au milieu de la scène' (centre-stage), with ensemble interjections:

Tous, en ce jour de gloire	Let us all, on this glorious day,
Chassons les noirs courroux!	Drive away our black anger!
L'astre de la Victoire	The star of Victory
Rayonne encor[e] sur nous.[3]	Still shines over us.

The quatrain, curiously enough, is based on lines that many years earlier Boito had assigned to Otello at the end of one of the earliest versions of the *concertato* text: 'Che? nel dì che consacra la vittoria', etc. (see p. 33 above). Their varied revival here (they are repeated by part of the chorus) fits well enough with the surging, cornet- and trumpet-led reprise, also altered to include new suspensions, and the sudden change of mood is less troubling in the mouth of Iago than in that of the desperate Moor: after all, he is deceitfully making a 'public' proclamation to pacify the crowd and is simultaneously driving home its irony to Otello.

Considered as a whole, the 1894 *concertato* is a serious, well composed, aesthetically based revision that addressed what Verdi believed to be flaws in the 1887 version. But is it a definitive change?

Apparently not, for we hear nothing about it after 1894. Although for *Falstaff* Verdi had clearly told Ricordi to include in future Italian scores several revisions made for the 1894 Opéra-Comique production (e.g., 19 January 1894: 'Translate [the new lines] now into Italian, without, understand, adding anything' (Hepokoski 1983: 80ff)), we know of no similar request for this *Otello* revision. Even though Verdi had composed the *Otello* revision in Italian and had given the manuscript score to Ricordi, no Italian edition prepared after the 12 October 1894 performance includes the change. Ricordi did print it, however, in the second edition of the French vocal score – again, pl. no. 51635, but now with 366 pages, including the ballet – which he released for sale in October 1894, simultaneously with the French premiere. But this published appearance cannot be considered definitive: having not yet seen the revision performed, that is, Verdi would not have had time to suppress its publication, should he have wished to do so. Complicating the whole issue somewhat, however, is Ricordi's 1894 French printed orchestral score for rental only, which also includes the revised ensemble. (A copy, apparently much-used – i.e., rented several times after 1894 – still exists in the Ricordi Archives.)[4]

Notwithstanding these 'special' French scores, and given Ricordi's concern during the same period about the variants for the Italian *Falstaff*, the most plausible supposition is that on the basis of the Parisian performance Verdi decided to retain the original version in subsequent Italian scores – the definitive scores – and told this to Ricordi during a personal meeting (one thus undocumented by correspondence): he may, for instance, have been reluctant to give up its monumentality. Without question, however, the revision – in Verdi's original Italian, of course – deserves to be more widely heard and made more easily available to conductors and singers as a reasonable, valid alternative (even if not, perhaps, a demonstrably definitive one). It is, after all, the last piece of sung stage drama that Verdi ever wrote.

In every respect the 1894 ballet was a less significant change that merits less attention. It was not written as an improvement – indeed, Verdi had resisted the idea of a ballet in *Otello* from the beginning. While in Montecatini in early July 1894 he continued to ask Ricordi for more old dances as models. Over the next two weeks the Verdi–Ricordi correspondence is amusingly larded with references to Greek melodies, *furlane*, farandoles (including one by Bizet, probably from *L'Arlésienne*), popular Venetian songs, national anthems, futile consultations with various scholars, and the like. (Many of the letters are translated in Budden, III, 400–1.) Nothing satisfied the crotchety Verdi. Back at Sant'Agata, on 26 July he remembered the orientalisms in Félicien David's 1844 *Le désert*, particularly in a portion that was 'a Hymn to Allah or a Song of the Muezzin' (Abbiati 1959: IV, 550; he had first heard and been impressed by the '*ode-symphonie*' in 1845: see Conati [1980]: 5, 7, 11). Thus he requested Ricordi to send him extracts from it, one of which he in fact used (Budden, III, 401).

Throughout this eccentric summer correspondence one can sense the ballet taking ever clearer shape in Verdi's mind, and it seems likely that he was simultaneously sketching out some musical ideas for it. The whole process must have condensed into some sort of draft in late July 1894, for on the 30th of that month Verdi asked Ricordi to have sent to him 'ten *cahier*[s] of 20[-stave] music paper like the [enclosed] sample' (unpublished; Ricordi Archives) – as usual, paper manufactured by the French company Lard-Esnault. On 5 August he wrote to Tornaghi, Ricordi's secretary: 'I received the Parisian paper, and I thank you. Now (not having the full orchestral score here) I would need a few measures of the full score in order to be able to insert the ballet into it' (*CVB*, II, 456). Within sixteen days the ballet was completed. On 21 August he wrote facetiously to Ricordi:

Today I am sending the registered package of the *Otello* ballet for Paris. Your Doctors of music did not know how to find anything for me – but I found a Greek song from 5000 years before Christ! If the world did not yet exist, so much the worse for the world! Then I found a Muranese that was composed 2000 years ago for a war between Venice and Murano – the Muranese won. It doesn't matter if Venice didn't yet exist.

With this find I composed my splendid ballet, imagining how it must be performed, and I drew up the outlines for it and sent it along attached to the score. In sending the ballet, please send these outlines to Gailhard along with a large orchestral score, so that the Dance Master won't make many people dance when the orchestra plays *piano*, and not many people in the *forte* passages, etc.   (Ab., IV, 552)

Verdi had timed the ballet at 5′ 59″ (the precision is surely intended humorously) and had written this duration on the front cover of his autograph score, above the moderately detailed scenario to which he was referring in the above letter (see Ab., IV, 552–3; facsimile in Weaver [1977], pl. 257). While by no means faultily composed, the ballet is something of an offhand piece, re-evoking earlier ballet styles (such as that for *Aida*) and mining once again the vein of French exoticism. The essential problem, of course, is that its somewhat strained local colour and Gallic diffusion of intensity seem out of place in *Otello*. The new music for the ballet starts as the ambassadors begin to arrive, three measures after Otello's closing order to Iago, 'Sì, qui l'adduci' (256/3/2). New stage directions have informed us that both Iago and Otello exit from the stage a few measures earlier (not Iago alone, as before). With the sounding of the (still 1887) off-stage trumpet fanfares, pages enter bearing gifts into the completely illuminated hall of the castle. They are quickly followed by Lords and Ladies, 'drawn by the fanfares to see the Ambassador disembark'. In the 1894 version the trumpet fanfares last only four bars (the last is recomposed as a C_2^4 transition), and the first of the six sections of the ballet splashes forth with four bars of new fanfares in A major. Heard as a whole, the ballet's sections articulate a broader, fast–slow–fast gesture that is not tonally rounded: the three 'tempo gestures' gravitate around A, E, and G respectively. (A discussion of the individual dances may be found in Budden, III, 402–6.) With the final G-major cadence an off-stage cannon shot leads to a sounding of a unison B♭ triplet in the off-stage trumpets, which dovetails with the original score four measures before the 'Viva! Evviva!' chorus (256/4/1). Thus the entire ballet has replaced a single measure of the 1887 version (256/3/2). New 1894 stage directions direct that 'After the dances Otello and the Ambassadors enter from backstage, preceded by the cortège'.

Surely nobody would claim that the ballet represented anything approaching a definitive change in *Otello*. It was a concession, nothing more, and it does not raise the aesthetic questions posed by the revision of the Act III *concertato*. Even as late as 17 September 1894 – a month after its composition – Verdi complained to Ricordi about its inclusion: 'Ah! It wasn't I at all who asked me to compose a ballet with such a hailstorm of notes! And indeed, *à la rigueur*, as far as I am concerned and for my use, I can do without it!' (Ab., IV, 554). After a few days more of the obligatory Verdian grumbling – for instance, to Ricordi, 19 September: 'I won't go to Paris only to have *my snout* seen, nor to read *my name* in the journals' (Ab., IV, 555) – the composer departed on 26 September to help supervise the rehearsals. The premiere – a great success with Albert Saléza, Victor Maurel, and Rose Caron, and conducted by Paul Taffanel –

took place on 12 October. While in Paris he was also delighted to see another performance of *Falstaff* at the Opéra Comique. He left Paris for Genoa on 22 October 1894. His career in the theatre had now ended.

5 Of singers and staging: Verdi's ideas on performance

Verdi composed *Otello* with concrete images of its realization in mind. From these often detailed conceptions he would admit no exceptions: it is clear that his compositional thinking was 'global', that is, along with purely musical considerations it included the envisioning of an ideal performance (cf. Degrada [1977]: 88, 100–4). For the composer this was the real *Otello*. All of the performances and interpretations that he saw fell short of it, like shadows on the cave-wall – shadows that caused him considerable anguish. He expressed the solidity of this envisioned *Otello* most clearly on 1 January 1889, almost two years after the premiere, as Giulio Ricordi was preparing the first La Scala revival of the work. By no means, he insisted to the editor, can one agree with 'those who claim that one must give in a little to the differing qualities of vocal timbres. No: the interpretation of a work of art is *one thing alone* and cannot be anything but *one thing*' (Ab., IV, 366). Thus in planning for the first *Otello* and in commenting on subsequent performances, at least those with which his name could in some way be linked, he was a dictator to whom all were obliged to pay homage – the *summum judex*, as Ricordi called him (24 August 1887; *VR*, 61).

Many of Verdi's most direct remarks on the performance of *Otello* are critiques of singers or descriptions of the way in which he feared certain roles would be misinterpreted. Preserved in dozens of letters, these comments are best understood within the contexts of the careers and abilities of the three principal singers for the 1887 premiere: Romilda Pantaleoni (Desdemona), Francesco Tamagno (Otello), and Victor Maurel (Iago), all of whom studied their parts with the composer, and the last two of whom recorded excerpts from the opera after Verdi's death. Other comments deal with matters of staging, scenery, and practical performance. Somewhat more oblique, but still authoritative, is the 1887 production book (*disposizione scenica*) compiled by Giulio Ricordi and based on the

(Boito- and Verdi-supervised) La Scala premiere. It includes a brief, important introduction, written by Boito with the warm approval of Verdi, that sketches each character's essence. (A translation of the entire preface may be found in Budden, III, 326–9.) The following discussion of these sources is more exposition than analysis: the typically late-nineteenth-century, Mediterranean character of the ruling ideas, many of which contrast markedly with today's literary, dramatic, and production values, will be dealt with in Chapter 8.

Verdi began thinking about singers for *Otello* in early 1886 following a visit to Genoa from Ricordi and the La Scala impresarios, the brothers Cesare and Enrico Corti, on 17 January. With the opera entirely drafted and Act IV orchestrated, it was evident that its completion was near. The Cortis were eager not only to secure it for their theatre but also to seek advice about which singers to sign for the 1887 *Carnevale* season. As usual, Verdi was cautious, but within two weeks the newspapers were announcing that *Otello* had been promised to La Scala. Because it bore more directly on personalities and reputations, the issue of the singers was to be handled more guardedly. During their January meeting Verdi, the Cortis, and Ricordi had mentioned Angelo Masini and Francesco Tamagno as possible Otellos (*VR*, 64) and, in all probability, Victor Maurel as a likely Iago. Ricordi recalled that he had asked whether Desdemona's part was similar to Aida's, and Verdi had replied, 'Less dramatic' (19 January 1886; *VR*, 64). The keynote for Desdemona had been struck. It was to be a graceful, lyrical role – honest simplicity beautifully sung – and its chief risk would be that of overdramatization. Ricordi had suggested Elena Teodorini or Gemma Bellincioni (Verdi had just abandoned his earlier consideration of Ernestina Bendazzi-Secchi: see his letters of 11 and 14 January 1886, in *CVB*, I, 93–5; II, 337). On 19 January, two days after the Genoa meeting, the editor began strong lobbying for Bellincioni, who was currently singing at La Scala in *Roberto il diavolo*, and about whom he had written to Verdi even earlier. But Verdi received the opposite advice from Boito on 20 January: '[Bellincioni's] voice is pleasant and thin like the person, but it is not a real theatrical voice . . . A shame! but I don't think that Bellincioni was born to be strangled on the island of Cyprus. A shame!' (*CVB*, I, 97–8). Nevertheless, Ricordi persisted in praising her, to the point where Verdi felt obliged to come unobserved to La Scala to judge for himself in mid-February.

In the meantime another candidate for Desdemona had emerged. Romilda Pantaleoni, intimately involved with Franco Faccio, hoped that she would be selected, and her candidacy was also warmly supported by Teresa Stolz and the Cortis (Ab., IV, 291–2; *CVB*, II, 344). Pantaleoni's chief virtues lay not so much in her voice, which could apparently become harsh and penetrating in the upper register – Verdi was also to object to her intonation (29 April 1887; *VR*, 59–60) – but in a solid intelligence governing an ensemble of passionate acting, singing, and nuancing abilities. She had known Boito and Praga during the *scapigliatura* days of the 1860s, and Boito had judged her 1876 Turin performance of Margherita in *Mefistofele* to be 'meravigliosissima' (Nardi 1942: 415). She had more recently sung in *La Gioconda*, in an 1884 La Scala *Les Huguenots* (with Francesco Tamagno), in the revised version of *Le Villi* at La Scala in 1885, and she had created a sensation in the 1885 La Scala premiere of Ponchielli's *Marion Delorme* (again, with Tamagno), a passionate, Hugo-based opera in which, as in *La traviata*, the protagonist is a reformed courtesan. (In 1891 Pantaleoni would triumph as Santuzza in the first La Scala production of *Cavalleria rusticana*.) From the beginning Verdi, with Ricordi, was suspicious, and he frankly told Faccio (as he recalled later) that Pantaleoni was 'an excellent artist in, I'll say, nervous parts, but I [don't] think her suited to the part of Desdemona' (20 April 1887; Ab., IV, 333).

After Verdi had listened to Bellincioni in Acts I and V of *Roberto il diavolo* – those acts alone were performed at La Scala along with a ballet, *Amor*, on 20 February – he immediately authorized the signing of Pantaleoni for the next La Scala season: 'With her and Tamagno you can make up a repertory even without *Otello*' (Ab., IV, 333). Although Verdi felt that he had not yet pledged the role, Pantaleoni felt otherwise: 'So I shall be Desdemona', she wrote to her brother on 27 February (*CVB*, II, 344). Her further Ponchiellian successes did little to encourage Verdi. To Ricordi on 28 June: 'Everybody coming from Rome tells me *Mirabilia* about Pantaleoni in *Delorme*. Everybody! Everybody! A real, extraordinary fanaticism! Alas! The larger the fanaticism, the more I fear for Desdemona!! How can such a passionate, ardent, violent artist be moderated and contained in the calm and aristocratic passion of Desdemona?' (Ab., IV, 282). Ricordi offered reassurances, and a month later, on 27 July, Faccio came to Sant'Agata for one or two days for his first hearing of *Otello* and to examine the soprano part to determine whether Pantaleoni could actually succeed in it. But the future conductor equivocated, urging the *maestro* to listen to her himself. After absorbing a lightning bolt of frustration from Verdi, Ricordi demanded more information from Faccio and received a generally positive, but still vague, reply. Eventually Ricordi himself brought the singer to Sant'Agata on 29–30 August for something of an audition, probably with the actual part, and Verdi accepted her at this time. His 2 September instructions to Faccio, with whom she was now to study the part, show us much of his essential conception of the role:

The Willow Song presents enormous difficulties for the composer as well as for the performing artist. The latter, like the Holy Trinity, must produce three voices, one for Desdemona, another for Barbara (the maid), and a third voice for the 'Salce, salce, salce' [cf. Verdi's related comments on 22 January 1888, Chusid 1979: 160–1].
Signora Pantaleoni's voice, accustomed to violent parts, often has high notes a bit too biting. I would say there is something too metallic. If she could accustom herself to sing a little more with a head [voice] she would more easily manage the softening down (*smorzato*), and her voice would also be more certain and more accurate.
. . . It is not always true that her D is, as she says, a very bad note. There is a passage (*canto*) in which it comes out very well.
This phrase is repeated three times. The last time she succeeds nicely, the other two less so . . . The part of Desdemona does not perfectly suit her manner of feeling and her voice, but yet with her considerable talent, her stage instinct, and with good will and study she will manage very well. And notice that many, many things suit her perfectly.
(Morazzoni 1929: 44–5; trans. adapted from Chusid 1979: 159–60)

Having worked with Faccio and learned the part 'almost by memory' (*CVB*, II, 353), Pantaleoni visited Verdi at Sant'Agata from 17 to 28 October for intensive study. (The composer's reshaping of some phrases of her Willow Song at this time has been mentioned on p. 66 above.) She was elated by the experience. On 29 October she gushed to her brother, 'And at the end how happy he was with me, after I had understood him and had sung the part just as he wanted, with all of that finesse, those *sfumature* and nuances (*accenti*) that he indicated to me!' (*CVB*, II, 354). Verdi's reaction was mildly positive and hopeful. He wrote Faccio at once, on 29 October:

One can say that she will produce effects everywhere. Excellent [ones] in

2. Romilda Pantaleoni as Desdemona: Milan, 1887 (Act III)

the Quartet and more in the Duet and Finale of the third act, and in all of the fourth . . . They will all be very good if she will make them less biting and all with a *head* [voice]; moreover, I've advised her to sing that way in many other places. If there is anything to mention, it is in the [love] scene from the first act. One would need something lighter, more ethereal (*vaporoso*), and, let's say it, more voluptuous as the situation and the poetry require. She delivers her solo passages very well but with too much nuance and too dramatically . . . Tell her to sing with a head [voice] as much as she can.

> (Morazzoni 1929: 45; trans. adapted from Chusid 1979: 160, in which the letter is misdated.)

He repeated these remarks to Boito on the same day and added a final point: 'But we'll have other rehearsals, and I shall insist until I manage to find the proper nuance for the situation and poetry' (*CVB*, I, 116–17).

Two months later, on 4 January 1887, Verdi came to Milan for the *Otello* rehearsals. The piano rehearsals were to begin shortly thereafter, but the *maestro* first wished to work privately with Pantaleoni. (This almost certainly concerned the final Willow Song changes: see pp. 71–5 above.) What he heard disconcerted him. Her voice was less secure than it had been at Sant' Agata: he now sensed a 'breaking-up (*spezzarsi*) of the voice', as he later described it (29 April 1887: Ab., IV, 333). Seriously alarmed, Verdi determined that at this late date the wisest course was to say nothing to anyone and to hope for the best. Particularly because she was also singing in *Aida*, the gruelling *Otello* rehearsals wore her voice down further. Stories were told of her returning home with Faccio, slumping motionless into a chair, with her coat still on, and groaning, 'Oh! if only I could rest a little! When will it end? (De Rensis 1934: 232–3). Her initial reviews were favourable after the 5 February premiere (Plate 2), but her health and voice weakened seriously during the ensuing twenty-four *repliche*. At great personal cost and suffering she gave up her contract for the subsequent *Otello* tour in Rome and Venice. The incident was well publicized and was followed by unpleasant legal ramifications with the Cortis, all of which prompted a flurry of frank, but concerned, correspondence from Verdi to Pantaleoni herself (*CV*, IV, 86) and to others, advising her to rest. 'Let's have no illusions', he wrote to Faccio on 29 April 1887, 'Pantaleoni was not good . . . Her voice . . . has always been waning (*calante*) by nature, but [in the past] it restored itself when she went up to the high notes, which became ringing and beautiful. It's not so

now. Even in the high notes her voice remains narrow and thin'
(Ab., IV, 333–4).

In Rome (16 April 1887, eight performances) and Venice
(17 May, six performances) she was replaced by Adalgisa Gabbi, of
whom Verdi never approved, continuing to prefer Pantaleoni and
urging Ricordi – in vain – to have the latter signed for the future performance in Brescia (11 August). The Desdemona-crisis persisted
for several months and provoked not only a search for a new
soprano but also some of Verdi's most penetrating remarks on the
role. The most celebrated comes from a letter to Ricordi on 22 April
1887:

> I don't think that Gabbi is right for a delicate (*fine*) part like Desdemona . . .
> Judging the character of Desdemona *terre à terre*; a female who allows her-
> self to be mistreated, slapped, and even strangled, forgives and entreats,
> she appears to be a stupid little thing! But Desdemona is not a woman, she's
> a type! She's the type of goodness, of resignation, of sacrifice! They are
> creatures born for others, unconscious of their own *ego*! Beings that exist in
> part, and that Shakespeare has poetized and deified, creating Desdemona,
> Cordelia, Juliet, etc., etc., types that have never been encountered, except
> perhaps in Antigone of the ancient theater.
>
> (Ab., IV, 331–2; trans. Chusid 1979: 161)

(Similarly, in Boito's instructions for the performance of
Desdemona, part of the preface to the *disposizione scenica*, the
librettist called for restraint, simple and gentle gestures, to evoke 'a
feeling of love, purity, nobility, docility, ingenuousness and resignation': see Budden, III, 328–9.)

More specifically, Verdi wrote to Ricordi on 5 May 1887: 'Ah,
this Desdemona is really a difficult part . . . [From Rome] Muzio
writes me that Gabbi (good as a voice) delivers the Willow Song
badly. She speeds up (*stringe*) the first triplet too much and overly
prolongs the final C [sharp] that makes the cadence to the F [sharp].
The usual provincialisms of those who have no talent . . . Poor
Desdemona!' (Ab., IV, 335). And finally, on 11 May 1887, to
Ricordi, once again stressing the idealized-lyrical aspect of the role:

The true Desdemona is yet to be found . . . Desdemona is a part where the
thread, the melodic line, never stops from the first to the last note. Just as
Iago must only declaim and snicker (*ricaner*). Just as Otello, now warrior,
now passionate lover, now cast down into the filth, now as ferocious as a
savage, must sing and howl; so Desdemona must always sing . . . I repeat,
Desdemona sings from the first note of the Recitative, which is still a
melodic phrase, until the last note, 'Otello non uccidermi . . .' . . . which is

still a melodic phrase. Therefore, the most perfect Desdemona will always be the one who sings the best.

(Ab., IV, 336–7; trans. adapted from Chusid 1979: 161–2)

The part of Otello presented a different set of problems, particularly because of the enormous range of expression that the role requires. After that initial 17 January 1886 meeting with the Cortis and Ricordi, Verdi wrote to the editor on the following day:

I'm frightened about the tenor part. For many, many things Tamagno would be wonderful, but in many others no. There are large, long phrases, legato ones that are to be said at half-voice (*a mezzo voce*), an impossible thing for him. What's worse is that the first act would finish coldly, and (what's still worse) the fourth!! There is a short but broad melody, and then some half-voice phrases (after wounding himself), extremely important . . . and we can't do without them . . . And if I could hear him . . . before deciding? (Ab., IV, 273–4)

Notwithstanding Ricordi's alternative suggestion of Angelo Masini, mentioned above, Francesco Tamagno was the chief candidate for the role, having sung both in the 1881 premiere of the revised *Simon Boccanegra* and the revised, 1884 *Don Carlo*. He possessed the most powerful tenor voice of his day – sheer sound, with ringing high notes – but, at least prior to *Otello*, his acting had been superficial and stiff, his vocal nuances cold, his general artistry and musicality lacking (Monaldi 1929: 223). In short, Verdi was reluctant to hand the role over to a massive voice unguided by a critical intelligence. He was more specific in his 21 January 1886 letter to Boito, with comments that also illustrate the unity of his musical and scenic conceptions:

Tamagno would be excellent in many points, but he would not do well in the Duo Finale of Act I; and much less well at the end of the opera . . . You do not know the first Duet, but you do know the finale of the opera. I don't think that he could deliver that short melody with full effect, 'E tu come sei pallida' and even less 'Un bacio un bacio ancora'. All the more that between this second kiss and the third there are four bars for the orchestra alone [*sic*], and these must be filled with a delicate, moving stage action that I was imagining while I was writing the notes. A very easy action for a true actor but difficult for . . . another. (*CVB*, I, 99)
[The 1887 *disposizione scenica*, p. 107, calls for the wounded Otello to struggle to raise himself at Desdemona's bedside to kiss her; he succeeds twice in kissing only her hand; on the third attempt 'his voice fails and he pronounces the final syllable in a weary sob', whereupon he dies, rolling down the steps of the bed.]

He wrote similar remarks to Ricordi the next day, adding only that in the final scene Otello, totally undone, 'neither can nor must sing in more than a veiled, semi-spent voice: this is a secure quality, which Tamagno does not have. He [Tamagno] must always sing in a full voice; if he doesn't, his tone becomes ugly, his intonation uncertain' (Ab., IV, 274).

In the meantime Tamagno had got wind of this *Otello* bustling – much to Verdi's displeasure. Ricordi thought it best to ask Tamagno at once whether he could visit the composer for an audition. The singer was more than delighted – he may already, clumsily and far too hastily, have asked Verdi for the part in February 1880 (Corsi 1937: 75) – but was obliged to postpone the audition because of a 'slight indisposition' and an engagement in Madrid (29 January 1886: *Cop.*, 342). Fearing that the overeager tenor was assuming too much, Verdi responded coolly to the 'embarrassing and compromising' letter on 31 January 1886, agreeing, however, to meet with him in Genoa to 'discuss it all frankly and honestly' after the Madrid obligation (*VR*, 65; Ab., IV, 268). Tamagno, in fact, did come to Genoa, on 26 April (datable from unpublished correspondence), accompanied by his little daughter Margherita, who always travelled with him. (Much later, Verdi expressed privately to Ricordi his surprise that to save money the two had travelled second class: Ab., IV, 298.) While Giuseppina entertained Margherita, Verdi and Tamagno are said to have worked with *Otello* for several hours, apparently to the composer's satisfaction (the story, with misleading dating, appears in Corsi 1937: 85–6).

By early September 1886 the impulsive Tamagno was already pressing to begin formal study. Verdi's strategy for taming him was to delay the delivery of his part, then to have him study the notes meticulously with Faccio. His instructions to Faccio on 29 October 1886, sent along with his advice on rehearsing Pantaleoni, deal frankly with the tenor's weaknesses: 'I ask you warmly to have Tamagno study his part after he arrives. He is so inexact in the reading of music that I would really like him to study the part with a true musician in order to get him to sing the notes with their true value and in time. With regard to the nuances, the pitch-levels (*coristi*), the *allaplin* [?], we'll do them later, after I've revealed all of my intentions about the singing, the staging, etc. etc.' (Morazzoni 1929: 45). Two days later Faccio vowed to oversee 'the *musical precision* above all' (Ab., IV, 295), and the tenor began study on 6 November. Even before the sessions began, however, on 4 November, Verdi was worrying that Tamagno would need study beyond Faccio's coaching, that he would have to be singled out during the January rehearsals, a potential ego-blow to the 'tenor of the 5000 Lire!!' (Ab., IV, 289). He admitted that he would like to invite Tamagno to study the part with him in Genoa for several days – he was planning to make his habitual winter transfer there within a couple of weeks – but did not relish the thought of entertaining him during the non-rehearsal time, when there was so much else to do (Ab., IV, 298; Budden, III, 323). Despite Faccio's studies and Ricordi's optimistic reports, he insisted on 11 November that 'I'll still have many things to say about the scenico-musical interpretation' (Ab., IV, 299). As it turned out, Verdi's transferral to Genoa was delayed until 9 December by an outbreak of cholera in that city. He was able to rehearse Tamagno, however, in Milan – in a room of La Scala itself – during a three or four days' trip beginning on 24 November (*CVB*, II, 355–6; Ab., IV, 300).

Verdi's guidance of Tamagno, both here and later during the January rehearsahs, apparently worked wonders. Recalling it many years later, Gino Monaldi described it as a 'miracle', a 'complete metamorphosis' of Tamagno into a true artist (1929: 223–4). A few stories of the January rehearsals survive: of the seventy-three-year-old Verdi, still intent on that Otello Death Scene, showing Tamagno precisely how to stab himself and die by miming the action himself, while all of the onlookers were stunned; of Tamagno practising his death-falls over and over again to achieve something 'à la Salvini' (see Chapter 8 below); of the tenor's missing several sessions in mid-January because of a throat inflammation, but of his continuing to rehearse *Otello*, and particularly the murder-scene, in his apartment, with seven-year-old Margherita as Desdemona; of Ricordi – and Verdi himself – substituting for Tamagno during this period; of Verdi showing Pantaleoni what he had meant by a 'fervent, passionate embrace' during the Love Duet (Pesci, 'Rehearsals' [1887]: 185; Monaldi 1929: 226; Corsi 1937: 105). At the premiere Tamagno's Otello was a triumph (Plates 3 and 4). The first applause heard was for his resonant, celebrated 'Esultate!' Said the reviewer for *Il capitan fracassa*, 'This phrase was said . . . with stupendous tragic effect: Salvini-like' (*OG*, 54). For *La perseveranza* Filippi wrote, 'I don't recall ever having seen Tamagno play a role so dramatically as that difficult one of the protagonist' (*OG*, 85). Verdi himself is said to have asserted, 'Ah! that *Miseria mia*! Nobody will ever know how to howl it like he does!'

(Monaldi 1929: 227). Tamagno, with Verdi's help, had conquered the role.

Considerably after his retirement – and after Veırdi's death – Tamagno recorded three *Otello* excerpts apparently five times each: 'Esultate!', 'Ora e per sempre addio', and the Death Scene, 'Niun mi tema'. (It now seems that the multiple takes, not all of which survive, may all stem from 1903: cf. the dating in Bauer 1947: 434–5.) Notwithstanding the decline in Tamagno's health, they are obviously valuable documents – resonant and uncompromisingly theatrical, somewhat deliberate in tempo, rhythmically quite free, and highly nuanced, by today's standards (see, e.g., Crutchfield 1983: 44, Ex. 171) – that repay several close listenings. Generally considered, they give the impression of dramatic pieces as much freely declaimed and acted as 'sung', and this seems likely to be the type of performance that Verdi had in mind. (See also Ashbrook 1985.)

Verdi's initial conception of Iago was forged with the assistance of the Neapolitan painter Domenico Morelli, whom he had asked at the beginning of 1880 for a sketch of Iago gloating over the fainted Otello. Naturally enough, the composer, imagining something Mephistophelean, had mentioned Iago's 'hellish smile' (6 January 1880; Ab., IV, 111; misdated in Budden, III, 302). Morelli, however, thought differently and proposed an 'Iago with the face of an honest man. I've found a priest who seems just like him' (Ab., IV, 111). Verdi agreed at once: 'You've struck home! Oh, I knew it; I was sure of it' (7 February, Budden, III, 302). Thus emerged the essence of the opera's Iago: a Satanic soul concealed in a normal exterior – and any performer would have to project both of these 'contradictory' aspects in interpreting the part. In mid-September 1881 Morelli mentioned the 'Jesuitism' that he wished on Iago's face (Ab., IV, 182–3), and Verdi responded on 24 September with a synoptic and famous description of the role (not yet composed):

That Iago should be dressed in black, as black as his soul, nothing better . . . But if I were an actor and had to play Iago, I would rather have a long and thin figure, thin lips, small eyes set close to the nose like a monkey's, broad, receding brow, and the head developed behind; an absent, *nonchalant* manner, indifferent to everything, witty, speaking good and evil almost lightheartedly, and having the air of not even thinking of what he says; so that, if someone were to reproach him: 'What you say is vile!' he could answer: 'Really? I don't think so . . . we'll say no more about it! . . . '
A figure like this can deceive everyone, and even up to a point his wife.

3. Francesco Tamagno as Otello: Milan, 1887 (Acts II and III)

4. The death of Otello. Francesco Tamagno: Milan, 1887 (Act IV)

A small, malicious figure arouses everyone's suspicion and deceives nobody! *Amen.* (Ab., IV, 183–4; trans. Chusid 1979: 157–8)

From the beginning Verdi conceived the role of Iago for Victor Maurel. One of the leading French baritones of his day and known particularly in Italy (his career is summarized in Budden, III, 323–4), Maurel capitalized on acute intelligence, gifted acting, crystal-clear pronunciation, and an extraordinary ability to colour his voice with subtle *accenti*. Verdi had been impressed with him in the title role of the revised *Simon Boccanegra* at La Scala on 24–30 March 1881. In his enthusiasm he had even remarked to Maurel at that time, 'If God gives me health, I'll write *Iago* for you', a remark of which Maurel reminded him almost five years later, on 22 December 1885 (misdated in *Cop.*, 330; see also Verdi's cautious 30 December response, *Cop.*, 331, trans. but misdated in Budden, III, 323). In the following month Verdi began considering singers with Ricordi and the Cortis, but in early February Emanuele Muzio, from Nice, reported that he had heard bad reports about the current state of Maurel's voice. Muzio suggested instead Jules-Célestin Devoyod (Ab., IV, 277–8), who, in fact, made a brief, uninvited (and fruitless) visit to Verdi in Genoa on 6 February 1886. On 10 February Verdi responded to Muzio: 'I am unhappy to hear what you tell me about Maurel, because nobody could do that part as he could. Nobody pronounces so clearly as he; and in this part for Iago there are so many things spoken *sotto voce* and said rapidly that nobody could do it better than he' (Ab., IV, 278). To clear up the matter Verdi went to Paris from ca. 20–21 March to 11 April to hear and speak with Maurel – and, doubtless, to have him read through some passages of *Otello*. Thus Maurel was probably the first singer to see and sing portions of the new opera. In early April Muzio was able to report to Ricordi: 'The maestro is no longer worried. His face is serene again; he is of excellent humour and sounds and sings and repeats and declaims some passages of Iago's part, which, he says, will be interpreted admirably' (Ab., IV, 280).

Over the next few months Verdi remained buoyantly confident about Maurel. On 4 November 1886, to Ricordi: 'Once Maurel has studied the music, he will guess the rest [i.e., about dramatic interpretation, *accenti*, etc.] and . . . for him there will be little or nothing to do [at the January rehearsals]. It's not like this for Tamagno' (Ab., IV, 298). A week later Verdi wrote the editor some well-known lines: 'Iago is not performable and it is not possible without pronouncing extraordinarily well, as Maurel does. In that part it is necessary neither to sing nor to raise one's voice (save in a few exceptions). Were I an actor-singer, for instance, I would say everything at the tip of the lips, *mezza voce*' (11 November 1886; Ab., IV, 299). As Maurel studied the part he became convinced that he would need to shave off his beard to play Iago. Muzio explained his reasoning to Ricordi on 22 November: 'He says that a full beard will make his face too mild, but he'll talk about this to the maestro and Edel [the costume designer]. In the second act he's joking, humorous, ironic, but terrifying from the Credo onwards, and he says that they need to see the movements of his face' (Ab., IV, 296–7). The issue of the beard surfaced again in late December – see *VR*, 56–8 – and early photographs and engravings of Maurel's Iago show him clean-shaven (see Plate 5), an appearance confirmed by Filippi's review of the premiere: 'beardless as he now is, [Maurel] is unrecognizable' (*OG*, 6). (The 1887 *disposizione scenica*, p. 37, also makes much of Iago's facial gestures, illuminated by footlights, in the 'Credo'.)

Having finished with the Opéra-Comique in Paris, and before arriving in Milan for some *Aida* rehearsals, Maurel stopped in Genoa to study the part of Iago with Verdi from 12 to 14 December (Ab., IV, 301; precise dating from unpublished correspondence). The work with Maurel resulted in a small addition to his part (see p. 71 above), but now Verdi again felt the clash of the 'real' opera in his mind with the limitations of any given realization. 'The recent meeting with Maurel', he wrote to Ricordi on 15 December, 'has convinced me (although he will do it well) that nobody will ever perform and sing Iago as it should be done . . . And I deeply regret having written that part! And also . . . the opera!!' (Ab., IV, 302). On 18 December, more anxieties followed as Maurel, Ricordi, Pantaleoni, Tamagno, and Edel went to a Milanese performance of the play *Othello*, with the celebrated 'realistic' actor Giovanni Emanuel as the Moor (*VR*, 55–6; see p. 169 below). Boito disapproved of Emanuel and refused to attend. Moreover, he seems to have convinced Verdi that it was an error for the singers to have attended the play (*CVB*, I, 119; Ab., IV, 303–4). The everoptimistic Ricordi, however, believed the experience to have been excellent for both Pantaleoni and Tamagno: 'At least you will be spared the highly ungrateful task of explaining to Tamagno who Othello was!' (to Verdi, 25 December 1886, in *VR*, 56–8).

Maurel's Iago could not have been more successful at the

5. Victor Maurel as Iago: Milan, 1887 (Act I)

5 February premiere. The reviews were filled with impressive praise. 'Handsome, dark, Satanic' (G. Gavazzi-Spech, *Corriere di Roma*, *OG*, 46). 'In many places he was so effective as to call forth shouts of admiration' (A. Gramola, *Corriere della sera*, *OG*, 13). '[A] stupendous interpretation . . . One simply must see and hear Maurel, when he says, with long pauses [in the 'Credo'], "*E poi?* . . . *E poi?* . . . *La morte è il nulla*"' (F. Filippi, *La perseveranza*, *OG*, 78, 80). 'Maurel sang that long blasphemy [the 'Credo'] with an admirable, strident power. Moreover, it is the only passage in his part where he opens up. All the rest he says with his elbows at his sides (*les coudes au corps*), without gestures, without *éclat*, and his talent consists precisely in producing dramatic emotions through a sort of interior force' (*Le matin*, *OG*, 105). Boito's later counsels for the role of Iago in the preface to the *disposizione scenica* (pp. 4–5) essentially echo those of Verdi, filtered through the positive experiences of Maurel. Boito emphasizes that it would be an error 'to play him as a kind of human demon; to give him a Mephistophelean sneer [throughout] and make him shoot Satanic glances everywhere . . . He must be handsome and appear genial and open and falsely bonhomous', but he changes his personality rapidly 'according to the person to whom he happens to be speaking' (Budden, III, 328). Indeed, it appears that some of the independent-minded Maurel's ideas may have filtered down into the details of the *disposizione scenica* itself, as Ricordi confessed to Verdi on 24 August 1887 (*VR*, 61). And, not content with that, Maurel produced his own elaborate set of performance directions in the following year: the 148-page 'A propos de la mise-en-scène du drame lyrique *Otello*'.

In 1905 Maurel, now past his prime, made a well-known recording of 'Era la notte' (he had also recorded it with French text two years earlier: Bauer 1949: 307), a piece for which he was praised at the premiere and succeeding performances. Its most notable features are its two supposed 'quotations' from Cassio, which, according to the *DS*, p. 53, should be performed in a voice whose sound differs from that of Iago's. Maurel not only alters his voice into a *cupo*, throttled sound but also breaks with the existing, rather slow tempo to underscore the fatal words in a slow, free declamation : they emerge in high relief as a fantastic vision. As in Tamagno's recordings, particularly those of the Death Scene, Maurel is concerned less with 'singing' than with intense acting – declamation and nuance. 'Who has not heard the "Dream

Racconto" sung by Maurel', affirmed Gino Monaldi, 'cannot have any idea of the wonderful artifice of the sung word' (1929: 218).

To judge from his correspondence, Verdi had little to say about the selection of the remaining singers and delegated this responsibility to Ricordi: Giovanni Paroli (Cassio), Vincenzo Fornari (Roderigo), Francesco Navarrini (Lodovico), Napoleone Limonta (Montano), Ginevra Petrovich (Emilia), and Angelo Lagomarsino (The Herald). He was keenly interested, however, in the costumes, the sets, and the special effects. Managing these matters throughout the last half of 1886, Ricordi kept Verdi informed about them. But the initial impulse here was given in May 1886 by Boito, who first determined the epoch to be depicted. Reasoning that Giraldi Cinthio's Prologue to the *Hecatommithi* (Venice, 1566; see p. 25 above) describes its narrators as fugitives from the 1527 Sack of Rome, Boito concluded that *Otello* should be set just before this date, in the years prior to 1525. Because the premise of the staging was to be literal, historical fidelity, Boito suggested to Verdi on 16 May that the costumes should be designed after a study of 'the Venetian painters from the last years of the fifteenth century and the entire first quarter of the sixteenth. Luckily for us the two great documents of that span of years are Carpaccio and Gentile Bellini! From their paintings will emerge the clothing of our characters' (*CVB*, I, 106–7).

Thus the costume and prop designer, Alfredo Edel (who had done similar work for the 1881 *Boccanegra* and the 1884 *Don Carlo*), was packed off to Venice for much of the summer to study in the Museo Correr and elsewhere. As he later reported to the *Corriere della sera* in late October, his designs were 'no fantasy at all, but exact reproductions of the truth for everything, from the protagonist's costume all the way to the last of the props' (*CVB*, II, 354). Verdi inspected most of Edel's fifty-eight designs (*figurini*), along with some of Carlo Ferrario's early sketches for the sets (*scene*) and probably some of the special effects, on his trip to Milan from 14 to 16 or 17 October 1886. At this time he probably demanded that a few costume designs be altered (*VR*, 52). Desdemona's Act I costume, for instance, was too 'splendid' (letter to Boito, 29 October 1886; *CVB*, I, 116–17). And, most important, he objected to Otello's Act IV costume, planned in exotic (Moorish?) style featuring bare arms and a long white tunic, according to the *Corriere della sera* report of 27–28 October. 'It's beautiful, but it's not true!', insisted Verdi. In it the character resembled a 'Cetivayo' (a Zulu King: *CVB*, II, 354–5), and 'not an Otello in the service of Venice. One has to search with a lantern in that *figurino* to find any traces of a Venetian costume' (letter to Ricordi, *VR*, 51; cf. *CVB*, I, 116–17). In his judgment one may see that Verdi had reversed his initially more 'foreign' conception of Otello, probably under the influence of Domenico Morelli, who in mid-September 1881 had mentioned the ideal Otello-image as 'not dressed in Turkish costume – that's an error. He has something oriental about him, yes, but he's dressed in Venetian style, and he's very handsome; with bright colours – Moors always choose bright colours for their clothes, never black' (Ab., IV, 182–3). Verdi had at first been surprised: 'I don't understand why Otello should be dressed in Venetian style . . . Why wouldn't it be all right for him to dress as an Ethiopian, without the usual turban?' (24 September 1881; Ab., IV, 183–4; see Chusid 1979: 157). But, clearly, by September 1886 he had come around to share much of Morelli's view (cf. Chapter 8 below). In any event, Edel redid the *figurini* but still failed to please Verdi. Desdemona was still 'too rich' in Act I and Otello 'too savage' in Act IV, as he again wrote to Ricordi on 3 November 1886. 'It attracts too much attention and distracts. Once the public starts saying, "Oh, what a beautiful costume" [in Act IV], we are lost. Artists must have the courage to *efface themselves*' (*VR*, 54). Once again, Edel was forced to reconceive these costumes. Similarly, Ferrario, with Verdi's approval, finished painting the La Scala sets of *Otello* by late December (*VR*, 58).

There were dozens of other details that passed under the *maestro*'s consideration. Some dealt with musical matters and sonority. Ricordi, for instance, informed Verdi on 20 September 1886 that the Chorus would number 104 voices, 64 men and 40 women, and that there was to be a special group of children (*coro ragazzi*) in Act II (*VR*, 50). The editor was also concerned about the twelve off-stage trumpets for the fanfares in the Act III Finale. After consulting with Faccio and Romeo Orsi (a La Scala clarinettist and instrument maker) and, of course, reporting the results to Verdi on 23 October (*VR*, 51–2), Ricordi had twelve special trumpets, uniform in sonority, made by the Mahillon firm in Brussels. On 24 October Verdi suggested that some of the twelve be pitched an octave higher than the rest to facilitate the playing of the high notes – for example, the c^3 required in the highest of the three trumpet-groups (Ab., IV, 293–4). Verdi also insisted that the La Scala orchestra – and, more to the point, all subsequent orchestras (since La Scala already employed it) – play at 'standard pitch (*corista normale*)'. By this he probably meant the official 'French' pitch (and Viennese pitch since November 1885) of an a^1 at 435 – eventually adopted in Italy as official by government decree on 30 October 1887 – or, less likely, the 432 endorsed by the Congress of Milan in 1881. In practice, either would do, since both were suitably low, and produced, as he had put it on 10 February 1884, a sound 'more noble, fuller, and more majestic' than could be obtained from the higher pitch level (ca. 450) still found at that time in parts of Europe (*CVB*, II, 334–5; Righini 1981: 543–5). Ricordi was also concerned with some of the special sound effects, particularly how the thunder of the opening storm was to be produced. Eventually, taking the idea from the Paris Opéra, he obtained a huge bass drum, some two metres deep and 1.25 metres in diameter, which was to be placed strategically backstage and beaten with timpani sticks (see, e.g., Ricordi's letters of 23 October and 4 December, *VR*, 51–2, 55, and *DS*, p. 9). Other concerns dealt with the special visual effects, to be supervised by the *macchinista*, Luigi Caprara. These included Caprara's construction of three movable ships to be seen ploughing through the stormy waves of the first scene of Act I and his solution of how to produce the fire in the same act (Ricordi's letter of 4 December, *VR*, 55, and the *DS*, pp. 18–20). For the latter, Caprara devised the raising of a box of branches covered with alcohol-soaked sponges through a trap-door. The branches were then to be lit, as Ricordi put it in the *disposizione scenica*, p. 20, by 'an intelligent chorus-member'.

The premiere was a grand and glittering success, an international event of splendour and magnitude (see, e.g., Budden, III, 324–6). The four-hour affair (*OG*, 10) spilled over with frequent applause, lengthy and prolonged curtain-calls, and frenzied ovations for Verdi himself. Three pieces were encored that first evening – and surely even this must have been pre-planned by the *maestro*: the Fire Chorus in Act I, Desdemona's 'Ave Maria' in Act IV, and – strangely enough – the extended solo for the contrabasses at Otello's Act IV entrance immediately thereafter (apparently Otello exited and entered a second time at the premiere: *OG*, 170). The second performance, on 13 February, was equally significant. The reviewers were now more 'profoundly moved' than stunned, as they had been at the first performance (*OG*, 168). No encores were

6. 'O sulla tua testa / S'accenda e precipiti il fulmine / Del mio spaventoso furor che si desta' (Act II, 178/4/1–179/5/2): engraving by A. Bonamore, 'Scena V dell'Atto II', in *Verdi e l'Otello*, a special number of the *Illustrazione italiana* (February 1887)

permitted, and at the end, amidst the ovations, the entire hall was 'electrified', went wild with enthusiasm, when Tamagno's little daughter, Margherita, appeared on stage to present Verdi with a silver crown (*OG*, 170, 174).

Following the premiere, however, Verdi had a number of doubts and began to complain about the Milanese sets and performances. It appears, in fact, that all of the sets were redone with slight modifications – although still based on Ferrario's originals – by Giovanni Zuccarelli for the subsequent tour. (Ferrario's designs no longer exist and are restorable only in part through contemporary engravings and photographs: see Plates 1, 4, and 6. The Zuccarelli materials, however, are still largely available in the Ricordi Archives: see Plates 7–10.) The sets for Acts II and III were especially problematic, and even as the La Scala performances were continuing Verdi was being consulted about modifications. In a letter to Ricordi on 14 March 1887, critical of the overly elaborate Act II set that Zuccarelli was proposing, Verdi singled out an unsatisfying moment of the Milanese staging – the Homage Chorus – and wrote that he had discovered his ideal Act II stage set quite by chance in the lobby of the Eden Hotel in Nervi, where he was work-ing on the French translation with Boito and Du Locle:

[The lobby] has three large windows; outside, a garden (still young); and beyond the garden, the sea.

Therefore, for *Otello*, a shallow set almost at the curtain and in the fabric many windows separated by slender columns, Moorish or Venetian, etc., etc. Beyond the windows a huge park with a large open space and a broad avenue, and others, smaller, crossing . . . Thus the desired dramatic action would take place, and the public would understand, rather would sense the fact that two events, two actions are taking place simultaneously at that moment: a *festivity* for Desdemona [and] a *conspiracy* between Iago and Otello.

Zuccarelli's [newly proposed] set may also be beautiful, if you will, but it is still wrong . . . There is nothing to be done but a large window.

(Ab., IV, 328; trans. Chusid 1979: 162)

Ricordi communicated the information to Zuccarelli, who promptly modified this and other sets. On 15 March the editor reported back in his usual mode of hopeful pacification: 'I also saw the plan of the last set, with the modifications that you suggested, and I think that it will be fine: just as the Act III set pleased me when he presented me with a prepared representation (*maquette*) of it' (*VR*, 17).

But Verdi, it seemed, was never to be appeased. In the following years he repeatedly charged – with increasing rancour and speci-

7. Giovanni Zuccarelli's set for Act I (1887, based on the original set by Carlo Ferrario: cf. Pl. 1, p. 2 above.)

8. Giovanni Zuccarelli's set for Act II (1887, based on the original set by Carlo Ferrario)

9. Giovanni Zuccarelli's set for Act III (1887, based on the original set by Carlo Ferrario: cf. Pl. 6, p. 110 above)

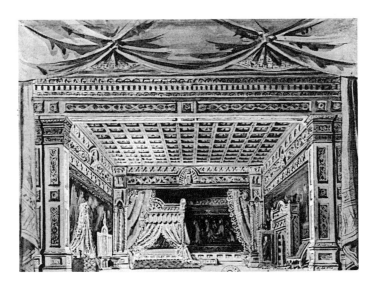

10. Giovanni Zuccarelli's set for Act IV (1887, based on the original set by Carlo Ferrario: cf. Pl. 4, p. 102 above)

ficity – that the opera had been poorly launched at La Scala. On 29 April 1887, in the midst of the 'Desdemona-crisis', the *maestro* vented more spleen to Ricordi: 'At La Scala itself not everything was good: decorations poorly conceived; *mise-en-scène* poorly directed; the *Fire* [in 'Fuoco] di gioia'; the *ship*; the *storm*; etc., etc. Many, many problems . . . Poor Otello! I deplore that you came into the world' (*VR*, 59–60). And in May 1887 he wrote to the celebrated bassist Giovanni Bottesini for fingerings in the contrabasses' solo to improve the bad intonation that he had heard in Milan (*VR*, 60; cf. Ab., IV, 366, 368).

On the occasion of the important revival of *Otello* at La Scala in early 1889 – a revival plagued with problems – Verdi complained to Ricordi again about the 1887 sets:

They may have been so many operatic masterworks, but they did not assist the development of the action of the Drama. The first scene lacked space and depth, therefore cramping the action. The garden scene was too deep. I would change the third [-act set] and make two: a small room inside for the first scene between Otello, Desdemona, Iago, and Cassio. Then, a set change in sight [of the audience] for the remainder . . . Then you must find something better for that wretched bonfire scene.

> (1 January 1889; Ab., IV, 366; trans. Chusid 1979: 162; cf. Verdi's similar – perhaps intensified – complaints for the 1892 La Scala revival, partially available in Ab., IV, 433–4.)

He went on to suggest, both here and subsequently in letters from 3 and 9 February 1889, a reduction in sonority for the Act II Homage Chorus' internal stanzas. Thus the instrumental forces were to be reduced to only one or two mandolins and guitars, and the stanzas were to be sung by soloists (a boy, a baritone, and a soprano) and accompanied lightly by eight choristers (Ab., IV, 371–2; Chusid 1979: 164–5). Whether these instructions were ever carried out is unclear, but since changes were made in neither the manuscript nor the printed scores, it is difficult to regard this proposal as more than a passing idea. As far as Verdi was concerned, the 1889 revival of *Otello* was doomed from the beginning, and for all of his grievances he blamed only himself. To Ricordi on 3 February: 'I've deplored and still deplore not having been more severe and demanding from the beginning [during the 1887 rehearsals for the premiere] . . . There were so many, many things that did not satisfy me, but I thought that at the age of 74 I ought not to permit myself to fly off the handle, as in the *Aida* years, and even more, in those of *La forza del destino* . . . ' (Ab., IV, 372). In the same period, it may be recalled, Verdi began to complain about the Act III *concertato*, which ultimately led to the 1894 revision of that piece (see p. 82 above). The February–March 1889 La Scala revival failed, foundering on poor planning, inadequate rehearsal, and severe problems with the tenor: the new Otello, Giuseppe Oxilia, had to withdraw for reasons of health after the first performance and was replaced after nearly a month's delay by a certain Signor Giannini.

Because the 111-page *disposizione scenica* (1887), a step-by-step description of the first La Scala production, 'compiled and ordered by Giulio Ricordi', is something of an abstracted, idealized document, it is probably exempted from the full force of these later Verdian criticisms. This production book, rich in practical advice far beyond the indications in the score, is too extensive to deal with in detail here. Basic descriptions and selected examples have already been provided by Harvey Bordowitz (1976), Doug Coe (1978), and Julian Budden (1983).[1] One's overall impression is that of a dictatorial pronouncement that forbids producers to alter a single significant stage detail. Throughout, one is reminded of Verdi's insistence in January 1889 that interpretation is 'one thing alone'. Several hundred blocking diagrams, copiously annotated, thus hoped to march future productions in lockstep with the La Scala production. Within the production book the key words are *naturalezza* ('naturalness', or relatively 'realistic' gestures freed from stiffness, or, especially, from conventional exaggeration – but for the apparent limits on this naturalness, see p. 169 below), *accento* ('accent', or better, 'nuance' – modifications in vocal timbre or delivery), *gesto* (physical gestures), and *fisionomia* (facial expressions, particularly with the eyes). The production book demands an intensely acted, coloured treatment of virtually every line, something borne out by the early reviews and recordings. From the book one may extract a whole repertory of standard (but still 'realistic', at least to Verdi) gestures: steps backward to express surprise or submission; steps forward for emphasis or frankness; covering the face with one's hands to display weeping, despair, or disgust; clasped hands in supplication; hands or arms raised towards others, or towards heaven, for supplications and oaths; and so on. Certain lines were to be stressed by addressing the audience, typically from a position ·close to the footlights: e.g., Otello's 'Desdemona rea!' (169/4/1; stage directions differing in *DS*, 50),

'Ah! morte e dannazione!!' (184/1/1; *DS*, 52), and 'Ah! mille vite gli donasse Iddio!' (191/1/1; *DS*, 53); Desdemona's 'E son io l'innocente cagion di tanto pianto!' (222/1/2; *DS*, 61) and 'le amare stille del mio dolor' (273/4/2–3; *DS*, 81); all of Iago's 'Credo' (*DS*, 37); and so on.

Coe (1978: 149–52) and Budden (III, 395) have pointed out several pantomimes called for in the production book, notably during the Act II Homage Chorus and Quartet, Otello's Act IV entrance, etc., but others, more subtle, are less well known: Cassio's 'new' entrance in Act I (33/1/1), ten bars earlier than indicated in the score, to chat gallantly with a group of young women, thus establishing his reputation as a womanizer from the beginning (*DS*, 17); Iago's bowing to Desdemona and miming words of consolation as she exits after the Act II Quartet (*DS*, p. 50; notice that in the score Iago never interacts with Desdemona); or Iago's leading of Desdemona by the arm onto the stage for the Act III Finale (*DS*, 73). Similarly, the production book alters a few important scenic details. Thus we learn that the sky is to become completely serene by the end of the Fire Chorus, not, as indicated in the score (89/2/2), just before the Love Duet (*DS*, pp. 15, 20). And we learn a few details about performance; the organ pitch-cluster is now to sound *through* the 'Esultate!', all the way up to 'Si calma la bufera' (*DS*, 15); and Iago does not laugh at the end of the 'Credo' but merely shrugs his shoulders.

The critical question is to what extent does all of this reflect Verdi's and Boito's intentions? Recently published correspondence establishes as certain that both men examined and approved the *disposizione scenica* in summer 1887. The key letter is from Ricordi on 14 July: 'I have completely finished the *messa in scena* of *Otello*, and the manuscript was reviewed by Boito. When it's ready, I'll send you a corrected proof (*prova*) so that you can see whether there are modifications to be done' (*VR*, 59). By 13 August Verdi had received the proofs of the four pages of Boito's preface, which delineates the essence of the characters. On that date he returned it to Eugenio Tornaghi, Ricordi's secretary, with a response, 'Excellent! Nothing better! But . . . those gentlemen . . . will they read it and understand it . . . will they follow its advice? In any event, it's good that it was done' (Ab., IV, 343). On 24 August Ricordi announced, 'I'm sending you this [letter] of mine through our friend Muzio, along with the last complete proof of the *messa in scena*. Please read a little of it each day, and if you have any observations to make, write them in the margin. Boito has already corrected it; we lack now only the inspection of the *summum judex*.' And he added casually, but significantly, 'Maurel made a few observations to me. I found some of them excellent. You will hear about this from Muzio' (*VR*, 61). What appear to be three scattered suggestions, undated but in Verdi's hand, still survive (*VR*, 61), and it is easily demonstrable that the relevant passages of the *disposizione scenica* incorporate these changes. With the proofs now returned, Ricordi noted to Verdi on 6 September: 'The indicated corrections on the *messa in scena* are very fine. I thank you heartily for it' (*VR*, 62).

Moreover, the closer one reads the document the more one is convinced that it is not merely a record of the La Scala production (albeit idealized, and perhaps in some places altered) but also a catalogue of what Ricordi remembered Verdi and Boito to have said during the rehearsals. Some of these details are easily confirmable. Ugo Pesci's February 1887 account of 'Rehearsals for *Otello*', for instance, tells of Verdi's dominance, of his insistence on 'naturalness (*naturalezza*)', of his idea for Desdemona's arm-gestures in the third strophe of the Willow Song, of his stressing the actions of Otello's Death Scene (in Conati [1980]: 184–7): all of these appear, without explicit attribution to Verdi, in the *disposizione scenica*. Tamagno's and Maurel's recordings are congruent with the document, even when it conflicts with the score. And Ricordi alone, eager to please a testy Verdi, would never have included so many interpretative – and penetratingly analytical – details on his own. Although no document is infallible, it is clear that the composer's voice and intentions, along with those of Ricordi and the fussily precise Boito (and also, it appears, a few problematic suggestions of Maurel),[2] riddle the production book. With modest caution, it may be considered a reasonably authoritative production statement.

6 *A brief performance history*

WILLIAM ASHBROOK

In the wake of the historic and enormously successful *prima* of *Otello* at La Scala, 5 February 1887, every major opera house was clamouring to stage Verdi's most recent work. Giulio Ricordi and his organization obliged by arranging for the prompt and efficient dissemination of *Otello* both throughout Italy and abroad. After the twenty-fifth and concluding performance of its initial run at La Scala, the whole production moved to Rome, where it was given with the original cast, except with Adalgisa Gabbi instead of Romilda Pantaleoni as Desdemona, on 16 April 1887. On the 17th of the following month, the troupe, again with Gabbi as Desdemona, introduced the score to Venice.

The impact of Francesco Tamagno's stentorian tenor had contributed in no small degree to the public excitement over these first performances, however difficult (and tactless) it might be to suggest that this enthusiasm could add some fillip to the interest and reverence aroused by the novelty of *Otello* itself. Yet it is clear that the public was more eager to encounter the opera with Tamagno than without him. Verdi deplored this state of affairs, particularly since, to his ears, the *torinese* tenor's instrument was less reliable when used softly than at full volume, a shortcoming that left the duet that closes Act 1 in some jeopardy whenever the idol of the hour sang it. In an effort to introduce a more dependable element in the title role, the composer espoused the substitution of Franco Cardinali, in those days an Italian Lohengrin of some repute, as Otello when the opera was first given at Brescia on 11 August 1887, but the box-office receipts proved disappointing. Still another, and a more durable, replacement for Tamagno was brought forward the following month, when *Otello* moved on to Parma. Here the title role was assigned to Giuseppe Oxilia, who flourished briefly as one of the *epigoni* of Tamagno, and he was matched with Gabbi once more singing Desdemona and a French Iago, Paul Lhérie, who had some-

118

thing of Maurel's finesse but whose voice was on the wane. Some idea of Lhérie's sound as Iago may be gathered from the fact that he was a *ci-devant* tenor, having been the original Don José at the Opéra-Comique in 1875. At Parma, with Faccio again in charge of the musical forces, *Otello* received twelve performances between 15 September and 4 October 1887.

On 18 November 1887 in Mexico City, the opera attained its first performance outside Italy, but in a rather dubious fashion: it was put on in a pirated edition orchestrated from a vocal score by Paolo Villane. Considering the richness and subtlety of Verdi's instrumentation in *Otello*, Villane must have had more enthusiasm than judgment. There seems to have been no great viability in this misguided enterprise, however, an aberration that recalls the bad old days of the earlier nineteenth century when many an Italian *copisteria* harboured a potential black-marketeer in opera scores and when a composer's rights in his music could be as easily flouted as protected.

A legitimate *Otello* opened the 1887–88 season at the Teatro Regio in Turin on the traditional date of Santo Stefano, 26 December. Here the score was conducted by Giovanni Bolzoni, and the principal roles were entrusted to Elvira Colonnese (Desdemona), Giovanni Battista De Negri (Otello) and Ottorino Beltrami (Iago), who was soon replaced by the more experienced Lhérie. During the first decade of *Otello* performances, De Negri came to be valued as second only to Tamagno in the arduous title role, even though by 1896 his career was abruptly terminated after an ineptly performed operation on his vocal chords. *Otello*'s initial run at Turin achieved the resounding total of thirty performances. While De Negri was establishing his claims to the role of Otello in Turin, Tamagno was in Naples, where he introduced his famous characterization to the stage of the San Carlo.

Tamagno and De Negri soon came into direct competition with their interpretations of Otello on the stage of the Carlo Felice at Genoa. At first the field belonged to De Negri, who sang all six performances in a special pre-Carnevale series that began on 24 November 1888, conducted by Gaetano Cimini and supported by Valentina Mendioroz as Desdemona and Senatore Sarapani as Iago. According to Vallebona, the chronicler of the first century of the Carlo Felice, De Negri produced 'a deep impression with his stupendous voice and his artistic spirit' (1928: 123). So eager were the Genoese to hear Verdi's work again that a further six performances were scheduled in the latter part of the Carnevale season of 1888–89, and in these De Negri sang the first four, and Tamagno, fresh from having introduced his Otello at the Teatro Carolino in Palermo, appeared in the last two. According to Vallebona again, this second series was an 'immense success', but 'especially' those performances in which Tamagno participated. Cimini was again the conductor and Mendioroz repeated her Desdemona, but the chronicle does not specify who sang Iago. The local appetite for *Otello* continued so unabated that the score was revived on 24 January 1891 for eight further performances, in which De Negri was joined by Cesira Ferrani and Ramon Blanchart (Iago). In Genoa the following year the quadricentennial of Columbus' voyage was celebrated at the Carlo Felice with a *Feste Colombiane*, a special season that opened on 23 August 1892 with Tamagno, surrounded now by Ericlea Darclée and Leone Fumagalli, for ten more performances. While the De Negri performances of 1891 are recorded as attaining that pitch of excitement known to the Italians as *fanatismo*, those of the following year with Tamagno are reported to have evoked delirious enthusiasm.

Before glancing further at Italian *Otello* performances, let us consider the introduction of the score abroad. The extraordinary interest and anticipation aroused by Verdi's newest opera produced the phenomenon that it was first put on in the United States and in England by special Italian touring companies, underwritten by local entrepreneurs. New York first heard *Otello* at the Academy of Music on 16 April 1888, produced by a company under the musical aegis of the twenty-seven-year-old Cleofonte Campanini, who had first come to the United States to serve as a répétiteur for the opening season of the Metropolitan Opera House. The star of the company was the conductor's elder brother, the tenor Italo Campanini, born in 1845 and, therefore, five years older than both Tamagno and De Negri. Campanini was a singer with a solid reputation in New York, having been in the cast of the *Faust* that opened the Metropolitan's doors on 22 October 1883; indeed even prior to this he had been a regular for a decade at the New York Academy of Music. Unfortunately, for some reason he did not appear in the first New York performance of *Otello*. His place was taken by the unsuitable (at least for the title role) Francesco Marconi, a well-endowed lyric tenor who had been singing in such operas as *La sonnambula* and *I puritani* and one who found anything more taxing than Enzo in *La Gioconda* heavy weather. Surrounding the frequently inaudible Marconi were Eva Tetrazzini – the elder sister of the more famous Luisa and later to become Signora Cleofonte Campanini – and Antonio Galassi (Iago), who was a veteran of many a Mapleson tour across the United States. Both Verdi's music and Marconi were harshly dealt with by the New York critics, then of a decidedly Teutonic orientation and buoyed up by the seasons of German opera current at that time at the Metropolitan: the first American performances of both *Siegfried* and *Götterdämmerung*, for instance, had occurred there only a few months earlier. In this context, then, one is less surprised by their condescending conclusion that in *Otello* Verdi seemed to be making a valiant, if futile, effort to come to terms with Wagner and his Music of the Future. Matters improved appreciably, however, four days after the local premiere, when, on 20 April 1888, Italo Campanini was able to replace Marconi. Thus bolstered, the troupe went on to give the first local performances of the opera in both Boston (on 30 April) and in Philadelphia (on 4 May).

The English premiere of *Otello* took place under more favourable artistic circumstances than those in New York. This first London performance occurred at the Lyceum on 5 July 1889. With the co-operation of Ricordi an entrepreneur named Mayer was able to import Franco Faccio and the La Scala orchestra and chorus, along with Tamagno and Maurel in their original roles. Their Desdemona was now Aurelia Cataneo, who the previous summer had appeared in the Italian premiere of *Tristan*, as Isotta in Boito's translation. Twelve *Otello* performances were given that month, and the expensive project is reputed to have turned some profit. On the whole, the critical climate in London was less biased than in New York (where, in order to present Wagner's major scores, the leading operatic institution had temporarily been turned into a German-language theatre, performing its entire repertory, even Italian and French operas, in that language with German singers). G. B. Shaw may have been a professed Wagnerian, but he had a sharp ear and a keen repertorial eye. He reviewed one of this series of London performances on 12 July 1889:

I have just paid my first visit to *Otello* at the Lyceum. The voices can all be beaten at Covent Garden: Tamagno's shrill and nasal, Maurel's woolly and tremulous, Signora Cataneo's shattered, wavering, stagy, not to be compared to the worst of Mr Harris's prima donnas. On the other hand, Maurel acts quite as well as a good provincial tragedian, mouthing and ranting a little, but often producing striking pictorial effects; Tamagno is original and real, showing you Othello in vivid flashes; and the interpretation of Verdi's score, the artistic homogeneity of performance, the wonderful balance of orchestra, chorus, and principals, stamp Faccio as a masterly conductor. The work of the orchestra and chorus far surpasses anything achieved under Signor Mancinelli at Covent Garden. The opera is powerful and interesting: immeasurably superior to *Aida*: do not miss it on any account . . .   (Shaw, rpt. 1937: 167)

To put this review in some perspective, it should be noted that it was a postscript tacked onto a diatribe about inept singing teachers and an account of Goetz's *The Taming of the Shrew* performed by students at the Royal College of Music; furthermore, Shaw makes no reference to *Otello* in his résumé of that London season that appeared in *The Star* later that month. To be sure, this was the time when he was an ardent partisan for the introduction of Wagner performances in German as part of the regular Covent Garden seasons; there is some comfort in noting, however, that in 1894 Shaw included Faccio's *Otello* along with Richter's *Meistersinger* and Mottl's *Tristan* as forming the triad of the most memorable performances in his experience (Shaw, rpt. 1932: III, 232).

These first London performances of *Otello* were not without their repercussions in New York, for Henry Abbey, a venturesome impresario, had perceived the *reductio ad absurdum* apparent in the final seasons of the Metropolitan's German phase and decided the time had come to reassert the claims of Italian opera. And what better drawing card to realize that ambition than Verdi's *Otello* with Tamagno in the title role, particularly if it were balanced by Adelina Patti in her bel canto repertory? Abbey's tour opened in Chicago, where his company inaugurated the just-completed Auditorium. Following a dedicatory concert on 9 December 1889 and Patti in Gounod's *Roméo et Juliette* the next night, Tamagno made his North American debut in *Guglielmo Tell* on the 11th, building anticipation for what by now had become his *cheval de bataille* by further appearances as Manrico and Radamès. *Otello* was premiered in Chicago shortly thereafter, on 2 January 1890: Tamagno was joined by Emma Albani and Giuseppe Del Puente, along with the veteran conductor Luigi Arditi. With the solitary exception of one Desdemona sung by Lillian Nordica, the cast of the first performance would remain the same for the fourteen performances of the tour. Abbey's forces gave Mexico City its first 'legitimate' performance of *Otello* on 18 January 1890, and then brought the opera to San Francisco (12 February), Denver (28 February) and Louisville (6 March). Now moving still further east, Abbey's troupe invaded the territory covered by Campanini's not altogether happy campaign of nearly two years before. After a week in Boston, where *Otello* was played twice, this company moved on to New York, taking over the Metropolitan Opera House, which only two days earlier had brought down the curtain on the final all-German season. Abbey opened there on 24 March 1890 with *Otello*, sung by his regular cast, and he repeated his repertory for the next four weeks. Although Abbey's company had its ramshackle features – particularly since Arditi, the composer of such vocal trifles as *Il bacio*, *Parla!* and *The Melba Waltz*, was scarcely an ideal conductor for *Otello* – this enterprise had at least furnished a broad cross-section of the North American public with its clearest notion so far of Verdi's opera, thanks to the efforts of Tamagno, who more than once performed his taxing role on two successive days.

In both London and the United States the most prominent Otello of the following year, 1891, was Jean de Reszke, who hoped to per-suade his public that there was another approach to Verdi's great role than Tamagno's stentorian one. After several postponements, de Reszke sang the first Otello of his career at Covent Garden on 15 July, when the other leading roles were sung by Albani and Maurel, with Mancinelli conducting. There was some unruliness on the part of a segment of the audience who missed Tamagno during the first two acts; this took the form of applauding Maurel at almost every phrase and disparaging de Reszke, who for his part had the support and vociferous encouragement of his good friend, the French baritone Jean Lassalle, strategically located in a proscenium box (Shaw, rpt. 1932: I, 235–6).

After scolding the tenor for his 'petulant laziness' in not under-taking Wagnerian roles, Shaw gives a none too flattering descrip-tion of de Reszke's acting, while remaining silent on the vocal characteristics of his impersonation:

His acting as Otello was about equally remarkable for its amateurish ineptitudes and for its manifestations of the natural histrionic powers which he has so studiously neglected for the last fifteen years . . . His reluctance to determined physical action came out chiefly in his onslaught on Iago, which he managed in such a way as to make the audience feel how extremely obliging it was of Maurel to fall. And at the end of the third act, in simulating the epileptic fit in which Otello's fury culminates, he moved the gods to laughter by lying down with a much too obvious solicitude for his own comfort.   (Shaw, rpt. 1932: I, 236)

Shaw goes on to compare the newer Otello with the former.

> His Otello will never be like Tamagno's, but he need not regret that, as the same thing might have been said of Salvini. The Italian tenor's shrill screaming voice and fierce temper were tremendously effective here and there; but the nobler side of the Moor, which Salvini brought out with such admirable artistic quietude and self-containment, and which de Reszke shews a considerable, though only half cultivated, power of indicating in the same way, was left untouched by Tamagno, who on this and other accounts is the very last man a wise tenor would attempt to imitate.
>
> (Shaw, rpt. 1932: I, 237)

That Covent Garden season of 1891 saw Jean de Reszke's Otello four times. On 25 July Albani was replaced by the twenty-six-year-old American soprano Emma Eames, who later would develop into one of the finest Desdemonas of her generation. Maurel sang three of the four Iagos. On the first night of this new Otello, Shaw had judged the last two acts of his performance to be superior (except for the ill-contrived fall at the end of the third act); at the subsequent ones, when there was no disturbance during the first half of the opera, his singing of the Act I Love Duet was judged to be the best that London had heard. Still, he could not eradicate the memory of the powerful impact of Tamagno in such moments as the 'Esultate' and the duet with Iago that closes the second act.

In the autumn of 1891 Jean de Reszke came to the United States for the first time. He was engaged by Abbey, who had entered into a triumvirate with Maurice Grau and Edward Schoeffel to run the Metropolitan. The New York season was preceded by a month-long tour that opened in Chicago on 9 November 1891 with the de Reszke brothers and Eames making their American debuts in *Lohengrin*, sung in Italian. Two weeks later, on 23 November, Jean sang his only *Otello* of the pre-season tournee. The cast was an exceptionally strong one, including Albani, Sofia Scalchi (Emilia), a debutante Iago in Edoardo Camera, and the veteran French tenor Victor Capoul as Cassio; the conductor was Louis Saar. There was likewise only one *Otello* performance in New York, on 11 January 1892, with the same singers heard in Chicago.

These six performances in London and New York mark the end of Jean de Reszke's association with this role; within a short time he became involved in mastering in German most of the leading Wagnerian roles. Before turning to other performers, however, it may be helpful to add an anecdote that gives some insight – besides that in Shaw's tone compounded of mockery and begrudging admiration – into the tenor's approach to this role. In her worshipful biography of the singer, Clara Leiser recounts an incident whose general flavour agrees with the comments of a number of Jean de Reszke's pupils:

One afternoon a friend was sitting in the room while Jean was going over a certain phrase in *Otello* again and again, the phrase 'E stanca, e muta, e bella', in the last scene. Curious as to why this great artist spent half an hour repeating nine syllables, he asked Jean what he was working for. 'Well', came the answer, 'I am standing here, gazing at the strangled Desdemona. She is very near me; that is, her body. But the soul of her is already far away. When I sing, "So pale, so still, so beautiful", I want to convey not only the sense of paleness and stillness and beauty, but the feeling that soon all that will be far away too. I am trying to convey the sense of distance through my tone.'   (1934: 245)

While Jean de Reszke experimented with *Otello* at Covent Garden, Tamagno continued to sing the role in Italian theatres, among others in Palermo, where he performed it for a second season and his Desdemona was Teresa Arkel. Tamagno's identification with the role was further reinforced in 1894, when both the Metropolitan and Covent Garden were thinking of combining revivals of *Otello* to coincide with their first performances of *Falstaff*. But even before Tamagno embarked on these ventures, he found a new port of call for his interpretation at Monte Carlo, where he was the favourite singer of the Princess of Monaco and could command a prima donna's *cachet*. He first sang his Otello there on 20 January 1894, in the company of Frances Saville and Gabriel Soulacroix; Léon Jehin conducted, and it was repeated three additional times within a ten-day period. (Tamagno would return to Monte Carlo in 1897 and would open both the 1898 and 1899 seasons in *Otello*; he would sing it yet again in 1900 and 1901). When *Falstaff* received its English premiere during the summer of 1894, it was without Maurel, who was involved in Paris with the lengthy preparations for the introduction of the French *Otello* at the Opéra; and indeed, as things turned out, there was no *Otello* in London that summer at all, since Tamagno was occupied elsewhere.[1] The desired conjunction first occurred in New York that winter. On 3 December 1894 the Metropolitan revived *Otello* with Tamagno and Maurel (his debut with that company), joining Eames as Desdemona and Luigi Mancinelli as conductor. There were three additional performances by 2 January 1895; this left Maurel free for a month of rehearsals before the introductory *Falstaff* on

4 February. On the post-season Metropolitan tour of 1895 Tamagno and Maurel participated in eight further presentations of *Otello* and introduced their now-famous interpretations to Baltimore (19 February), Washington (22 February) and St Louis (2 April). Back in England, on 13 May 1895 Tamagno opened the Covent Garden season with his Otello, now in the company of Albani and Arturo Pessina as Iago, the baritone who had sung Falstaff there the previous year. *Otello* received five performances in all, with Margaret Macintyre taking over for Albani and Maurel donning his doublet as Iago. As in New York, the conductor was invariably Luigi Mancinelli.

The scenic aspects and the stage direction of these performances, particularly those at which there was no carry-over from the 1887 production at La Scala (as at the English premiere in 1889), were at no very high level: clearly, audiences were more tolerant of these features than they would later become. Jean de Reszke reported that when he sang *Otello* at the Metropolitan in 1891, none of the three stage directors then employed by that company knew the opera at all, with the result that the tenor, abetted by his brother Edouard and Albani, were forced to take over that function (Leiser 1934: 119). Such a situation was not without precedent in those 'carefree' days, when the demands of the more volatile singers had to be observed. For instance, when in 1897 Tamagno appeared at the Paris Opéra as Otello as a special guest, it would have been surprising had he relearned his role in French for this isolated occasion.

In 1898 the forty-eight-year-old Tamagno began to suffer from heart trouble, but he continued to pursue his career for three more years. Besides the above-mentioned performances at Monte Carlo between 1897 and 1901, he returned to La Scala on 27 December 1899 for the first of nineteen performances that season under Toscanini's direction, appearing in all of them with Emma Carelli as Desdemona and either Delfino Menotti or Tieste Wilmant as Iago and Oreste Luppi as Lodovico. In the summer of 1901 he bade farewell to Covent Garden with, among other things, a series of six Otellos, in which he was joined by either Emma Eames or Phoebe Strakosch as Desdemona and Antonio Scotti or David Bispham as Iago, with Mancinelli again assuming musical control.[2]

With the retirement of Tamagno and Maurel, the first phase of *Otello*'s performance history – that part of it in which some glimmers of Verdi's direct influence might have survived – may be said to have terminated. (In the pit, however, the situation was otherwise: Arturo Toscanini, who had been a cellist in the orchestra under Faccio's leadership in 1887, claimed that his memories of it remained fresh.) But before we leave the two singers from the original cast, there are still a few points worth making. Tamagno's Otello, for instance, might well have changed during the fourteen years in which he performed the role. The New York critic W. J. Henderson, who had heard Tamagno in 1890, found in 1894 that his interpretation 'has lost some of the dignity that the severe restraint of [Verdi] imposed upon it in earlier years, [but] it has lost none of its tremendous power, its sweeping expression of fierce, over-mastering passion, and its superb vitality of declamation' (Seltsam 1947: 69). And after his health began to wane, it seems that Tamagno began to husband his resources and – perhaps a result of his experience with Toscanini at La Scala in 1899–1900 – even found a way to sing *mezza-voce*, a refinement that had eluded him earlier (Lauri-Volpi 1955: 120). Of his final appearance in London, one critic went so far as to claim that 'Tamagno as actor and singer was head and shoulders above every other artist alive' (Rosenthal 1958: 294).

Of Maurel's Iago, the critics, with the exception of Shaw, were generally enthusiastic. Henderson reacted to him at the time of his Metropolitan debut as Iago, as a singer 'with some of the freshness gone from his voice – never a great one – but with his art at its maturity . . . a truly great singing actor. His work . . . was charged with vitality and significance. His vocal work was full of finesse . . . ' (Seltsam 1947: 69). In 1891 Shaw had objected to Maurel's Iago as not being human enough and wanting some touches of realism. He then went on to make an illuminating distinction:

The excessive descriptiveness which is the fault in [Maurel's] method, and even in his conception of the actor's function, resulting in a tendency to be illustrative rather than impersonative, occasionally leads him to forget the natural consequences of the actions he represents on stage.

For instance, when Otello half throttles Iago, it is a little disillusioning to see the victim rise from a faultless attitude, and declaim [']Divina grazia, difendimi['], with his throat in perfect order. Nothing is easier to produce than the *voce soffocata*; and there are not many operatic passages in which it is more appropriate than here. (Shaw, rpt. 1932: I, 238)

When Maurel returned to London in 1895, his inventiveness had been subjected to a renewed dose of Verdi's chastening, both from the rehearsals of the French *Otello* at the Opéra in 1894, and even before that from the composer's anger at the cuts that Maurel had insisted on introducing into the French *Falstaff* at the Opéra-Comique (Hepokoski 1983: 123). Maurel's presence in these productions was not of long or consistent duration, since when the baritone departed for the United States near the end of 1894, Francisque Delmas took over as Iago at the Opéra, and Lucien Fugère became the Falstaff at the Opéra-Comique. In sum, the available evidence suggests that Maurel shared with certain other singers of pronounced dramatic gifts a tendency to deflect attention from his waning vocal endowment by inserting distracting bits of action. But it is Shaw, once again, who supplies what is probably the fairest estimate of Maurel's genius.

> He challenges criticism as a creative artist, not as a mere opera-singer. In doing so he at once arouses antagonisms from which his brother artists are quite exempt, since his view of the characters he represents may conflict with that of the critics – a risk obviously not run by eminent baritones who have no views at all. (Shaw, rpt. 1932: I, 169)

To turn to the subsequent stage history of *Otello* is to note a strange phenomenon. In the German-language theatres, where the opera was customarily sung in the German translation of Max Kalbeck, himself a librettist as well as a translator, the opera was introduced with considerable dispatch. It first reached Hamburg on 31 January 1888, followed in fairly rapid succession by Munich (5 February), Vienna (14 March), Cologne (3 April), Bonn (23 April), and the list continues, although its introduction in Berlin did not occur until 1 February 1890. The success of the opera on these stages was in direct proportion to the suitability of whichever singers were appearing in it. In Hamburg, for instance, it maintained itself with considerable regularity, averaging about twenty performances a decade; the number of performances experienced a marked increase, of course, in the wake of the German Verdi revival that began about 1930. In Vienna, too, it fared well, launched by a cast that included Antonia Schläger (Desdemona), Hermann Winkelmann (Otello) and Theodor Reichmann (Iago), with the Intendant Wilhelm Jahn conducting. From Vienna would come the leading Otello of the next generation of the international circuit, Leo Slezak, who studied the role of Otello in Paris with Jean de Reszke. It remained in Slezak's active repertory for much of his lengthy career, near the end of which he was sometimes partnered with

Lotte Lehmann as Desdemona. *Otello* did not really take root in Dresden until it was revived there in the late 1920s with Meta Seinemeyer (Desdemona) and Tino Pattiera (Otello). In the 1930s there was a notable revival in Berlin with Tiana Lemnitz (Desdemona), Franz Völker (Otello) and Heinrich Schlusnus (Iago). At that time the emergence of a number of tenors with sufficient vocal power to produce an impression as Otello assured the opera's continued presence in German theatres; perhaps the most prominent of these were Helge Roswänge, Marcel Wittrisch and Max Lorenz.

It was no doubt due to the fame of Tamagno's powerful impersonation of the title character that up until about the time of World War II most of the general public regarded *Otello* primarily as a vehicle for a tenor with special vocal attributes. Otello's brief but gruelling *sortita*, the notorious 'Esultate!', came to be regarded as a classic test of a tenor's powers. This singling out of the *sortita* was largely the result of Tamagno's own example: on more than one occasion admiring crowds, having followed him to his hotel after an *Otello* performance, would raise a clamour sufficient to draw the tenor out onto his balcony; then, when the cheering seemed interminable, he would be obliged to deliver an impromptu, unaccompanied 'Esultate!' from on high. Once, when the enthusiasm seemed boundless, he is reported to have even added an encore, transposing the passage up a half step. Apochryphal or not, such legends were told and they were enough to make his would-be successors in the part quail.

The relative paucity of performances of *Otello* in Italy for the two decades following Tamagno's retirement is in some measure due to the panic lesser tenors felt in the face of the competition with an unassailable myth. For instance, at the Carlo Felice in Genoa, following those Tamagno performances at the *Feste Colombiane* of 1892 there were no subsequent performances until 1902, when Orazio Cosentino (with Maria Farneti as Desdemona and Wilmant as Iago) managed to survive ten performances, modestly described as 'buono'. Ten more years elapsed before the opera appeared again on 22 February 1912. On this occasion, the Puerto Rican tenor Antonio Paoli was whistled at so derisively during the opening performance that he withdrew, to be replaced in the ensuing seven by Nicola Zerola. *Otello* did not reappear until it opened the Carnevale season of 1923–24 on 26 December for a series of eight performances. Now the title role was in the hands of Jean Brumet, later supplanted by Giovanni Zenatello, and the Desdemona was Linda Canetti; the Iago, Giovanni Inghilleri. At La Scala the once-a-decade record of the Carlo Felice of these years was not even approached. Between the Toscanini-led performances of 1899–1900 with Tamagno and his revival of 1927, there was but one, not particularly happy, attempt to revive *Otello*. On 6 November 1913, under Tullio Serafin's direction, Icilio Calleja sang in the company of Linda Canetti and Mario Sammarco, in a new production with sets designed by Parravicini, Rota and Rovescalli and new costumes by Chiappa. Three performances with this cast formed part of a special Verdi centennial series at La Scala, but there followed thirteen more with much the same cast – Claudia Muzio and Enrico Nani appeared at least once as Desdemona and Iago, respectively – to open the regular season of 1913–14.[3] La Scala heard *Otello* no more until the Toscanini revival of 22 November 1927, when there was another new production, this time with scenery by Edoardo Machioro, costumes from Caramba's famous atelier, and a designated producer – Giovacchino Forzano. As if to break completely with the prevalent notion of *Otello* as a tenor's opera, Toscanini imported from France a singer unknown to Italy, one with an unspectacular voice but capable of retaining the conductor's musical instruction – Antonin Trantoul. In 1927, he appeared in the role eleven times, with Bianca Scacciati as Desdemona and Mariano Stabile as an outstanding Iago. Trantoul returned as Otello to open the 1929–30 season, but this time he and Stabile were joined by Rosetta Pampanini as Desdemona in five further performances. Infused with Toscanini's powerful sense of Verdi's score and cast with singers who did not deflect attention away from it onto themselves, this 1929–30 La Scala production is a significant milestone in the history of *Otello*. Unfortunately for Trantoul, nothing in his subsequent career matched his participation in this notable revival: a Buenos Aires audience, for example, would later force his withdrawal in the middle of a presentation of Boito's *Nerone*, and his few New York appearances left Metropolitan audiences wondering why he had been engaged to appear at all.

Otello would never again remain away from La Scala for an extended period after this fortieth anniversary revival by Toscanini. From 7 March 1935, it returned in three successive seasons for a total of fourteen performances, first with Gino Marinuzzi conducting; Francesco Merli as Otello and Maria Caniglia as Desdemona remained as constant figures in this series. The role of Iago was sung in 1935 by Stabile, but in the next two seasons it was performed by Piero Biasini, and in 1937 the musical direction was assumed by Victor De Sabata. Marinuzzi returned to the helm on 14 February 1941 for four more performances, at which time Caniglia and Stabile were joined by the mannered Lauri-Volpi in the title role. There was another new production to open the post-war season of 1947–48, with scenery and costumes by Nicola Benois. On this occasion De Sabata conducted (as he would again in 1949 and 1951), and Ramon Vinay made his Milanese debut as Otello in the company of Caniglia and Gino Bechi (Iago). In the opera's next two appearances at La Scala the role of Desdemona was entrusted to Renata Tebaldi. In 1953 Mario del Monaco took over as the Moor, first with Leonard Warren and then Paolo Silveri as his antagonist, but now the conductor was Antonino Votto. From this account it can be seen how at La Scala the pattern of presenting *Otello* had changed from a relatively large number of performances in a few widely spaced seasons to a smaller total each season but repeated with a certain regularity as a central monument in a well-balanced repertory.

As the other house besides La Scala where Verdi had been personally involved in preparing his opera, here in French translation and with a ballet divertissement, the Paris Opéra presents a pattern similar to La Scala. The original 1894 Paris cast of Rose Caron, Albert Saléza (Otello), Maurel (Iago) and Albert Vaguet (Cassio) did not remain long intact. Before the year was out Delmas had replaced Maurel, who had left for the Metropolitan, and Hector Dupeyron had substituted for Saléza. On the occasion of what would be its thirty-sixth performance at the Opéra, *Otello* was revived on 6 November 1903 with a largely new cast – Louise Grandjean (Desdémone), Albert Alvarez (Otello), Delmas, and Léon Laffitte (Cassio) – again the baton was in the hand of Paul Taffanel, who had led the local premiere in 1894. This series ran for some twelve performances, and then the French *Otello* lay dormant until 1919, when it was revived again, now with Madeleine Bugg (Desdémone), Paul Franz (Otello) and Maurice Renaud (Iago), with Arturo Vigna conducting, but seven performances were all this effort produced. *Otello* was not put on again until 6 May 1931, for its fifty-fifth hearing at the Opéra, now with Yvonne Gall and Eidé Noréna alternating as Desdémone, Franz again as Otello, but Lauritz Melchior also sang the role that year, in German, while

Vanni Marcoux and Arthur Endrèze shared the part of Iago. The conductor was Philippe Gaubert. From this time until the reorganization of the Paris opera houses, the rate of performance of the French *Otello* more than doubles what it had been before 1931. By 1955 the regular Paris cast had become Régine Crespin, José Luccioni (Otello) and René Bianco (Iago). Among the Cassios of the Opéra are at least two that gained greater renown in more taxing assignments: Raoul Jobin, who sang the role in 1931, and Nicolai Gedda in 1957.

The decade of the 1920s, at least until the Toscanini revival of 1927, was a relatively dry period for *Otello* in most opera houses. (It appeared in several Covent Garden seasons during this period: see below.) An outstanding exception to this generalization is the Chicago Opera Company, which gave several performances every year during that decade in its relatively short season. The reason underlying this uncommon activity was the presence of Charles Marshall, an unknown tenor who had a brief, undistinguished career in Italy and had been rescued from the relative anonymity of vocal pedagogy in Philadelphia by Rosa Raisa, who remembered him from his Italian days as a singer of untapped potential. Marshall's Otello endured for eleven seasons and nearly thirty performances as the cornerstone of this venture. Before he undertook this assignment, the company had given only a single performance, on 11 January 1911, with the unlamented Zerola as the Moor. In his first outing Marshall had the strong support of Raisa as Desdemona and Titta Ruffo as Iago, while the baritone of the next two seasons was Raisa's husband Giacomo Rimini. In 1924–25 the conducting chores of *Otello* were assumed by Roberto Moranzoni, who retained them through 1931. Later Desdemonas in this continuing production were Anna Fitziu, Marion Claire, and, after the move to the new opera house in 1929, Claudia Muzio; the role of Iago was variously entrusted to Joseph Schwarz, Richard Bonelli, Montesanto, Cesare Formichi and Vanni Marcoux. During this period of dedicated and repeated service to Verdi's score in Chicago, the Metropolitan gave not a single performance of the work. Less persistent than Chicago, perhaps, but contrary to the prevailing pattern elsewhere, was the Kungliga Teater in Stockholm which gave *Otello* nine times in five different seasons during the 1920s.

At Covent Garden following Tamagno's last appearance there as Otello in 1901, the opera returned in 1903 with the French tenor Alvarez as the Moor and Scotti as Iago; it was given twice under the leadership of Mancinelli. The following autumn it came back once again to present Maurel in an exceptional late appearance in the role he had created. There was to have been a second performance that autumn, but it was cancelled when Valentin Duc, the Otello of the season, contracted a persistent hoarseness from his first outing in the part and no tolerable substitute was available. In 1908 Melba returned in her first London Desdemona in fifteen years to sing five performances with Giovanni Zenatello, with whom she had recently appeared at Hammerstein's Manhattan Opera Company. Scotti was the Iago, and Cleofonte Campanini conducted, as he would the following season when Louise Edvina was the Desdemona to Leo Slezak's Otello in three performances. The following season Melba returned to take her place in the cast, but Nicola Zerola's rough approach to the title role proved too much for London's sensibilities, and the opera was dropped after a single performance. During the last pre-war season of 1914, *Otello* was given four times, again with Melba, although Muzio replaced her at the second performance, with the veteran Scotti back as Iago, and Giorgio Polacco at the helm. The Otello this time was Paul Franz from the Opéra, who was, however, appearing in a part he would not sing in Paris until five years later.

When *Otello* returned to the stage of Covent Garden after World War I, it was to open Beecham's winter season on 3 November 1919, performed now in English, with Frank Mullings winning considerable credit for his admirably earnest performance. Mullings appeared in the role three times that season and three more in 1924; in most of these the Desdemona was Miriam Licette. *Otello* in Italian was brought back in 1926 in a fondly remembered revival, in which Lotte Lehmann partnered the now well-seasoned Moor of Zenatello. More performances were projected for the following season with James Joyce's favourite tenor, John O'Sullivan, but abruptly dropped after his poor showing in a dismal *Les Huguenots*. In 1928 Renato Zanelli made a favourable impression as Otello and strengthened it further two years later. In between Zanelli's two seasons, there had been another intended series in 1929, but this plan was dropped when Nicola Fusati had failed to please as Pollione. When *Otello* next came back in 1933, it was with the anomaly of Lauritz Melchior singing the title role in German, in contrast to the efforts of Rosetta Pampanini and Giacomo Rimini singing the original Italian; this mixture was tolerated for only two performances. Having relearned his role in Italian, Melchior was back as the Moor the following season, partnered now by non-Italians like Viorica Usuleac (who, however, was not liked as Desdemona and was therefore replaced by Joan Cross) and John Brownlee, but the Wagnerian's way of distorting vowel sounds to gain resonance and his uncertain command of legato left audiences no more enchanted with him than they had been the season before. For the Coronation season of 1937, the four performances of *Otello* were led again by Beecham, but now the title role was sung by Giovanni Martinelli, whose success seemed in even greater contrast with the showing of his immediate predecessor, and Noréna's Desdemona was preferred to Fernanda Ciani's, as Lawrence Tibbett's Iago was to Formichi's. In 1939 there were two more performances in the last season before the outbreak of World War II, once again with Melchior, now appearing with Caniglia and Mario Basiola, under the guidance of Vittorio Gui. One explanation for Melchior's tenacity in appearing in this role at Covent Garden is that he had been repeatedly denied an opportunity to sing it at the Metropolitan.[4]

After the war, *Otello* was brought back to London by the visiting La Scala company; De Sabata conducted three performances featuring Tebaldi, Vinay and Bechi. The next re-emergence of *Otello* was in the 1955–56 season, when Rafael Kubelik conducted seven performances with Gré Brouwenstijn, Vinay and Ottokar Kraus. The Iago had originally been intended to be Tito Gobbi, but his late arrival in Britain for rehearsals was disciplined by his being replaced by Kraus. In 1956–57 the previous season's forces were reassembled for another seven performances. Again, the pride of place of Verdi's score had been reasserted as a *sine qua non* of a balanced repertory.

To revert now to the Metropolitan, following the twelve performances of the 1894–95 season with Tamagno and Maurel, four in New York and eight on tour, several years elapsed before its return. Albert Alvarez, who would later sing Otello in London and later still in Paris, sang the title role on 31 January 1902, when he was joined by Eames (Desdemona), Louise Homer (Emilia), Scotti (Iago) and Marcel Journet (Lodovico), with Armando Seppilli conducting. W. J. Henderson thought Alvarez 'sang the music with brilliant power and eloquence'; Scotti's Iago he found 'well conceived', if 'not wholly subtle', but 'crafty, malignant, intense'; while Eames was 'gentle, graceful' and 'her voice showed again its perfect suitability to the music' (Seltsam 1947: 126). The opera received three performances in New York and one on tour, both for this season and the next, with the important difference that *Otello* was chosen to open the 1902–03 season at the Metropolitan; Manicelli, who had been absent from the United States the previous season, returned to conduct the score.

Six years would elapse before *Otello* was heard again at the Metropolitan, but one of the promises offered by the new Gatti-Casazza regime had been that of performing Verdi's last two operas as soon as worthy casts had been assembled. The second evening of Gatti's second season saw the revival of *Otello*, conducted by Toscanini. In the title role, Slezak, fresh from his coaching with de Reszke, made his memorable New York debut, accompanied by Frances Alda, Scotti, and that peerless comprimario, Angelo Badà as Cassio. The night of the revival was only the twelfth performance of *Otello* by the company in New York, but by the end of this season and the three succeeding ones that total had grown to thirty. With the exception of Pasquale Amato, who functioned as a regular alternate for Scotti, the first cast was usually maintained intact; however, during the 1910–11 season, when Alda did not appear with the company in New York, the role of Desdemona was filled by Marie Rappold. The last performance of this revival, on 31 January 1913, was the last *Otello* for twenty-four years by the resident company.

It was not intended to have worked out this way. Caruso rehearsed the role, but decided that he would be wiser to postpone it until later; but when *Otello* had been tentatively projected for a revival with Caruso in the early 1920s, his untimely death intervened. During this long hiatus when the Metropolitan did not perform Verdi's penultimate opera, the gap was to some extent filled for New York audiences by the activity of touring companies. In the spring of 1921, the Chicago company gave it at the Lexington Theater, with Raisa, Charles Marshall and Titta Ruffo, on which occasion Henderson observed that Pietro Cimini conducted with 'as much authority as the singers would allow' (Kolodin 1966: 296). Near the end of September 1922, the American San Carlo touring company gave it in New York with Anna Fitziu, Zerola and Vincente Ballester, conducted by the estimable Carlo Peroni. For the four succeeding seasons this company performed *Otello* once a year in New York with such Otellos as Manuel Salazar and the veteran Paoli. In 1933 they brought it back once more, this time with Aroldo Lindi. Although these San Carlo performances were indelicately cut and performed in front of odds and ends of scenery, their service to the New York public was estimable.

An *Otello* of an altogether different order returned to that city when the Metropolitan at long last revived the opera on 22 December 1937. Ettore Panizza conducted, and Giovanni Martinelli was cast as the Moor, having prepared himself for this assignment by performances within the preceding year in Chicago, London and Paris. His associates were Elisabeth Rethberg (Desdemona) – Panizza had previously rehearsed Eidé Noréna and Gina Cigna in the part before deciding upon Rethberg – Lawrence Tibbett was the Iago. There was a new scenic investiture that was functional rather than evocative by Donald Oenslager; the producer was the experienced Herbert Graf. Although Martinelli was past fifty and his voice showed signs of wear, he phrased his music with great art; for a comparable nobility of declamation one would probably have to go back to Tamagno himself. Martinelli managed to sustain himself in the role during the next four seasons, despite the undeniable signs of the passage of time. Rethberg and Tibbett were often associated with him in the cast, but on occasion Desdemona was sung by Maria Caniglia or Stella Roman, whose best role it was, and Iago was sometimes taken over by Carlo Tagliabue and Alexander Sved. As we have seen in the case of other theatres, *Otello* during the 1930s came to assume a more central position in the repertory.

After a four-year lapse, *Otello* rejoined the Metropolitan on 23 February 1946, when it was conducted by George Szell and sung by Torsten Ralf, Leonard Warren and Stella Roman. The following season it was back with the same principals, but now the conductor was Fritz Busch, and at the sixth and final performance of the season Ralf was succeeded by Ramon Vinay (on 12 March). *Otello* returned to open the 1948–49 season, again conducted by Busch, but now Vinay and Warren were joined by Licia Albanese as Desdemona. It was out of the repertory until 1951–52, when it came back with Fritz Stiedry conducting Vinay and Warren, with Eleanor Steber as Desdemona. At the second performance of *Otello* this season (15 February 1952), Mario del Monaco sang the title role for the first time with the Metropolitan. One of the best balanced casts of this period was first heard on 31 January 1955 when Renata Tebaldi made her company debut as Desdemona, with del Monaco and Warren, the latter continuing to grow into his role of Iago. When the opera was next performed, during the 1957–58 season, two newcomers to Desdemona's music were Victoria de los Angeles (27 February) and Zinka Milanov (17 March), the latter enjoying one of the more notable successes of the final stage of her career. On 10 March 1962, James McCracken returned to the Metropolitan as Otello; this was his second stint with the company, for he had sung Roderigo in the 1954–55 revival of *Otello*, along with other comprimario roles. It was an imposing impersonation, if not always completely convincing. To mark this occasion there was new scenery by Eugene Berman to replace the Oenslager settings that had seen service both in New York and on tour for nearly thirty years. Solti conducted, and Gabriella Tucci and Milanov shared the assignment of Desdemona, while Merrill was a vocally apt Iago. McCracken grew in confidence throughout the seven performances of the balance of that season. On 27 February 1967, the opera returned again, now conducted by Zubin Mehta, with Montserrat Caballé as Desdemona; Tito Gobbi resumed the role of Iago, which he had first sung in New York in 1958 (see his remarks on the role in Gobbi 1980: 106–12), and McCracken again was Otello. During this season, Jon Vickers offered his first Metropolitan Otello on 3 April 1967, in the company of Tucci and Gabriel Bacquier. There were no more performances of *Otello* until the final year of the Bing regime, 1971–72, when there was another new production, this one by Franco Zeffirelli, to take the place of the Berman sets that had not pleased, although they were far from worn out by Metropolitan standards. On this occasion Karl Böhm conducted McCracken, now joined by Sherrill Milnes, new to Iago, and Teresa Zylis-Gara as Desdemona. This production was maintained in the next two seasons, but with Jon Vickers gradually assuming increasing prominence as Otello, particularly after McCracken left the company in 1973–74. Another series of *Otello* performances began in the 1977–78 season, conducted by James Levine, with Vickers joined by Katia Ricciarelli or Renata Scotto and with Cornell MacNeil as Iago. The latest contender to the title role has been Placido Domingo, who first experimented with it in Hamburg in 1975. If this name-packed chronicle has a major point to make, it is that the Metropolitan in its second half-century will not allow more than a few seasons to pass without *Otello*, whereas in its first half-century the opera was given in but eight of the fifty seasons.

As a performance history of *Otello*, the preceding remarks make no pretence to be anything more than representative. As such, I believe, it illustrates three distinct phases of the opera's career during its first century. In the first phase, although Verdi clearly intended his opera to make its way on its own magisterial merits, it became, at least in the awareness of the public, a vehicle that turned both Tamagno and Maurel into international stars in a way that neither of them had quite been before. Its first round of successes were brightest when they appeared in it. This was followed by a second phase when *Otello* was more highly regarded as a great work than performed with any regularity, a situation that was encouraged by the trepidation felt by the next generation of singers to compete with the memory of their formidable predecessors. The attitude that *Otello* was a necessary part of the central repertory, a third phase more clearly promulgated in London and Chicago than in New York in the inter-war years, received a most beneficial reinforcement from the Toscanini revival at La Scala in 1927. The fruits of this attitude, along with the general readiness of audiences to go to the theatre to see a particular work rather than some well-advertised star, have been quite generally apparent since World War II. The signs look bright for the second century of *Otello*.

7 An introduction to the musical organization: the structures of Act II

With the unmistakably 'progressive' *Otello*, which pushed formal freedoms well beyond the *Aida* point while strengthening the role of the orchestral motivic work in the interests of increased musical continuity, Verdi had crossed a significant aesthetic line. For the first time in a complete Verdian opera one may seriously question whether the larger formulaic *ottocento* structures are consistently relevant: they not infrequently seem to exist more as memory – or as implied, but distant, referential points – than as current reality. In *Otello* each act now comprises a series of 'formal' pieces (or *pezzi*, as they shall be called here) – often relatively static and set in relief through a variety of procedures – that are smoothly approached and left by freer, more dramatically active connectives. The opera flows from one stratum of lyrical-dramatic formality and intensity into another, and all of the levels respond in their own ways to the exigencies of the drama. In the most basic, poetic sense – and there are significant exceptions within this complex work – the *pezzi* are usually recognizable through their use of *versi lirici* (rhymed, regular verse), while the connectives are normally written in one of two types of recitative verse (a characteristically Boitian complication): unrhymed *endecasillabi* (11s), implying a recitative-like setting that may be referred to as a '*scena*'; and a more heightened, rhymed mixing of *endecasillabi* (11s), *settenari* (7s), and *quinari* (5s), implying a similarly free setting, or 'rhymed *scena*'.

In brief, the normative structural unit in *Otello* –the 'modern' substitute for the old 'numbers' – is now one that passes through three phases: (rhymed) *scena* / *pezzo* / (rhymed) *scena*, or, in terms perhaps more directly relatable to dramatic and emotional effect, entrance (transition-in) / set piece / exit (transition-out). With some leeway for flexibility and variants, and with a certain sympathy for the process of inductive abstraction, the opera may be understood to consist largely of a string of these three-phase musical-dramatic units. The set piece, the core (set in high, often lyrical musical relief), typically unfolds a separate system of musical relations within itself, although, of course, it participates in larger organizational systems as well. Embedded within a freer, more generative husk, these *pezzi* are the portions that touch the conventions of the Italian past most decisively. In many ways they are the principal 'Italian' identifiers around and through which the more 'progressive' motivic drama is spun. To be sure, the three-phase model itself is eminently derivable from past Verdian practice (for instance, from duets or ensembles with omitted *cabaletta* or *stretta*): it is its consistent and freely varied employment here that makes a notable break with Verdi's past operas.

The abstract model embraces a variety of actual realizations, dramatic exceptions, and subtle complications, the detailing of which would require more space than is available here. Some types of variants, however, include highlighted and expanded *scene* (for instance, the lengthy stretches of the ambassadors' entrance and Otello's reading of the parchment in Act III – an expanded entrance-*scena* – and the entire Murder Scene in Act IV); motivically rounded *scene* (the exit-*scena* from the Duel in Act I, 89/2/1–92/4/4); omitted *scene* (before 'Dio! mi potevi scagliar' in Act III); a self-standing *pezzo* without a significant, poetically contrasting entrance or exit (the 'Ave Maria' in Act IV, but here, curiously enough, the 'poetic' set piece itself seems to be cast in a 'miniature', rounded three-phase form, its centrepiece being, of course, 'Prega per chi adorando a te si prostra'); a self-sufficient *scena* without *pezzo*, having the effect of a separate recitative introduction to a subsequent, more normative entrance-*scena* (the opening dialogue of Act II); the addition of a 'static', *stretta*-like fourth phase (the Act I Victory Chorus), unusual in *Otello* but clearly evoking a common, earlier structural convention; and so on. The discussion of Act II below, which I have subdivided into 'numbered' three-phase units, will illustrate how the model is consistently used and varied throughout an entire act.[1]

As is often mentioned, an important element of continuity throughout *Otello* is provided by the grounding of the *pezzi* and *scene* in a network of developing orchestral motives – often clear, contrasting motives dramatically juxtaposed with one another. This is the 'symphonic' aspect of the opera, and it often provides the smooth, at times almost imperceptible transitions between many of the units (in a kind of late-Verdian 'art of transition'); more generally, the motivic work can produce the effects both of spinning unorthodox shapes out of the interplay of much smaller elements and of purposefully interconnecting the various larger structural units. More than ever in Verdi, the forms, both large and small, seem the products of the motives (see, e.g., Kerman 1956: 137–9). A number of specific instances will be apparent in the discussion of Act II below.

Before proceeding to that discussion, however, we might ask the general question, to what extent are some of the central *pezzi* and their supporting structures still related to conventional *ottocento* formulae? At times the relationship – or better, the 'evocation' – is clear, and this occasional lingering of the traces of past procedures is the most markedly traditional aspect of *Otello*. The most problematic area here is that of duet-structure: the duets – worthy of a full-length study in themselves – range from the notably 'traditional' (the '*cabaletta*'-like ending of Act II, 'Sì, pel ciel') to the extremely free (the heightened, *scena*-like setting of the first Otello–Iago Duet in Act II). In between are the freely sectional but rounded Otello–Desdemona Act III Duet (a provocative, but problematic, analysis of which is provided in Nicolaisen 1980: 46–50), and the much-discussed Act I Love Duet, which approaches – but still radically modifies – aspects of the conventional duet structure (see Archibald 1974; Lawton 1978; Parker and Brown 1985; and especially Powers 1987).

Some of the most 'traditional' structures in *Otello*, however, occur in the shorter forms within individual *pezzi*. These briefer melodic paragraphs often play on the simplicity of the old Italian 'lyric form', aa'ba'' (or aa'bc, etc.), with its several possible extensions and variants (Budden 1973: 14–15; Kerman 1982) for effects of naiveté or, particularly, to evoke the bitter irony of loss. Thus the music for the chorus, a consistently honest, ingenuous, and direct group throughout the opera, sometimes falls quite naturally into the aa'ba'' (as in the final two of the three interior episodes of the Act II Homage Chorus) or aa'bc (as in the Act I Victory Chorus) schemes. Similarly, Desdemona uses the aa'ba'' pattern to shape her 'Prega per chi adorando a te si prostra' within the 'Ave Maria', and the simple trust that she bears for this time-worn emotional contour carries a special poignancy. As we shall see, Otello evokes the structure to bid it farewell in 'Ora e per sempre addio'. Iago taunts Otello with shameless distortions of the 'naive' structure – or a close variant – in 'Era la notte'. And Otello and Desdemona begin their Act III Duet, 'Dio ti giocondi, o sposo', by caressing the purest of aa′ba″ patterns (which is then immediately extended with an episodic interpolation, 'Eppur qui annida', and ultimately rounded a few bars later). For Desdemona the initial, simple aa′ba″ shape reflects the smiling, frictionless give-and-take of a love-ritual; for Otello it is savage irony, because he interprets her ingenuousness as debased sham. It is important to keep this 'naive' shape in mind, for in the Duet's brief reprise, 'Datemi ancor l'eburnea mano' (224/3/1, beginning with a′), Otello liquidates the structure midway through to shout his frenzied 'vil cortigiana' accusation. Otello's desecration of the form parallels his now-explicit rejection of Desdemona's innocence, and the orchestra, in a short exit-passage, responds with primitive convulsions.

Finally, one might call special attention to Verdi's (and Boito's) apparent favouring of poetic and musical stanzas with concluding refrains. The convention most probably evoked here is that of the French operatic *couplet*, particularly appropriate for genre pieces, inset songs, songs performed by characters of common, or less noble, blood, and so on. The structure's natural habitat seems to have been within 'artless' songs, but Verdi had been experimenting with offshoots, elevations, and elaborations of the genre in several of his past operas (for instance, in Aida's 'O patria mia'). Astonishingly, in *Otello* the *couplet*-structure is evoked no fewer than four times. Moreover, three of them bear marked formal resemblances despite their differences of emotional tone and structural nuance: the Act I *Brindisi* ('Inaffia l'ugola!', 59/4/3), the first portion of the Act III Terzetto ('Essa t'avvince coi vaghi rai', 236/3/1, up to the appended *stretta*-substitute, 'Questa è una ragna', 245/1/1), and the Act IV Willow Song. Each is built from three strophes of poetry, the first two of which are parallel and the third of which 'disintegrates' in one way or another – in drunkenness, in frustratingly inaudible whispers, or in morbid anxiety. For each of these three '*couplets*' Verdi suppresses radical variations in the first two strophes (although text-motivated variants do occur, the overriding principle is *reculer pour mieux sauter*), then distorts the third. The remaining '*couplet*', the interior episodes of the Act II Homage Chorus, provides a different but no less ingenious pattern, and it will be discussed within its proper place below.

The Music of Act II

The second act is the most dramatically pivotal of the four. It is here that the essence of Iago's plot is unfolded; it is here that Otello sinks from the *miles gloriosus* to the raging cuckold. With a few exceptions the first act had been largely decorative: a 'setting of the scene' in a succession of genre pieces. Indeed, the *tableau vivant* quality of the Act II Homage Chorus (an image even framed by a window) impresses us as an incursion into the second act of the principles of the first. The second act may not properly be said to be 'in' a single key at all, even in the limited sense in which E major as a frequent goal may be said often to dominate in Act I. In Act II individual keys hold sway over smaller areas and subdivisions, but no single pitch governs the entire act to produce a contained, tonally 'unified' whole. This is not to say that the tonal choices within the act are irrelevant, much less without dramatic significance. In fact, Act II seems grounded in the free clash and juxtaposition of two different key-systems: the resolution of the two at this point in the drama is not a significant factor. On the one hand, we find at the most general level an F-major–minor system (including arpeggiations of the upper and lower fifths, e.g., including such keys as a, A♭, C, d, and B♭), which Iago appropriates as his own at the opening of the act, and into whose fatal orbit fall both the B♭ Quartet and, possibly, Otello's A♭ 'Ora e per sempre addio'. On the other hand, one finds an E-major system (including E, g♯, B, c♯ and A) with clear associative links to Act I as an expressive region of stability, Venetian victory, serenity, the 'Bacio' ('Kiss'), and so on. Its evocation in the Homage Chorus is clear, but once Otello's mind has been poisoned this system tends to return only ironically, as in the suggestions of E in 'Era la notte' (a piece nominally in C and closer to Iago's Act II key-system), or, perhaps ferociously 'resolved' to its own subdominant, A major, as in 'Sì, pel ciel'. That there are important retentions of contrasting sonorities and tonalities throughout the act is beyond doubt. Because we are dealing, however, with the rather free interaction of entire complexes, indeed, systems that can overlap ambiguously, any attempt to demonstrate a rigorously 'inevitable' tonal plan throughout the details of the act – or to involve the various keys in a remorseless system of nuanced, psychological symbolism consistent throughout the opera – seems unwise. *Ne cherchons pas midi à quatre heures.*

1a Scena *Cassio–Iago (109/1/1–113/1/1)*

This *scena*, in some senses an introduction to – or a separable first part of – the first entrance-*scena* proper (No. 1b below), provides a classic illustration of a method of construction often encountered in mature and late Verdi that has little to do with the standard *ottocento* conventions. The basic principle is that of varied phrase- (or phrase-group-) repetition, in which the most characteristic variations involve dramatic interruptions, interpolations, truncations, or extensions of an initial model. (The Act IV 'Prelude and *Scena*' before the Willow Song is built similarly, but there the model is a smaller, five-bar phrase, hauntingly repeated and varied a greater number of times; see also Otello's 'Dio! mi potevi scagliar'.) In this instance the model is a sixteen-bar orchestral statement clearly divided into two asymmetrical parts (4 + 6) + 6, that share the same F-major cadence (Example 14); it concludes with a seventeenth bar, a brief orchestral tag (110/3/2) that recirculates into its opening, rotary-triplet motive. The rest of the *scena*, then, consists of a varied repetition of the model, now with text and with dramatic interpolations where desirable. The first part of the model recurs (beginning with its 'D-minor' fifth bar, its opening spins having been evoked in the tag) as Iago's words begin to be accompanied (110/5/1) and concludes eleven bars later, 'e il tuo perdono è certo' (112/1/2), but only after Iago has sinuously interpolated a new, gently rocking passage through a secretive-sounding G minor to plant the idea of Desdemona as intercessor into Cassio's ear. (Noske [1971]: 155–7 refers to the contour of this three-note ascent followed by a descending interval, here a fourth, 'Tu dêi saper', as Iago's 'designing motive', part of his general musical language. Notice here the perfection of the nuances: having delicately peered into the door of opportunity, Iago flings it wide open with the descending minor seventh of 'Pregala tu' – 'Importune her' – 111/4/1.) The varied second part of the model follows (112/2/1), even including the flickering, motivic tag, now doubled in length after Iago's dismissal of Cassio with his first 'vanne'. One might also notice that the model and its varied repetition are linked by the 'early' dovetailing of Iago's first words, 'Non ti crucciar' (110/3/2).

The dramatic intent of the structure is clear. Iago has 'preconceived' the scene, composed his gestures in advance, if you like, in the largely closed-curtain prelude. He smoothly carries out his plan in what follows, even as we break into the conversation *in*

Ex. 14

medias res. Indeed, the insistent motivic growth of the rotary-triplet upbeats, unrolling inexorably into larger, compound-metre phrases, suggests the gearing-up of a grand scheme. The F major of the opening initially appears to be a key with positive associations: we have just heard it prominently in the Love Duet (although Iago's final words in Act I, 'Oh! mio trionfo!', also in F major, 93/1/1, were scarcely positive). From the beginning measures of the second act, however, even before his first words, Iago has been colouring the 'benign' F major – manipulating it – with his own nuances: the move through D minor (109/3/1); the descending chromatic scale (e.g. 109/4/2), perhaps tinged with memories of his bellowed 'Beva' in the *Brindisi*; the important 'spoiling' of the F major with machinations in F minor for the second half of the model (110/1/1); and so on. This is all craftiness and miniature work. One can visualize Iago moulding every bar with his fingertips – always to return, of course, to the semblance of utter guilelessness, the seeming honesty, frankness, and *bonhomie* of his *dolce*, F-major cadence (Example 14).

1b Rhymed Scena *with Embedded Credo (113/1/2–123/4/4)*

Verdi now develops further the musical image of Iago as deceitful manipulator. Among the usual Iago-identifiers (orchestral trills, 'chromaticism', clearly enunciated declamation, interspersed triple-time rhythms or triplet-figures, rapid downward orchestral leaps often decorated with acciaccatura or triplet upbeat – see Noske [1971]: 148–57; and 1981: 149–50), a special type of harmonic and tonal practice becomes crucial here. Dramatically the two central aspects of Iago's self-image are his nonchalant confidence in the ease with which he can control and use others and his conviction that, through his own ability to mislead, nobody will be able to divine his true purposes until they have been carried out: Iago as puppeteer and trickster. Tonally, the first aspect translates as an *ad libitum*, almost anarchic wrenching of tonal levels in unpredictable and unprepared ways: keys become casually pliant, easily malleable in his hands. And the second, related aspect, suggests that Iago cunningly conceals his actual tonal goals. One is never quite certain where he is headed. At times the listener (with Cassio – and, later in the opera, with Otello) can only hang on dizzily to see how it all turns out.

The brief, seven-bar entrance-recitative, Iago's unmasking, begins by violently jolting the seemingly innocent 'tag' of the preceding *scena* into a *fortissimo*, nastily grinding idea on the Neapolitan, G♭ (113/1/2). Characteristically, the recitative leads not to the tonic of the 'Credo', F minor, but to an emphatically false goal, D♭, 'Inesorato Iddio' (114/1/1). This shifts immediately to the celebrated unison-pillars of negative affirmation (cf. Budden, III, 358) that uphold the set piece. The 'Credo', with its unusual, rhymed-*scena*-like text so metrically appropriate to this theatrical monologue, is structured in three distinct parts, ABA', for Verdi a French design (Kerman 1982), with important internal subdivisions. The initial section, lasting through 'quest'è la mia fè', is itself framed by the F-minor unison pillars, but its internal texture is declamatory and unpredictably modulatory. Thus Iago obscures the tonic F minor – as if commanding pungent clouds of hell-smoke – with diminished sevenths and, while carefully probing the sonorous space between c^1 and e♭^{1}, he produces – *voilà* – an emphatic cadence in the subtonic, E♭ major ('e che nell'ira io nomo', 114/3/3). This E♭ he then casually shifts up a step, to E major (that is, back towards F), for the second important motive of the piece, played *aspramente* (114/4/1), within which Budden acutely senses the flavour of a Lisztian or Boitian 'infernal dance' (III, 358). Iago regains F minor with 'Vile son nato', but promptly abandons it (chromatically, of course) for a decisive cadence on the dominant (and a plunge downwards into the 'fango originario' – 'primal mud' – of the lowest note of this part, C, before the F-minor pillars return.

The second part, B, reflecting the anaphora of its text, divides into three subsections. Each begins with the word 'Credo' or 'E credo', and each begins vocally a half-step higher than its predecessor (c^1, d♭^{1}, and d^1), as one unspeakable tenet is added to another. The entire second part is cast as a set of radical phrase-variations subjected to progressive disintegration – a typically late-

Verdian treatment. Thus the first subsection (itself a variant of material and sonorities from the last portion of the A section) rounds tonally in C minor. Its motivically important iv–I plagal cadence under 'Per mio destino adempio' (116/4/1–2), producing the 'C-major' Picardy third, will return, varied, at the conclusion of the piece. The second, 'D♭' subsection, 'Credo che il giusto', evades closure by jamming a seventh under the final 'tonic' chord, 'Sacrificio ed onor' (117/4/2). The third subsection, 'E credo l'uom', begins with menacing, tonally ambiguous diminished sevenths, then suddenly erupts with an unforeseen B$^6_4$ chord, 'Dal germe della culla' (118/2/1), a nihilistically sensational diminished fifth away from the reigning F minor of the set piece – with sinister aftermath in B minor, 'Al verme dell'avel'.

The final section, A', brings back the pillars of negative affirmation (119/1/2), now sounded *poco più lento* and chromatically harmonized (including some low parallel fifths in the strings). Besides its obvious rounding and synthesizing function, this section devotes itself to preparing and executing one of the most spectacular tricks in music: gulling the listener to believe in one tonic, the 'vecchia fola' of D♭ major, then cruelly slapping him across the face with the real one, F major (F minor with Picardy third). Much of the deception lies in the tantalizing text-setting. With each sneeringly stroked word Iago invites us to focus on textual meaning while, 'behind our backs', he manipulates the tonality. His first words, 'Vien dopo tanta irrisïon', are tellingly set over a submediant chord ('deceptive resolution') in F, but with 'Morte' the music decays into a murky diminished seventh. The 'pillar' motive returns, *ppp*, to cadence this time in D♭ before 'E poi?' (again via parallel fifths), thence to move fleetingly and ambiguously through F minor ('e poi?', preceded by a iv^6 in F minor, with the critical D♭ as bass, and a return to that D♭ bass, *ppppp*, two bars later). After the crucial 'La Morte è il Nulla' the orchestra rushes in, shrilly articulating what appears to be an asserted tonic with a clear plagal cadence ('Amen') in D♭, 'È vecchia fola il Ciel'. The D♭ tonic illusion is all the more believable since the IV–I cadence clearly echoes the parallel ending of Subsection I of Part B (116/4/1–2). But, no, the 'Amen' cadence in D♭ was but a cynically cruel joke, like heaven itself in Iago's text. On the next available beat the full orchestra gleefully, and with wicked satisfaction, pounces on the true tonic, F major – by now, Iago's F – to stun the listener, who has been looking elsewhere.

What better way for the spectator to understand Iago's capacity for deceit than by experiencing it personally – in effect, to find himself mocked by 'Iago's' orchestra, now exulting in ecstatic triplets?

An exit-transition ('Eccola'), rhythmically evolved out of the 'infernal dance' idea at the end of the 'Credo', permits Iago to arrange the details of the next stage of his plot. This is free action-music in late-Verdi's 'steathily busy' vein: a similar, scurrying-staccato texture would be used at the beginning of Act II Part ii of *Falstaff*. Although modulatory, the transition is texturally rounded, swelling in its centre into more melodic phrases for Iago (the A-minor–C-major section beginning with the diabolic invocation, 'aiuta, aiuta / Sàtana il mio cimento!', 12/3/3). With his final words, 'all'opra' ('to the task', 123/3/2), Iago sets in place the key he needs – a seemingly pure D major not clearly related to anything that we have heard thus far – and nudges the staccato motive forwards (including two malevolent *pianissimo* octave leaps in the horn) to begin the next section.

2 'Duet' Otello–Iago ('Scena') and Homage Chorus (124/1/2–154/1/1)

Notwithstanding its text in *versi lirici* (rhymed *doppi settenari*, 7 + 7, but disposed here in active dialogue), Verdi treats this critically important Duet, Iago's first set of direct operations on Otello, as a free, heightened recitative, now melodic, now declamatory, the better to underscore every line of text. It falls into six modulatory subsections – tempo and texture changes. The first three are centred around D major–minor, and the last three gravitate towards the E major of the Homage Chorus. The sustained opening chord of Subsection I could not more perfectly colour the situation. Having bustled about in modulatory *staccati* to get everything in order, Iago now gazes at Cassio and Desdemona and lays down a wide-eyed, 'innocent' D_4^6, ripely in need of resolution, while above it he leans with skilfully feigned anguish on the dissonant g ('Ciò m'accora'). He dangles this prolonged, lurid dominant (cadential $_4^6$–V^7) in front of Otello for fourteen tantalizing bars. In the first ten the violins, almost imperceptibly, trace the outline of a fourth-ascent and return, a–b–c♯^{1}–d^1: this intervallic shape, once inverted later in the act, will become an explicit symbol of Iago's control and Otello's downfall. This opening phrase of the 'Duet' plays on carefully gauged, provocative nuances. Gingerly resolving his dominant,

Ex. 15

Iago asks Otello in an insinuatingly undular phrase about Cassio's early acquaintance with Desdemona (125/3/1; Example 15). The interrogative melodic lift on 'conosceva' is pointed with a pizzicato V$^6_5$/V, the only altered chord in the phrase and an uncanny musical question-mark. (By way of contrast, try the phrase with G♮ in the bass at this point, a standard ii$^6_5$.) Otello responds, 'Si', and repeats the question-mark, now V$^4_3$/V ('Well?'), which instantly changes to the cocked head of genuine puzzlement, the single 'foreign' e♯[1] in the cello. Iago – always the obscurer of keys and intentions – denies the importance of his request by playfully leading the next two bars through F♯ minor and its dominant, before Otello returns to the main interrogative point, V of D major: 'Di' il tuo pensiero, Jago' ('Speak your thoughts, Iago', 126/2/2, shaped from Iago's earlier 'designing motive', which now lingers as accompaniment to several of the ensuing bars – see p. 144 above). This artfully shaded manner of mincing motivic insinuation continues until the exasperated Otello bursts into the faster, *forte* Subsection II, demanding an explanation (128/1/1). This is the first of the Moor's several rages. It begins with a keening chromatic wail ('nel chiostro / Dell'anima', etc.), modulatory shifts , rising sequences, and a tonal 'collapse' into *fortissimo* diminished-seventh chord bluster: the typical musical apparatus of his fury. At the end he hands the V^7 of D major back to Iago, 'Suvvia, parla se m'ami' ('Go ahead, speak if you love me'), and Iago chillingly resolves it to D minor, 'Voi sapete ch'io v'amo' ('You know that I love you'). Iago's original point in proffering the bright D major at the beginning of the Duet is now clear: it was to wrench it into the parallel D minor, to set the hook, here at the beginning of Subsection III (129/4/1) – a tonality within the sinister orbit of his F-major axis. But, characteristically, the keys, under Iago's spell, are soon unpredictably twisted elsewhere – through A minor, then through B-flat (130/3/2). Within nine bars, after Otello's exhortations, Iago arrives at the pivotal words of the opera, with whose utterance Otello's life changes, 'Temete, signor, la gelosia!' – landing on another unforeseen chord, V^7 of F♯ minor. Verdi's extraordinary setting, appropriately enough, indulges in explicit sensationalism with its flagrant, 'monstrous' reliance on parallel triads.

The F♯-minor Subsection IV (it will function as ii of the eventual E major) is the celebrated serpentine setting of Iago's 'dark hydra' lines (131/1/1) – the most powerful melodic image in the Duet – with their characteristic, bestial vocal trill. It may derive from the rise-and-fall idea of Iago's 'designing motive' (Noske [1971]: 155–7), and, of course, the melody will recur as a poison-motive in the Prelude to Act III. Subsection V, 'Miseria mia!!' (131/3/3), is Otello's second rage-passage, again modulatory (but aiming at E minor) with motivic, upward sequences in the orchestra, much diminished-seventh colour, and the like, and Otello now pushes his line up to a desperate, high b^1, 'Amore e gelosia vadan dispersi insieme' (133/1/1), only to have his E-tonic goal delayed and ushered in two bars later by Iago. Subsection VI (133/3/1), finally in the goal-key of E (now major), introduces the distant, off-stage chorus in anticipation of the set piece to follow. Iago, 'the seal of his lips' now broken, lets the poison flow freely in rapid recitative. The *idée fixe* here is 'Vigilate', the melodic leap from dominant to tonic and back again. Its psychological point is to stain with suspicion the most innocent of appearances, and its cruel implications echo through the unguarded simplicity of the tonic–dominant ostinato in the 'cornamusa' that accompanies the chorus. Iago's appropriation of the innocent $\hat{5}$–$\hat{8}$ (V–I) sonority deflowers everything that Otello will subsequently see and hear.

The E-major Homage Chorus proper, beginning 135/2/1 (launched with one final 'Vigilate' from Iago), is a simple pastel *tableau*. Its static, symmetrical arch structure could not contrast more markedly with the wily fluidity preceding it: x / A / B–C–D / A' / x (6-bar string introduction / full chorus / three interrelated 'solo' choral episodes / full chorus, with Desdemona-led coda / 6-bar string conclusion). The use of children's voices and rustic instruments – bagpipes (cornamusa), mandolins, and guitars – are central aspects of this piece's naiveté, as are the internal forms. Moreover, the choral episodes evoke the entrenched barcarolle genre, thus providing a recognizable Venetian stamp – a kind of local colour – on the scene, despite the stage directions that identify the townspeople, sailors, and so forth as Cypriots and Albanians: the point, of course, is that they are honouring Desdemona in the accents of her native city (Salmen 1976 provides a discussion of the barcarolle as an operatic genre). The full chorus, 'Dove guardi', already heard at the end of Subsection VI of the preceding Duet, unfolds in a simple aabb' setting, contentedly diatonic in the 'secure' key of E and rhythmically reflecting the unusual trochees of Boito's *senario* verse. The episodes of the middle section are grounded in the *couplet* principle, always fitting for inset songs of a popular or folklike nature: three successive strophes, each with a four-line refrain ('Mentre all'aura vola / Lieta la canzon / L'agile mandòla / Ne accompagna il suon'). Responding to the textual sense of 'constant accompaniment' in the refrain-lines ('While the happy song flies in the breeze, the nimble "mandolin" accompanies its sound'), Verdi keeps them exquisitely ever-present as background: they are sung not separately from, but simultaneously with the three episode-strophes. Although the episodes are in contrasting keys, they are all clearly governed by the fundamental E major of 'Dove guardi'. Following the through-composed, but safely foursquare and periodic, first episode (the children's 'T'offriamo il giglio'), modulating from A back to E major, the second episode, in B major (the baritones' 'A te le porpore'), falls back on the 'naive' Italian structure, aaba', as does the third, in G♯ minor (the women's 'A te la florida'). Desdemona's echo of the E-major full chorus later on, in the coda, 'Splende il cielo' (150/2/1), identifies her fully with this pure *tableau* (see p. 180 below). Even the 'poisoned' Otello can scarcely believe her to be false, as he confesses in a line and a half of *doppi settenari*, the Duet-metre (thus, poetically, the Homage Chorus is embedded in the middle of a line of poetry – a clear interpolation or an extravagantly expanded caesura), while Iago below, in new, rhymed *endecasillabi*, vows to pursue his essence: to untune the concordant.

3 Rhymed Scena with Embedded Quartet (154/1/1–171/3/1)

This section, so clear in its entrance / set piece / exit shape, so motivically coherent throughout, may be considered a paradigm of the three-phase model, a touchstone of the late-Verdi style. (For a closer analysis, see Hepokoski 1987, upon which the following discussion is based.) The entrance-*scena* begins gracefully with the now 'beatified' Desdemona's intercession for the 'groaning man', Cassio, 'D'un uom che geme', begun with a motivically important and recurrent fourth (Example 16a). Her music of gentle petition proceeds by smooth parallelism and suave chromatic inflection – Desdemona-identifiers throughout the score – and its ductile shape and breadth are masterly. She clearly intends to make a simple request, pre-planned as a graceful, embellished $\hat{6}$–$\hat{5}$–$\hat{4}$–$\hat{3}$–$\hat{2}$–$\hat{1}$ descent in G major (from e^2 to g^1). As if testing her husband's mood, she feints twice at her main linear point but each time evades the closure of a cadence ('La preghiera ti porto', 154/2/1–3; and 'e il suo dolor che in me s'infonde', 154/4/2–155/1/2). At last, now confident, she makes her final, impassioned appeal and moves to her direct request, again essentially $\hat{6}$–$\hat{5}$–$\hat{4}$–$\hat{3}$–$\hat{2}$–$\hat{1}$. 'Intercedo per lui', etc. She coyly withholds the precise point, 'Tu gli perdona', until the moment of her G-major cadence (155/3/1–2; notice the similarity here to the parallel petitions 'Dona eis requiem' and 'Dona requiem sempiternam' in the 'Agnus Dei' of Verdi's *Requiem*). The psychology is perfect – or would have been perfect had not Otello had his prior conversation with Iago. Unexpectedly rebuffed, Desdemona reactivates the cadence figure, 'Gli perdona', by touching on an embellishing chord, 'E♭$^{6}_{3}$' ('Non oppormi il tuo diniego', 'Do not oppose me with your refusal'), which, in the striking manner in which it is produced, by double chromatic inflection from a G chord followed by an immediate return to G (recalling the characteristic $^{5♭\,6♮\,5}_{3♭\,3♮\,3}$ sound that, for instance, is so important to the

Ex. 16a

154/1/3: DESDEMONA

D'un uom che ge - me   sot-to il tuo   di -

Ex. 16b

161/1/1: JAGO

Dam-mi quel vel!

Ex. 16c

165/1/1

el - la è per-du-ta   e ir-ri - so io so -no

Love Duet), is probably intended to carry with it an irresistible, if private, reminder of their love. Otello's second, sterner refusal precipitates a radical change of texture and key, plunging onto an E_4^6 (originally an F_4^6: see p. 66 above) launching the brief, agitated Subsection II of the rhymed *scena*, 'Perchè torbida suona' (156/1/1).

Subsection III, Desdemona's offer of the handkerchief, 'Quell'ardor molesto svanirà' (156/4/2), recalls aspects of the texture of Subsection I (insistent quavers, fragments of a linear, descending bass, etc.) and drifts towards a thwarted E♭ minor; it ends, however, with Otello's rough insistence on B♭ minor–major, 'Mi lascia! mi lascia!' Subsection IV (157/4/1), a direct, seven-bar B♭ pathway to the ensemble set piece, presents us with a classic example of Desdemona's bountiful musical language: diatonic lines enriched by functionally superfluous but expressively potent chromatic harmony, particularly secondary dominants – and these characteristically in second inversion (Example 17). Her line is a pure, 'humble' descent of a tenth and could easily be harmonized with common diatonic chords. Instead, before the cadence one finds the first four bars enriched, and the 'surplus' sharp-side alterations can move us as sacred rays of an inner devotion. (Cf. the *chiaroscuro* of her 'Prego per chi adorando a te si prostra', 339/1/1ff; and of Otello's impassioned farewell to this harmonic language in the almost unbearably moving phrase in Act III, 'Spento è quel sol, quel sorriso, quel raggio', etc., 229/4/3–230/2/2.) In this instance Desdemona's humility, descending to her lowest note in the score, could not be more affecting.

Her resonant, low b♭ launches the set piece, the Quartet (whose B♭ tonality belongs clearly to Iago's F-major system; originally,

Ex. 17

Verdi had written this Quartet in B, an expectant dominant of the 'secure' E major – see pp. 53–5 above). Iago's central act of obtaining the handkerchief divides the Quartet into two musical and dramatic subsections, the 'exposition' and the 'peroration' (the latter term is from Amintore Galli, *OG*, 19). The exposition is dominated by a single, expansive, periodic melody for Desdemona with dovetailed interpolations from the other singers, Otello in particular. It is thus a telescoping of the normal ensemble procedure – that found, say, in the Act III *concertato* – in which a solo exposition (*proposta*) or a group of successive solo expositions (*proposta* and *riposte*) lead to a separate, later expansion into ensemble texture. With touching irony, Desdemona's opening phrase (Ex. 17, bar 8) unknowingly echoes and varies Iago's repeated 'honest' cadence near the beginning of the act (i.e., that in Ex. 14 above). At one point the earlier fragment had set Iago's promise to Cassio, 'e il tuo perdono è certo' (112/1/1–2). By the time of the Quartet the person requesting parson is no longer Cassio, but Desdemona. The asymmetrically periodic exposition ends with Desdemona alone, floating downwards from a high b♭^{2} (and recalling 'Se inconscia', Example 17) in parallel $^6_3$ chords – her characteristic parallels – just at the moment that Iago steals the handkerchief from Emilia (164/2/1; *DS*, 49).

With Otello's 'Ella è perduta e irriso / Io sono' the second half of the Quartet – the 'peroration' – begins. This section shifts the dramatic focus largely towards Otello, who, unlike Desdemona, has not yet completed his ten-line stanza of *settenario* text. The peroration is a concise transformation of the conventional 'double-groundswell' sections of many of Verdi's earlier ensembles – those *concertato* wind-ups and eventual releases onto cadential six-fours (Grey and Kerman 1987; Budden, I, 19). Here the groundswell procedure functions as the Moor's personal cries of humiliation, 'She is lost and I, mocked', a direct commentary, even if he is unaware of it, on Iago's theft and a splendid use of a conventional device to serve dramatic ends. Most important, Otello's 'Ella è perduta' motive (Example 16c, foreshadowed in Iago's 'Dammi quel vel!', 161/1/1, Example 16b; cf. Noske [1971]: 161–2) varies and recalls as a reprise Desdemona's opening words of the rhymed-*scena* entrance: her first intercession for Cassio (Example 16a). Thus the *scena* and the ensemble are drawn together, cast as a whole. The *scena* / exposition–peroration succession takes on a subtle ABA′ shape, quite apart from the many other motivic interactions and cross-references. Perhaps more significantly, it is with the 'unmasking' of Otello at the peroration that he, even more than Cassio, stands revealed as the real 'uom che geme', the 'groaning man'. After a brief coda, creating yet another, overlapping order of rounding – that typical mid- and late-Verdian obsession – by bringing back the initial melody and first two textual lines of the Quartet (168/1/2), we merge into the exit-*scena* (perhaps about 169/2/2). This is a brief, nine-bar commentary on and echo of what had preceded: classic exit-functions. It is built on swirling transformations of the 'Ella è perduta' (or 'D'un uom che geme') motive – yet more rounding – now in C major. Iago's glib 'Non pensateci più' brings it to a close (171/3/1) before merging directly into the entrance of the next set piece.

4a *Rhymed* Scena *with Embedded Solo Piece*
(172/1/1–179/5/1)²

The first six bars of the entrance, 'Tu?! Indietro! fuggi!', energize the preceding C major into V of F minor, Iago's key, as Otello falls deeper into his web with weak-beat accents and pathetic orchestral squeals ('M'hai legato alla croce!'). The remaining twenty bars of the entrance ('Nell'ore arcane') clearly centre around F minor, now provided with a four-flat signature, although Otello's sequential ravings carry him momentarily through several different pitch levels. His final cries, 'Ed ora! ed ora' (173/5/2–3) mount upward over an inverted e diminished seventh, probably still interpretable as vii (diminished seventh) of f, before suddenly snapping into the resolute A♭ major of the set piece, 'Ora e per sempre addio' (174/1/1).

About the militaristic *pezzo* itself, as simple and direct as Iago's subsequent 'Era la notte' will be devious and convoluted, only three points need to be made here. The first is that we repeatedly encounter in the cellos the first definitive presentation of the rolling-triplet, descending-and-reascending fourth motive (174/1/1, 174/4/1, etc., with several variants) that will persist through the rest of the act as a symbol of Otello's downfall. (Its triplets, of course, grow out of the rotary-spinning rhythms of Iago's opening *scena* with Cassio and the ensuing 'Credo', while its particular intervallic shape was adumbrated at the beginning of the 'Ciò m'accora' duet.) Second, one might notice the shifting orchestral colours under almost every line. Rather than that of strict continuity the orchestral effect is one of textually appropriate refractions or juxtapositions. Finally, the entire piece relies essentially on a single structural effect: the brutal stifling of an implied reprise. 'Ora e per sempre' consists of an eight-line stanza (4 + 4) that Otello seems to set forth as if they were the first 'four-fifths' of a slightly expanded, but eminently old-fashioned, square-cut, Italian lyric form: a (two lines) a′ (two lines) b (four lines, sometimes divided into parallel halves). The old form (e.g., in *Ernani*, 'Oh tu che l'alma adora', 'Ernani! Ernani involami', 'Tutto sprezzo che d'Ernani') implies some sort of line-repetitions with a decisive return to a climactic restatement of the a melody, typically sung to lines 7 and 8 – although by middle Verdi a 'French' *da capo* effect, back to line 1, was also possible (cf., for instance, the ten-line 'Et toi, Palerme' from Act II of *Les vêpres siciliennes*; Kerman 1982: 51–3). Thus, to

Ex. 18

Cla -mo - ri e can- ti di bat-ta -glia, ad - di - o! Del-la glo -ria d'O- tel - lo è ques-to il

fin   O - ra e per sem -pre   ad - dio   san- te me - mo - rie,

savour the effect of the actual ending we must imagine the grand, unfurled reprise that might have been, following Otello's mighty expansion on the dominant – perhaps something like the (hypothetical) Example 18, in which two new lines (the nonexistent lines 9 and 10 of a longer stanza) might be even more effective. The whole point of the piece, however, is that such a possibility is violently choked off ('è questo il fin'). Not only Otello, but also Verdi bids farewell to a genre that had permitted such gloriously extroverted expression. It is a grand review not merely of Otello's, but also of Verdi's 'sante memorie' ('holy memories').

The fifteen-bar rhymed-*scena* exit consists of a mounting whirlwind of sequences on the downfall motive, the descending and reascending fourth. Thus although the reprise of the prior set piece is lacking, we do hear a significant motive of its accompaniment treated at some length in the exit. As Otello flails about, groping for security, the motive in various forms passes from A♭ major to E major and thence to several other pitch levels before ending up with Otello's final words, 'Del mio spaventoso furor che si desta!', on a violent V of C♯ minor. At this point Otello seizes Iago by the throat and casts him to the ground in a measure of ferocious orchestral unison that lands joltingly on C♮, 'Divina grazia, difendimi!' ('Divine grace, defend me!', 179/5/2). So continuous is the music throughout all of this that it is difficult to determine at what point we leave the exit from 'Ora e per sempre addio' and begin the entrance to 'Era la notte'. Because of the signature-change several bars earlier, at 'Sciagurato!' (177/2/1), a case may be made that the entrance has already begun: Verdi often signals entrances by adopting the signature of the eventual set piece (cf. the 'wrong' four-flat signature in Act III, at 'Vieni; l'aula è deserta', 233/3/1, the entrance to the A♭ Terzetto, which itself begins 236/2/1). Yet the poetic shift from rhymed-*scena* verse to *endecasillabo sciolto*, comes only later, with Iago's 'Divina grazia, difendimi!' This later line is also a moment of textural and dramatic articulation (and it stresses a unison C♮, anticipating the key of the forthcoming 'Era la notte'), and the entrance is probably best acknowledged to begin at this point. But surely more important than any taxonomic decision is the realization of the passage's functional ambiguity, a classic instance of Verdi's masterly 'art of transition'.

4b Scena *with Embedded* Racconto *(ca. 179/5/2–191/1/1)*

The shaken Iago at once picks himself up and begins again to manipulate the keys. He begins with a fleeting hint of his own F minor, 'Il cielo vi protegga' ('Heaven protect you', 180/3/1), then, characteristically, lifts the implied pitch-centre up a half-step (181/1/1) before indignantly asserting his honesty in a momentary D major (181/3/1). (The brief *tutti* outbreak of triplet exclamation points after 'Che l'onestà è periglio', 181/3/1, however, might remind us of the end of his 'Credo' – a reminder also underscored by the similar orchestration.) Otello accepts the 'honest' D major, 'No, rimani', and pointed woodwinds immediately pierce the tonality, along with the Moor's hopes of recovery. The second subsection, 'Per l'universo!' (182/2/1), shoots forward in F♯ minor and moves two notches down the circle of fifths to E minor. It is here, in the parallel minor of the Act I 'key of security', that Iago speaks his horrible words that suggest the possibility of incontrovertible, lascivious proof of infidelity, 'Avvinti / Vederli forse?' (183/4/1–3–184/1/1). He mouths each syllable over an obscenely suggestive tremolo in the flutes alone, and, most important, the words trigger a crucial sonority: *fortissimo*, doubled oboes producing a raw, goatish two-note motive, c^1–b♮ (6̂–5̂) in their lowest register. The sonority will reappear in slightly expanded form, but with full salacious significance, after the set piece, at the critical moment of Iago's handkerchief-proof, 'Quel fazzoletto, ieri / (Certo ne son)' (190/3/2–3). For the moment, however, Iago draws closer to Otello, as if initiating him into a hushed secret. The single, solo notes in the horn have the effect of a confidential 'Listen!': Iago actually utters this word at the end of the entrance, 'Udite', following a slippery-smooth E-minor cadence.

Although the set piece 'Era la notte' is one of the miracles of the *Otello* score, it is one of the most complex *pezzi* to summarize briefly: Iago deliberately distorts the traditional lyric-form rhetoric to tantalize, interpolate, and suggest double meanings. Moreover, sheer orchestral timbre is again elevated to the level of a prominent structural parameter. Indeed, one could organize a convincing, rounded analysis around timbre alone: the muted-string group underlying the first four lines and most of the final line, 'E allora il sogno', etc. (188/2/1), is juxtaposed with a high, then a lower, group of pure woodwinds enveloping the greater part of Iago's two direct quotations (187/1/2, 188/1/1). In addition, it is clear that much of the *racconto* hints at earlier passages in the opera. The rocking triple metre, of course, has been associated with Iago since the beginning of the act, but far more subtle, and far more goading to Otello, are the nearly explicit recollections of his own Love Duet with Desdemona (which, at least in an early version of the libretto, Iago was supposed to have overheard). These include the word 'soave' (187/1/2); the similarity of the text and music of the chromatic 'L'estasi del ciel tutto m'innonda' (187/2/2–3) with Otello's earlier, somewhat more diatonic 'e mi colga nell'estasi / Di quest'amplesso' (103/3/2–3); the obvious, varied echoing in the low-register woodwind chord-succession under 'Il rio destino impreco' (188/1/1–2) of the familiar $\flat\substack{6\natural5\\3\natural3}$ motion under, say, 'Già nella notte densa' (95/1/1–2); the ironically blissful E_4^6 at 'E allora il sogno' (188/2/3–4); and so on. This is expert, wicked torture.

Structurally, the *racconto* begins simply enough. A single c^1 in the solo horn introduces two parallel phrases, aa', leading to a half-cadence. The two phrases seem to be the antecedent of an implied double period, perhaps suggesting the initiation of some sort of expanded variant of the aa'ba" lyric form. In any event, the form breaks down with the sudden, rather baffling production of the tonic, C, as ♭VI of a newly implied E major, under 'con flebil suono' (187/1/1). This leads to the contrasting quotations, which, although in some senses an interpolation, have something of the typical function of a 'b section' within an Italian lyric-form structure. They produce a convincing dominant, that is ('Tutto m'innonda'), and imply an immediately subsequent reprise. What follows, however, is Iago's cruel prolonging and nuancing of the hanging dominant, while promising a reprise at any moment. Thus, the 'Seguia più vago' section (187/3/1) has elements of a reprise – the $\hat{5}$–$\hat{6}$–$\hat{5}$–$\hat{6}$–$\hat{5}$ oscillations of the accompaniment – but proves to be only a dominant prolongation. The second quotation, spoken entirely on the tonic pitch, c^1, moves to another quasi-reprise gesture, but one at the wrong pitch level – c^2–d^2–c^2–d^2 in the strings – before gliding into the potent 'dominant substitute', E_4^6, at 'E allora il sogno'. The 'correct' dominant is then re-produced as a single, open-string note on the violins and violas – clearly this reprises the 'initiatory' horn-note at the opening of the *racconto* – and the next two bars, 'in cieco letargo', finally provide a prosaic, telescoped reprise-substitute: they furnish the essential linear descent from dominant to tonic in almost unadorned form.

With the onset of the twenty-one-bar, modulatory exit, 'Oh! mostruosa colpa!' (188/3/1), the references to past music become more frequent. We have now clearly entered the 'rounding' phase of the act (and, needless to say, also of this No. 4a–c 'Finale'), in which nearly every bar recalls and varies something heard earlier: a tumbling-together of several important Act II sound-images. Thus the opening four bars of this exit, with the pedal c (here in the horns) and the recitations on c may remind us of the exit from the Quartet, 'Il mio velen lavora', etc. (170/3/1ff). Iago's B♭-minor 'Un sogno che può dar' (189/2/1) varies his earlier, honeyed words to Cassio in the opening *scena*, 'Tu dêi saper che Desdemona', etc. (111/2/1). The 'hark!' horn at 'Talor vedeste' (189/3/3) – Iago is now bringing up the subject of the handkerchief – of course, we have just heard before 'Era la notte' (and notice that Otello has thus learned of his cuckolding in a narrative surrounded by *horns* – the pun *corni–corna* also works in Italian, and Verdi would use it once again in Ford's II.i Monologue in *Falstaff*); and the fluid, parallel six-three chords that follow, 'un tessuto', etc. (190/2/1), moving through F, then through A♭, clearly pick up on characteristic textures of Desdemona in the 'Handkerchief' Rhymed *Scena* and Quartet. The critically important low-oboe, c^1–b bleat at the moment of proof, '(Certo ne son)' (190/3/1–2, here d^1–c♯^{1}–c^1–b), has already been mentioned above: for Otello it is the horrifying identifier of illicit sexuality, the explicit pronouncing of the unmentionable.

4c Rhymed Scena *with 'Cabaletta' (191/1/1–201/4/4)*

With Iago's mouthing of Cassio's name, ironically on the secure E major (which is immediately turned into the dominant of A), Otello, shifting now to rhymed-*scena* verse and a new tempo, erupts with one of his most important 'footlight' lines, 'Ah! mille vite gli donasse Iddio!' ('Ah! that God would give him a thousand lives!', 191/1/1), and the last entrance of the act is under way. The two opening chordal hammer-blows under 'Ah! mille vi-', E and G$\sharp^4_3$ (i.e., the second chord with a root a major third higher than the first), initially have the same third-related effect of the celebrated 'È vecchia fola il ciel' chords at the end of the 'Credo' (D$\flat$–F). Now, however, the second chord is an inverted seventh, and the two sounds are used as powerful springboards for a cat-like, savage pounce onto an attempted, but thwarted, A-major cadence ('donasse Iddio!', 191/2/2–3), followed by a mounting, uncontrollable fury: as with the Act I Love Duet, the initial gesture of the entrance forecasts the eventual key of the set piece. At the *più mosso*, 'Jago, ho il cor di gelo' ('Iago, my heart is ice'), the naked descending fourth (Otello's downfall) rolls freely forwards in intensifying sequences. One might also notice the raw, low c^1–b oboe sonority as Otello pronounces the name 'Iago' (191/4/2; cf. 192/1/2). In his frenzied sequences Otello brings the harmony to a 'remote' D$^4_2$ chord, 'L'idra m'avvince' ('The hydra is grabbing me!', 193/2/1–2), then, crying 'blood!', savagely clubs the harmonies four times ('Ah! sangue! sangue! sangue!') and vaults into the frightening high ground of A major (in some senses an unforeseen resolution of the 'secure' E). The shift into A is primitive indeed, and upon reaching the new key the strings seethe in tremolo at their new pitch level.

The '*cabaletta*' aspects of the large-scale structure of 'Sì, pel ciel' are obvious. A decisive *proposta*, or exposition, for Otello (shaped into an aa'b form, seemingly a lyric form denied its fourth, completing element – a structure somewhat analogous, that is, to that of 'Ora e per sempre addio') leads to a varied, but similar *risposta* for Iago (also aa'b). At the end the leading musical idea is heard yet a third time, *a due*, with repeated text (but now expanded into an aa'ba'' structure, thus completing the standard form; see Kerman 1956: 148–9). The *cabaletta* or *cabaletta*-substitute joint oath, of course, is no stranger to the earlier Verdian operas (cf., e.g., 'Dieu, tu semas dans nos âmes' in *Don Carlos*, Act II, Scene i). Its high-voltage evocation here may lack subtlety, but the raw-nerved theatricality is undeniable: its principal effects cannot be misconstrued. Although Otello begins the duet formally the whole piece is imprinted with Iago's image. It is clear, for instance, that the '*cabaletta*' is built from the descending-fourth downfall idea – with frequent upward-swelling inversions – which Iago has been producing ever more clearly since 'Ciò m'accora' early in the act. Thus the melodic bass under the opening lines not only recalls that under 'Ora e per sempre addio' – in a sense rounding this No. 4a–c 'Finale'

– but also summarizes the whole point of Iago's destructive activity. It is significant that the head-motive of the melody belongs to Iago. He sings it in both his *risposta*, 'Testimon è il Sol che miro' ('My witness is the Sun that I gaze upon', 195/2/1), and in the '*cabaletta*'-reprise (197/3/2), while Otello is largely reduced to primitive howling on the dominant above. Otello's lines, however, do permit a magnificent declamation, self-indulgently resonant with Boito's carefully modulated and potent 'ar', 'er', 'or', and 'ur' sounds, all in the elemental, antique poetic metre originally heard for eight lines near the beginning of the Act I Storm ('Lampi! tuoni! gorghi!' etc.; see p. 27 above). His *proposta* lines are harmonically 'open', since by their end he has fallen into Iago's F major ('Questa man ch'io levo e stendo!', 'This hand, which I raise and extend', 194/4/2–195/1/1). Iago hoists the key back up to A and begins a varied *risposta* pointed towards G major at its end ('s'armi il suo voler', 197/2/1–2). This G is then wrenched up a step for the varied reprise in the tonic, A major – a brutal harmonic effect similar in violence, if not precisely in key-relations, to Otello's earlier production of the '*cabaletta*'s' A major out of the D$^4_2$ that had preceded it by three bars.

The concluding orchestral effects of the last thirteen bars set the seal on Act II. They belong exclusively to Iago. Thus we hear two more explicit allusions to his demonically ecstatic, *tutti* triplets as forceful punctuation – which had first been heard at the end of the 'Credo' ('È vecchia fola il Ciel', 120/1/2) – after the final, joint 'ch'io levo e stendo' (201/1/1) and 'Dio vendicator!' (201/2/2–201/3/1: notice also that differing, but parallel conceptions of God are invoked both here (the 'Dio vendicator!') and in the 'Credo' (the 'Dio crudel')). The final orchestral *coup*, similarly, is Iago's: anarchic parallel major triads (cf. 'Temete, signor, la gelosia!', 130/4/1–4) underscore twice more a linear variant of the fatal fourth, A–G–F♯–F–E–A (the triad-roots, of course, are borrowed from the parallel A minor). Music has nothing more shocking to offer than that first, passing, *pesante* G-major sound. Once again, as spectators we directly experience the lawless audacity of the man who has controlled the entire act.

8 Shakespeare reinterpreted

In coming to grips with the dramatic content of *Otello* a reasonable starting-point would be to inquire what initial conceptions of Shakespeare and *Othello* Verdi and Boito brought to their work. A second, related line of inquiry would explore the differences not only between the content of the opera and that of the play but also between Verdi's and Boito's separate visions of *Otello*, for it is clear that the opera's Shakespearean images were conditioned both by their nineteenth-century Italian context and by Boito's idiosyncratic, post-*scapigliatura* treatment. Perhaps more to the point, many of these *ottocento* images have disappeared from the modern theatre and from current literary criticism. Native speakers of English, whose knowledge of Shakespeare is direct in a way that Verdi's and Boito's could never have been, may also profit from the reminder that the main streams of English-language *Othello* criticism (Rymer, Johnson, Coleridge, and so on, not to mention the imposing list of twentieth-century critics, Bradley, Eliot, Knight, Leavis, etc.) were not the principal streams in which Verdi and Boito swam. To permit the original play or the English-language critics to hold exclusive sway over one's study of *Otello* is to risk misconstruing the opera's intended effects. To address the images that the composer and the librettist probably had in mind, one must frequently invoke a different, Continental cast of characters: non-English translators, critics, and actors.

Otello was conceived during the crest of a general Italian enthusiasm for Shakespeare, a period when Shakespeare was the 'new' dominating and liberating force in the reform of the nineteenth-century Italian theatre (Gatti 1968: 175). It had not always been that way. Apart from a few scattered reductions and rather free dramatic adaptations – among them Rossini's *Otello* of 1816[1] and Salvatore Viganò's well-received Milanese ballet, *Otello*, of 1818 – the first truly Shakespearean *Othello* to be put on the Italian stage was the work of the reform-minded actor Gustavo Modena in Milan in 1842. It was a complete failure. As a bold, direct presentation of a foreign product written by the extravagant, reckless Englishman (albeit in Michele Leoni's translation, with cuts), it flew in the face of the current reality of the Italian stage, still hemmed in by the double constraints of a political and moral censorship on the one hand and a lingering, hidebound Classicism on the other: a marked insistence on the sacred 'rules' of the dramatic unities of time and place, the boundaries of theatrical propriety, and so on (Gatti 1968: 7–9, 37–51, 175; Busi 1973: 149–61). Before the mid-1850s (again, excepting a few operatic and balletic adaptations – including Verdi's audacious 1847 *Macbeth* – which helped to clear the path for the real thing: see also Weaver 1981) Shakespeare was essentially a literary, even a cultish phenomenon. Above all, he was a writer embraced by the rebellious Romantics and reformers as a symbol of liberty and individuality, immensity of conception and force, and penetrating, realistic psychological truth. Not surprisingly, enthusiastic Italian Shakespeareans at this time were obliged to proffer carefully reasoned defences and explanations of the plays. Even as late as 1847–48 Verdi deemed it advisable to preface the first *Macbeth* libretto with an explicit *apologia* for the nature of the plot and the supernatural intervention of the witches (Rosen and Porter 1984: 349–50). Nevertheless, many of the early Florentine critics barraged the new work with scorn, often on precisely these dramatic grounds (Pinzauti 1984). Ultimately, the Italian Romantic defence of Shakespeare, in which Verdi had been steeped, may be traced to two key documents by Alessandro Manzoni: the 'Preface' to *Il Conte di Carmagnola* (1820) and the related *Lettre à M. Chauvet* (1823). Here one finds a summation of the first strong Italian attacks on the dramatic unities along with the championing of internal, *ad hoc* criteria for assessing literary value, of mixed genres, of the striving for historical and psychological truth by any appropriate means (Beronesi 1979; cf. especially Tomlinson 1986–87).

The key figure behind Manzoni, and behind virtually all subsequent *ottocento* conceptions of Shakespeare, was August Wilhelm Schlegel, whose influential Viennese lectures *Vorlesungen über dramatische Kunst und Literatur* (Heidelberg, 1809–11) appeared in an Italian translation by Giovanni Gherardini, *Corso di letteratura drammatica*, in 1817. Schlegel's Romantic counsels – for instance, to avoid externally imposed, 'mechanical' rules of form in favour of internal, 'organic' form – would have a profound impact on the Italian Romantic literary mind and, ultimately, on Italy's music as well. But, most important, here was a fountainhead of specific Shakespearean commentary destined to be excerpted and disseminated in most of the principal nineteenth-century Italian Shakespeare translations. There were, of course, several translations of *Othello* in Verdi's lifetime: those by Michele Leoni (1814, 1819–22, 1825), G. C. Cosenza (1826), Ignazio Valletta (1830), Virginio Soncini (1830), Giunio Bazzoni and Giacomo Sormani (1830), Carlo Rusconi (1838–39, for years the standard translation, in prose, with several subsequent, revised editions), Giulio Carcona (1852, 1857–8), L. E. Tettoni (1856), and Andrea Maffei (1869) (see Busi 1973: 35–101, 309–10). We may be certain that Verdi owned copies of Rusconi's celebrated but problematic *Teatro completo di Shakespeare* – probably the composer's (but not Boito's) principal source for the play – along with copies of the translations of Carcano and Maffei.[2] Both Rusconi and Maffei – and, for that matter, Leoni – reprinted Schlegel's (and only Schlegel's) remarks on *Othello* as supplements to their own translations. It is evident that Verdi and Boito had ample opportunity and motivation to familiarize themselves with it. For Italian readers it was nothing short of the standard introduction to the play.[3] The crux of Schlegel's vision of *Othello* lay in his understanding of its protagonist. The essence of the hero's character, he insisted, was his primitiveness and barbarity, over which the aspect of a Venetian soldier was but a thin veneer. Embracing a facile racial stereotyping without a second thought, Schlegel argued that Othello's physical blackness is the key to his character. His remarks, translated here from their Italian version in Rusconi, merit a full quotation:

Othello is covered with dark shadows. It is a Rembrandt painting. But whatever kind of happy error was it that had Shakespeare mistake the Moor of North Africa, the baptized Saracen, as in the original story [by Giraldi Cinthio, 1566], for a real Ethiopian? One may see in Othello the savage nature of that burning (*ardente*) zone, which produces the most ferocious animals and the most poisonous plants. The wish for glory, the foreign laws of honour, sweeter and nobler customs, have only apparently tamed him. In him jealousy is not that delicate irritability of the heart that is one with an enthusiastic respect for the loved one; but it is the sensual frenzy that brought into the heated (*cocenti*) climates the unworthy practice of shutting women indoors and many other unnatural abuses. One drop of this poison put into his blood gives rise to the most fearful effervescence. Othello shows himself to be noble, sincere, full of trust (*fidanza*), fully aware of the love that he inspires; he is a hero who scorns danger, the worthy head of his soldiers, the solid supporter of the State. But the purely physical power of his passions demolishes his adopted virtues with one blow, and the savage supplants in him the civilized man. This same tyranny of the blood over the will is shown in the expression of his unrestrained desire to be revenged on Cassio. And after recovering from his deception (*acciecamento*) – when remorse, tenderness, and the feeling of offended honour suddenly reawaken in his heart – he turns against himself, with all the fury of a despot who punishes his rebellious slave. He suffers doubly; he suffers in both of the spheres into which his existence is divided.

The image of a seemingly noble hero quick to fall back into a more elemental, 'uncivilized' rage was brought to the Italian stage by the actor Ernesto Rossi in 1856. With his Milanese *Othello* and subsequent *Amleto* – and especially with the even more celebrated, more emotionally nuanced Othello of his rival, Tommaso Salvini – the floodgates finally opened for the Italian acceptance of staged Shakespeare. Rossi, whose volcanic, spectacular Othello interpretation was applauded in Italy for nearly forty years, was a dedicated actor who, before performing *Othello*, had gone so far as to demand a new translation – that of Carcano (Busi 1973: 163, 169–70). To judge from most accounts, Rossi's Othello emphasized the savage, barbaric conception of the hero. Although he is said to have begun his role in Act I clearly and ardently enough (even Salvini admitted that, generally considered, 'There has never been an artist who pronounced the phrase "I love you!" like Ernesto Rossi'; Busi 1973: 167), by the third act he gave way to bursts of unprecedentedly ferocious, 'uncontrollable' passion – doubtless inspired by Schlegel's 'one drop of poison' commentary. According to the theatrical historian Anna Busi, summarizing the effects that most lingered in the minds of the nineteenth-century critics – especially foreign critics – 'Rossi prowled around the stage with the impotent fury of a chained wild beast, alternating outbursts of wrath with sobs and suffocated groans' (p. 174). Several of Rossi's special 'savage' effects were notorious. His murder of Desdemona, for instance, was particularly cruel. Instead of suffocating her with a pillow, he strangled her with his hands, agonizingly, 'with refined slowness' – some reports say for five minutes (Busi 1973: 175). Similarly, the critic Raffaello Barbiera confessed himself fascinated by Rossi's desperate outcry of shock, rage, and incredulity ('Parve!', 'Seemed!') after Iago's words in *Oth.*, V.ii, 175–6, 'I told him what I thought, and told no more / Than what he found himself (*a lui parve*) was apt and true': 'At that point Rossi makes our blood freeze. T. Salvini, on the other hand, remains silent' (Busi 1973: 172).

For the highly critical Henry James, who saw Rossi in Rome in 1873,

Rossi is both very bad and very fine; bad where anything like taste and discretion is required, but 'all there', and much more than there, in violent passion . . . [In the last act] the interesting thing to me was to observe the Italian conception of the part – to see how crude it was, how little it expressed the hero's moral side, his depth, his dignity – anything more than his being a creature terrible in mere tantrums. The great point was his seizing Iago's head and whacking it half-a-dozen times on the floor, and then flinging him twenty yards away. (James 1948: 55)

English audiences – for Rossi toured much of the world with the role, always performed in Italian – similarly condemned Rossi's eruptive primitivism, although he obtained notable successes with it in several other countries, including the United States. Although Verdi obviously knew the Italian acting tradition well, it is unclear whether he actually ever attended a performance of Rossi's *Othello*, or one of his famous rival's, Tommaso Salvini – at least, I am unaware of any written document to this effect. Boito, however, seems easily familiar with and enthusiastic about these famous interpretations, and he addresses Verdi about them – clearly with the assumption that they were common knowledge – in his letter of 21 December 1886 (*CVB*, I, 119; see also below).

Tommaso Salvini's *Othello*, which also first appeared in 1856 (in Vicenza) after years of study and preparation, was more complex, the emotions no less powerful, to be sure, but more subtly graded. Above all, Salvini took a different view of the play. As he explained in an 1883 analysis printed in the Roman *Fanfulla della Domenica* (i.e., after Boito had written the *Otello* libretto), *Othello* was not so much a drama of violent jealousy as one of deep, idealistic love. Thus he portrayed the Moor not as a man wild and ferocious by nature, but as one who has staked all for a love that is 'lasting, aware, completely pure', not a mere sensual passion. For Salvini, the murder of Desdemona is an act of neither primitive violence nor savage revenge; rather, it is a premeditated, ritualistic sacrifice, one virtually owed to society (in Busi 1973: 189). The concept surely springs from Othello's 'Yet she must die, else she'll betray more men' (V.ii, 6). Salvini's great gifts as an actor, which included an imposing stature and a deep, resonant voice, permitted him to transform his concept of a love-drama into a memorable projection of carefully graded, intense emotion – a 'study of pure passion' (Gatti 1968: 163). His Othello, for instance, managed to earn the praise of Constantin Stanislavsky:

> [In Act I Salvini] opened for a moment the gates of paradise in his mono-
> logue before the Senate . . . [By the final portion of III.iii] Salvini seems to
> enter as if his inner soul is red-hot, as if burning lava has been poured into
> his heart . . . He throws Iago to the floor and is on him in one leap, pressing
> him to the ground, leaps up, lifts his foot above Iago's head to crush it like
> a snake's, remains in that pause, becomes confused, turns away, and with-
> out looking at Iago offers him a hand, lifts him, and falls himself on a couch,
> crying like a tiger in the desert when he has lost his mate. At that moment
> the likeness of Salvini's Othello to a tiger was self-evident.
>
> ([1924]: 268, 271)

Similarly, Henry James had written in praise of Salvini in 1883–4:

> No more complete picture of passion can have been given to the stage in our
> day, – passion beginning in noble repose and spending itself in black
> insanity . . . Some of his tones, movements, attitudes, are ineffaceable; they
> have passed into the stock of common reference. I mean his tiger-like
> pacing at the back of the room, when, having brought Desdemona out of
> her bed, and put the width of the apartment between them, he strides to and
> fro, with his eyes fixed on her and filled with the light of her approaching
> doom. Then the still more tiger-like spring with which, after turning,
> flooded and frenzied by the truth, from the lifeless body of his victim, he
> traverses the chamber to reach Iago, with the mad impulse of destruction
> gathered into a single blow.   (James 1948: 171–5)

And it is worth noting that Salvini made three notable alterations in
the play: he omitted the 'eavesdropping scene' in IV.i (the source of
Verdi's Act III Terzetto) as unworthy of the noble Othello; his
murder of Desdemona with the pillow was accomplished out of the
sight of the public, behind a lowered bed-curtain; and, although the
play is not specific here, he committed suicide by cutting his throat,
not by plunging a dagger into his breast (Busi: 190–2). The English
critics were somewhat kinder to Salvini on his tour than they were
to Rossi, although they still deplored the barbarism of his violence
and the pronounced 'orientalism' of his interpretation (p. 191).
Indeed, there was a Turkish cast to Salvini's costume, as there was
to Rossi's, which is why, one presumes, there is a prominent
scimitar in Act IV of Verdi's *Otello*. (See also the extended discussion of Salvini in Rosenberg 1961: 102–19.)

   In the special edition of the *Illustrazione italiana* brought out in
February 1887 in honour of the *Otello* premiere, *Verdi e l'Otello* –
something of an official commemorative publication, undoubtedly
prepared in collaboration with Giulio Ricordi – Ugo Pesci mentioned both Rossi and Salvini as excellent Othellos and singles out

the latter as the superior performer, 'for two entire generations of spectators the pre-eminent Otello'. Pesci includes an engraving of a turbaned, Turkish Salvini and praises his direct emotional impact and heightened 'scenic effect', along with his famous 'creeping, furtive tiger-steps in the sleeping Desdemona's chamber' and his frightening death-cry, the 'heart-rending howl that seems cut off in his throat by the curved dagger-blade'. Pesci concludes (perhaps tacitly evoking Schlegel), 'Tommaso Salvini will not easily be equalled in those [aspects] in which savage, passionate energy predominate – those things that the Moor of Venice personifies' (p. 34).

At the time of the opera it is clear that to the Italian theatrical public the subject of *Otello* immediately called to mind the Rossi–Salvini rivalry. As is already evident to the reader, aspects of both interpretations are reflected in the opera. One might finally point out that Boito strongly objected to the opera cast attending the new, more modern, lower-key, and much more naturalistic *Othello* of Giovanni Emanuel in Milan on 18 December 1886 – less than two months before the operatic premiere.[4] Although Boito (and Verdi) claimed to demand realistic acting from their own performers, this 'realism' and *naturalezza* appears to have extended only to the incipient theatrical realism of the mid-nineteenth century, that is, to the Rossi–Salvini manner, in which many of the grand gestures and large effects remained. According to Boito, who apparently kept up with these things as a literary man, Emanuel's interpretation was too cold. 'Rossi and Salvini, they are the two giants!' he wrote to Verdi on 21 December. 'From them Tamagno could have learned something, but from Emanuel he could have learned nothing at all' (*CVB*, I, 119).[5]

In addition to those of Schlegel, Rossi, and Salvini, the final mainstream of *Othello* interpretation flowing into the opera, with something of a counter-balancing effect, was that of François-Victor Hugo's French translation of the play – Boito's main source of the text (see pp. 24–7 above). Hugo prefaced his translation with a thirty-five-page introduction, and Boito marked off certain passages of it in his principal copy (that now housed in the La Scala Library), wrote comments in its margins, and so on. Much of this introduction, shot through with unstinted admiration for Othello-as-hero, is an undisguised attack on Schlegel's interpretation of the protagonist as a primitive. Early on Hugo aligns himself with an uncomfortably racialist passage that had impressed him in

Coleridge's *Literary Remains*: 'It would be something monstrous to conceive this beautiful Venetian girl falling in love with a veritable negro. It would argue a disproportionateness, a want of balance, in Desdemona' (Coleridge [1818] trans. in Hugo 1960: 53). Hugo goes on to insist that Othello's skin is tawny, not black, that he is a member of a noble race, 'artistic and industrious' (p. 56), an Arabic race with a glorious past, a 'rival of the Latin race' (p. 57). Othello is lauded as 'the son of Saracen kings' (p. 58) and therefore Desdemona's marriage to him was no misalliance, as Schlegel had suggested, but 'the sympathetic fusion of these two primordial types of human beauty, the Semitic and the Caucasian type' (p. 58). Boito was apparently unconvinced by the specifically racial aspects of Hugo's argument: shortly after this point he wrote into the margin 'And yet he is a black' ('eppure è un negro', p. 58). Four pages later, when Hugo mentions Desdemona's line, 'I saw Othello's visage in his mind' (I.iii, 248; Hugo, p. 62), Boito notes 'So then, he could also be a black' (dunque poteva anche essere un negro'), and the issue of race seems settled. (Boito was careful to work this line into the Act I Love Duet, although its full significance may be veiled by the somewhat contrived poetry: 'Ed io vedea fra le tue tempie oscure / Splender del genio l'eterea beltà', 'And I saw the ethereal beauty of genius shine between your dark temples', 101/3/1). In any event, having strenuously argued the fundamental nobility of Othello, Hugo proceeds to interpret the play as a tragedy of honour: as with Salvini, Hugo's Othello is 'an executioner beloved of the condemned' (p. 77), one who is 'sadly driven to murder and suicide through the demands of moral justice and revenge'. And what is the reason for his suicide? To speed up justice. 'The murder of Desdemona is there crying for revenge, and Othello is not the sort of man to grant a reprieve to a murderer' (p. 78).

It may be noted that in none of these 'passionate' interpretations – Schlegel, Hugo, Rossi, Salvini, and, ultimately, Boito and Verdi – do we find those lurking suspicions about Othello's sincerity, about his self-dramatizing theatricality ('Behold, I have a weapon') that characterize so much mid-twentieth-century criticism of the play.[6] As is well known, the modern attack on Othello-as-hero began in earnest with T. S. Eliot's observations of the Moor's capacity for egotistical self-deception, of his 'bovarysme', of his aim of 'cheering himself up' in his suicide speech ([1927]: 111). And the Romantic bubble finally burst in 1937 with F. R. Leavis' strong seconding of Eliot (and simultaneous attack on A. C. Bradley and his heroic conception of Othello) and his extended critique of the Moor, who

> has from the beginning responded to Iago's 'communications' in the way Iago desired and with a promptness that couldn't be improved upon . . . And it is plain that what we should see in Iago's prompt success is not so much Iago's diabolic intellect as Othello's readiness to respond. Iago's power . . . is that he represents something that is in Othello – in Othello the husband of Desdemona: the essential traitor is within the gates.
>
> ([1937; 1952]: 127–8)

The extent to which this crucial 'readiness to respond' might recall Schlegel's 'tyranny of the blood' – or, rather, might abstract and deepen it through appeals to modern psychology, while washing it clean from the earlier stains of its racialist axioms – is not our concern here. We might merely notice in passing that the tone and feel of the relatively recent ironic and ruthlessly objective critique of Othello was quite unknown to Verdi and Boito.

What, then, are we to make of the opera's hero? One must begin by observing that Verdi's and Boito's handling of the racial question, the wellspring of most of the interpretations that they knew, is commendably understated. Verdi's first thoughts in 1881 may have been of 'an Ethiopian, without the usual turban' (see p. 108 above), but by 1886, after the composing of the opera, he strenuously objected to any stage-costume that suggested the exotic or the primitive instead of the noble Venetian (pp. 107–8) above).[7] Whether consciously or not, Verdi's costume-choices seem virtually to echo the arguments of Hugo on this point. Boito's libretto is remarkably restrained in its racial references, and it is characteristic that the most explicitly racial remarks are either put into the mouth of an evil Iago ('Presto in uggia verranno i foschi baci / Di quel selvaggio dalle gonfie labbra', 'The dark kisses of that thick-lipped savage will soon grow tiresome', 32/2/1), 'transcended' by a somewhat overrefined 'poetic' reinterpretation (as in the treatment of Desdemona's 'I saw Othello's visage in his mind', mentioned above), or tucked into the by-ways of an ensemble (as in Othello's 'Haply for I am black' all but submerges – despite Verdi's telling setting within the Act II Quartet, 'Forse perchè ho sul viso / Quest'atro tenebror', 160/2/1). It might be added that no contemporary musical critics commented significantly on the racial issue within the opera.

There can be no doubt, however, that Verdi's Otello is governed by the larger-than-life quality of his emotions: the powerful rush of inner feeling consistently threatens to crack the vessel. This insistent pressure of penetrating, surging emotion may well have been suggested by Salvini's or Rossi's Othello – or by Schlegel – and there is no denying its suitability to a fully ripe, late-nineteenth-century musical treatment. It is, of course, a radical simplification of Shakespeare's character. In the opera there is not a single bar of music that so much as hints at that aspect of the play's hero that stood calm and self-controlled even as his brother fell under cannon-fire (III.iv, 128–31), of whom Desdemona even naively could believe 'I think the sun where he was born / Drew all such [jealous] humours from him' (III.iv, 26–7). And one notices that in the Act III Finale Boito suppresses this aspect of Lodovico's 'Is this the nature / Whom passion could not shake? Whose solid virtue / The shot of accident nor dart of chance / Could neither graze nor pierce?' (IV.i, 256–9) and gives us merely 'Quest'è dunque l'eroe? quest'è il guerriero / Dai sublimi ardimenti?' (266/1/2, 'Is this then the hero? This is the warrior of sublime boldnesses?'). Othello is conceptually diminished in the opera, and it is perhaps on this point that one most regrets Boito's suppression of most of Shakespeare's first act (perhaps suggested to Boito by Samuel Johnson's famous remarks on the 'regularity' of the last four acts of the play: see n. 3 above). So, if the opera were to rise to the full challenge of Shakespeare, what Otello lacked in complexity would have to be compensated by musical intensity (Cooke [1964]; Bradshaw 1983). Few would deny that Verdi rose to the task.

Verdi tends to depict Otello in two different modes, which seem to be directly analogous to Schlegel's 'two spheres' hypothesis, or even, understood with proper caution, roughly analogous to the Salvini–Rossi polarity. When 'summarizing' the character or defining the Moor's emotional essence – principally in the outer sections of the opera – the composer stresses the elevated and the grandiose: the Salvini-like centrality of the love-drama, or possibly a heightening and deepening of Schlegel's 'adopted virtues' argument. On the other hand, when Othello is required to act dramatically, for instance in responding and reacting to Iago, particularly in the middle two acts, Schlegel's primitive and – it would seem – Rossi's theatrical explosions overtake the drama (although, given the reports of Salvini's acting, we ought not to confine these traits too exclusively to Rossi). This general observation is at least casually supported by Ugo Pesci's 1887 report that Verdi insisted on something 'à la Salvini (*salvinesca*)' from Tamagno in the suicide scene and fatal death-falls, and by the reviewer in *Il capitan fracassa* who was reminded of Salvini in the tenor's delivery ('Salvinianamente') of the 'Esultate!' (p. 99 above). Similarly, in Act IV one could easily understand the light *staccati* and ominous, circling stops and starts of Otello's entrance-music into the bedchamber as recalling Salvini's cat-like steps. Moreover, the 'frightening calm' (*DS*, 96) with which he begins his dialogue with Desdemona (344/2/1–346/3/2) and the highly nuanced, intense final speech, 'Niun mi tema', also seem crucial points here. And it is evident that the *tema-cardine* of the opera, the recurring 'Bacio' theme that draws together the strings of Otello's character, stresses the generating force of the Moor as residing in his love – a Salvini-like, or Hugo-esque, point. (On the other hand, and characteristically, when Otello actually acts in Act IV – the murder – it is Rossi's barehanded strangulation that is momentarily summoned (*DS*, 99), not Salvini's behind-the-curtain smothering.)

The first act, more exposition than dramatic action, also gives us the 'elevated', shatteringly intense Otello. But here the situation is more complex: on the one hand, the magnificent 'Esultate!' entrance gives the opera's hero an unforgettable stamp of his own, whatever its superficial debts might be to Salvini; on the other hand, towards the end of the act we find explicit forebodings of the hero's inability to control the hot lava of his emotions. The impact of 'Esultate!' (21/2/1) has to be potent enough to resound in our memories throughout the rest of the work, for it is only here – and fleetingly – that we perceive an unflawed hero. Otello enters far less as what Boito called 'the brave, loyal figure of a man of arms' (*DS*, 4; Budden, III, 327) than as a demigod, produced out of the raging struggle of the earth, the air, and the water (and whose deeds are immediately celebrated by fire) – one who, as Peter Conrad (1977: 57) and Stefan Kunze (1981: 9) have pointed out, is in league with the elemental forces of nature. There is a typically Boitian metaphysical dimension to his appearance, just as the preceding storm-poetry had been tinged with the supernatural ('Fende l'etra un torvo e cieco spirto di vertigine, / Iddio scuote il cielo bieco, come un tetro vel', 'A menacing, blind vertigo-spirit splits the ether; God shakes the sullen sky like a dark veil', 8/1/3; see Degrada [1976]: 158). By sheer force Otello's music grasps, bends, and resolves music heard in the storm. 'Esultate!' responds heroically to the earlier, choral 'È salvo!' (18/1/2–3). 'L'orgoglio musulmano / Sepolto è in mar' seizes the poetic images and melodic-rhythmic contours of Iago's malevolent 'L'alvo / Frenetico del mar sia la sua tomba!' (17/2/2) and recasts them into a strident crow of victory. 'Nostra e del ciel è gloria!' may evoke aspects of the choral plea, 'Salva l'arca e la bandiera' (13/3/3). And 'Dopo l'armi lo vinse l'uragano' boldly reshapes the earlier, fearful 'Fende l'etra un torvo e cieco' (8/1/3) into a triumphant, E-major tonic resolution. Otello crystallizes god-like out of the elements and resolves the deepest fears (and, for the moment, hatreds) of those to whom he is responsible.

With his second entrance, 'Abbasso le spade!' (89/1/2), it becomes clear that the operatic Otello is to be essentially a man of ready emotion. This might not yet have been Boito's intention, for he insisted that this post-duel scene was pivotal in showing us the hero's principal virtues, 'simple in his bearing and in his gestures, imperious in his commands, cool in his judgement' (*DS*, 4; Budden, III, 327). Verdi's Otello may well be imperious here, but he is also enraged, as he will always be in moments of action. He soon erupts into the first of his habitual *forte* diminished sevenths (here in tremolo strings) after he learns that Montano has been wounded, 'Pel cielo / Già il sangue mio ribolle' (92/1/2; the line comes from Shakespeare, II.iii, 185–8, 'Now by heaven / My blood begins my safer guides to rule', etc., but it is given a high prominence in the opera: Schlegel's 'tyranny of the blood' may be lurking around the edges of Verdi's setting). More disturbingly, Otello's dismissal of Cassio immediately after – and only after – he sees that Desdemona has been awakened invites one to conclude that her awakening, as the last straw, is the proximate cause of Cassio's demotion. In the play Othello's action, 'But never more be officer of mine', II.iii, 230, had occurred just before Desdemona's entrance. While it is true that seeing her thus 'raised up' vexes him further, his prior, official action had been untinged by her presence. Whatever Boito might have intended by his curious reordering of events in the opera (the first clear indication of Otello's devotion to his wife?), it cannot contribute to the image of a man 'cool in his judgement'.[8]

Through extraordinarily beautiful poetry and music the ensuing Love Duet identifies the ego of Otello's military exploits with the lovers' bonds. Here the impulsive Moor exchanges one grand emotion for another; 'l'ira immensa' transmutes into 'quest'immenso amor' (95/4/2–4). Significantly, the most rapturous moments of the duet foretell Otello's future by exposing his flaws. The matter goes far beyond the Tristanesque 'Venga la morte!' (103/2/2; from *Oth.*, II.i, 181–2, 'If it were now to die' – once again, Boito approached the text principally via Hugo's French; see pp. 24–7 above). At the climactic music leading up to and including the kiss, we are presented with the startling image of the hero physically collapsing under the impact of his emotions. This is much extended from its poetic source in Shakespeare, Othello's lovely 'It stops me here; it is too much of joy' (II.i, 189). Boito begins the transformation into a far more *fin-de-siècle* physicality by rewriting Otello's lines as 'Ah! la gioia m'innonda / Si fieramente . . . che ansante mi giacio' (105/2/2, 'Ah! Joy so proudly floods me that, panting, I stagger') and adding stage directions to the effect that the weakened Otello must support himself on a projection of a nearby bastion ('un rialzo degli spaldi', 105/2/2). This in itself might be passed over lightly, for its superficial dramatic point is obvious. But the *disposizione scenica*, p. 34, records that much more occurred on-stage during the first performances:

At the peak of emotion Otello feels weak. Desdemona moves to the left, and while he steps backwards, she follows him, supporting him [!]. At the words 'Mi giacio' Otello supports himself on a bastion, sitting down, almost fainting, on the steps of a small practicable elevation. Desdemona bends down over him. Coming to, Otello turns to Desdemona and says 'un bacio'. Bending further down, she exclaims, 'Otello!' with an emotional, sweet nuance (*accento*).

Thus 'il Duce / Del nostro Duce' (111/3/1, 'our general's general') must take command, support him and lean over him in his excess – even though in context it is blissful excess indeed. As is well known, Boito, following Shakespeare, had originally planned to have the eavesdropping Iago vow at this point to ruin the lovers. Whatever its effect on the rapturous Love Duet might have been, at least one aspect of the idea would have been brilliant: an extended negative recurrence of this image of bending over the collapsed Otello appears at the end of Act III, Otello's sudden fainting and Iago's 'Ecco il Leone!' A far more explicit, 'reversed' re-evocation of the Love Duet image occurs at the very end of the opera, where Otello hovers over the body of Desdemona. She is motionless at that point not merely in a near-faint, as Otello had been, but in death: and once again Otello's crucial final rhyme is 'giacio' – 'bacio' ('lie down', or, poetically, 'collapse' – 'kiss').

Although, then, in the outer acts with their summations of character there may be much to remind us of the elevated interpretation of Salvini, the two central acts display the emotional equivalent of Schlegel's and Rossi's primitive – or perhaps some of the 'barbaric' side of Salvini's theatricality. Certainly Verdi's remark to

Ricordi on 11 May 1887, that Otello must alternately 'sing and howl' (p. 96 above), recalls the useful simplicity of Schlegel's 'two spheres' theory. Boito's explicit linking of Otello with 'Jealousy' and even 'a fearful jealousy' (*DS*, 4; Budden, III, 327) – instead of, say, with purity of love or Hugo's 'honour' – furthers the bonds with Schlegel and suggests the fundamental importance of this 'unrestrained' conception of the protagonist. Much of Boito's outline of the character, in fact, derives clearly from Schlegel and the 'one drop of poison' idea: 'From that moment [i.e., from Iago's 'S'anco teneste in mano tutta l'anima mia / Nol sapreste . . . Temete, signor, la gelosia!', 130/3/1–130/4/4] . . . the whole man changes . . . He was wise, sensible [where, one might ask?], and now he raves . . . Iago's words are like poison injected into the Moor's blood. The fatal progress of that moral blood-poisoning should be expressed in all the fullness of its horror . . . ' (*DS*, 4; Budden, III, 327). Hence also Verdi's early fascination with the poison image ('farmaco', 'medicine') in his 6 January 1880 letter to Morelli (Budden, III, 302); hence Boito's insertion of the word 'veleno', 'poison', into the 'idra fosca' passage (131/2/1, 'dark hydra', not 'green-eyed monster'; cf. *Oth.*, III.iii, 167–70); hence Iago's double statement of the pivotal line, 'Il mio velen lavora' ('My poison is working', 170/3/1, 321/1/3).

In Acts II and III Otello's rage responses are consistently convulsive and emotionally primitive, set off by hair-trigger releases. Such frequent, violent eruptions may provide one momentary musical *coup* after another, but even by mid-opera one is in danger of being left with a character who has prematurely weakened himself by overreacting in consistently similar ways. In the second act alone, for instance, Verdi's Otello responds with no fewer than seven 'kinetic' rages or despairs (128/1/1, 131/4/1, the area surrounding 157/2/2, 172/1/1, 176/4/1, 182/2/1, 191/1/1), not to mention the vehemence of 'Ora e per sempre addio' or his baying in 'Sì, pel ciel'. Even admitting the special force of the seventh outburst, 'Ah! mille vite gli donasse Iddio!' ('Ah! that God would give him a thousand lives!'), one might be hard put to demonstrate a careful gradation of emotion from the first to the last. In fact, the first, 'Pel cielo! tu sei l'eco dei detti miei' ('By heaven! You are the echo of my words'), gives us an already explosive Moor, with an alarming wrench of the key, *subito forte* (128/1/1), a despairing wail largely in descending chromatics ('Nel chiostro / Dell'anima', etc., 128/2/1), threateningly fearful hammer-blows on 'qualche terribil mostro'

(128/4/1, 'some terrible monster'), the characteristic plunge into 'chaotic', rising, sequential diminished sevenths ('Ma di che t'accoravi?', 129/1/1), the rise to the high g[1] on 'Suvvia, parla se m'ami' (129/1/1, 'Go ahead, speak if you love me'), and the desperate high a[1] on 'il tuo rio pensiero' (130/2/1, 'your most evil thought'). All of this happens *before* the poison is injected (that happens with 'Temete, signor, la gelosia!' at 130/1/1), before the moment when, as Boito claimed, 'the whole man changes'. That this initial outburst is without sufficient cause is evident. In the parallel section of the play one need not interpret Othello's response to Iago, 'By heaven, he echoes me' (III.iii, 107), as anything more than astonishment. Verdi's turbulent setting was doubtless intended to be accepted in a straightforward way, without probing too deeply, but he could have provided no clearer example of what Leavis called Othello's 'readiness to respond'. The traitor, indeed, is within the gates.

The danger in bringing up Otello's rage too quickly and too violently in Act II is that, emotionally, Act III has nowhere to go. This is the principal dramatic difficulty in the opera, and from its first performances Act III was considered the problematic act. After invoking some of Maurel's cautionary advice about the role of Otello, Budden prudently suggests that the solution lies in a carefully measured, nuanced interpretation by the tenor who sings the role (III, 413). No matter how one considers Act III, however, it is difficult to argue that it provides us with much information about Otello's character that we have not already learned – and perhaps overlearned – in Act II. The exception, the moment that most enlarges our understanding of Otello in Act III, is the monologue, 'Dio! mi potevi scagliar' – and of that, primarily the four lines beginning 'Ma, o pianto, o duol! m'han rapito il miraggio' (229/1/1, 'But, o weeping, o sorrow! They have stolen the mirage from me'). This is not only his most important utterance in the 'primitive' central acts, furnishing the painfully needed contrast: these lines may well be, with those of 'Esultate!', his most important in the opera. Here, finally, Otello lifts himself up and provides us a glimpse of his former potential for greatness. In the context of the whole monologue, largely derived from the 'Had it pleased heaven' soliloquy (IV.ii, 46), the four critical lines are clearly substitutes for the section beginning, 'But there where I have garnered up my heart' – the confession that he has now built his life entirely on his love for Desdemona, the crucial passage for Salvini's interpretation.

Although their general sense is identical with Shakespeare's, Boito's images differ at this point (Hueffer's translation in the vocal score, however, does not acknowledge this): they are apparently a conflation of Othello's longing for the 'miraggio', his earlier state of ignorance (e.g., 'What sense had I of her stolen hours of lust?', III.iii, 339–41, already used once in Act II of the opera, and 'I had been happy if the general camp', III.iii, 346–8) and his 'Put out the light' (V.ii, 7). Underscoring the importance of the final two lines, Verdi puts them twice on Otello's lips, 'Spento è quel sol, quel sorriso, quel raggio / Che mi fa vivo, che mi fa lieto!' ('That sun, that smile, that ray is extinguished, which gives me life, which gladdens me!'). With their repetition (229/4/3) Otello strides boldly and nobly up the span of a tenth, up to that high b♭^{1}, and even in his sorrow, for a glorious moment, we see what he must have been – before it all slides back, once again, to primitive chaos (cf. Bradshaw 1983: 155–6).

The two other principal characters, far simpler, can be dealt with more briefly. In the case of Desdemona the groundwork for the Romantic, *ottocento* conceptions of her character was again laid by Schlegel. Saintly images abound. She is 'a victim without stain', 'sweet, humble, simple, and so innocent that she cannot even conceive the idea of infidelity', an 'angelic being', 'Othello's good angel', propelled by 'the need to consecrate her life to someone else, this natural instinct in women', and so on. From all indications, the Desdemonas in Rossi's productions were similarly sweet, innocent, and passive (Busi 1973: 179), although Salvini's Desdemona, characteristically, was more complex and passionate (Gatti 1968: 122). That the simpler heroine was Verdi's model is clear from his letter to Ricordi on 22 April 1887, which virtually echoes, but secularizes, Schlegel's language: 'Desdemona is not a woman, she's a type! She's the type of goodness, of resignation, of sacrifice! They are creatures born for others, unconscious of their own *ego*!' (see p. 96 above). Boito's description of her in the *disposizione scenica* is similar (see p. 96 above). Once again, the one-sidedness of the interpretation is leagues away from mid-twentieth-century discussions of her character (some written by explicit non-admirers, such as Auden 1962 and, for the most part, Rice 1974; see also the summary in Rosenberg 1961: 206–8), and Jane Adamson, in a recent full-length portrait of Desdemona, quite properly insists that 'in the first three acts she seems active, resolute, confident – as decisive as Othello at the beginning' (1980: 220).

In the opera we see nothing of this adventurous, bold side – the side to which Iago could insidiously refer in his 'She did deceive her father, marrying you' (III.iii, 208). These words severely damage Othello's peace of mind, although Boito gratuitously dismissed them in an 1887 conversation with Blanche Roosevelt (p. 228). In effect, Boito has with considerable skill transformed Desdemona into a pure, guiltless passivity, closely related to the typically *fin-de-siècle* dramatic type that Ariane Thomalla has identified as the *femme fragile* (1972; cited in Kunze 1981: 30; see also Hinterhäuser 1977 and Bradshaw 1983: 153; on the other hand, Kerman (1956: 160–2), takes a strikingly different view). She is above all a selfless adorer of Otello. Needless to say, the musical advantage of this for Verdi was one of providing utter contrast with Iago's machinations, the opportunity to permit 'naive' melodic lyricism to counterpoint with an otherwise almost relentless, pointed declamation and motivic symphonism.

The keys to Boito's understanding of Desdemona lie in his pointed alterations of Shakespeare's text. It is significant, for example, that what was initially Othello's greeting of her, an acknowledgement, however nuanced, of her boldness, 'O, my fair warrior!' (II.i, 174), is taken out of his mouth to become her wide-eyed apostrophe of him, her first words, 'Mio superbo guerrier!' (96/1/1). And once her humiliation has begun Boito twists the knife by providing her with two parallel pleas that we do not find in Shakespeare: the 'helpless' Desdemona meekly asks Otello twice for pardon and mercy – indeed, in the opera these are two of her most telling moments. In the first, the Act II Quartet, 'Dammi la dolce e lieta / Parola del perdono' (158/1/4), Boito even heightens the image of childlike innocence, thus making its rejection doubly painful, by adding 'La tua fanciulla io sono / Umile e mansueta' ('I am your young girl / Humble and gentle'). All of this stems merely from the play's two simple exit-lines, 'Whate'er you be, I am obedient' (III.iii, 89) and, perhaps, 'I am very sorry that you are not well' (III.iii, 291). The second plea, in the Act III Duet, is even more typically Boitian and unmotivated by the play (cf. the continuation of her 'I understand a fury in your words, / But not the words', IV.ii, 31ff): 'Mi guarda! Il volto e l'anima ti svelo; il core infranto / Mi scruta . . . io prego il cielo per te con questo pianto', etc. (218/4/4, 'Look at me! I am revealing my face and soul to you; Study my broken heart; I am praying heaven for you with this weeping'). Once again we find innocence pleading before guilt and being rejected. Her tears here are in marked contrast with the play, in which the shocked Desdemona does not weep during her confrontation with Othello (although she does after he leaves; cf. IV.ii, 101–2, 'I cannot weep', and 123, Iago's remark to her, 'Do not weep, do not weep!'). Perhaps spurred on by Verdi in his search for a proper Act III finale, Boito 'invented' the image of Desdemona weeping before Othello yet one more time in Act III: within the prolonged spectacle of her public debasement in the *concertato* begun 'in the livid mud' ('nel livido / Fango', 271/2/1): 'Piango . . . m'agghiaccia il brivido / Dell'anima che muor' (271/3/2, 'I weep . . . am frozen by the shiver of my dying soul').

In characteristically late-nineteenth-century style, Boito also surrounds Desdemona with what Degrada has called a 'devotional iconology'([1976]: 159) that is most clearly seen in the (non-Shakespearean) Act II Homage Chorus. This *tableau* serves to offer distinctly Nazarene, pre-Raphaelite-like attributes to Desdemona (Kunze 1980: 29). One notices, for example, the references to the approaching of a 'chaste altar', to pure lilies, angels, heaven, the Madonna, the adorning of Desdemona 'like a sacred image', and so on. The Chorus was not part of the original libretto, and it is unclear whose idea it was to include it: apparently Verdi had at one point considered an opera with no chorus (*CVB*, I, 57; Budden, III, 312). More to the point, Verdi seemed to have interpreted this *tableau* in a straightforward, almost 'innocent' Schlegelian way; 'That chorus', he wrote to Boito on 23 June 1881, 'could not be more graceful, more elegant or more beautiful. And then, what a splash of light amidst so much darkness!' (Budden, III, 312). Boito's description of it a few days earlier was somewhat more pointed: 'It will be like a pure, sweet, apotheosis of songs and flowers encircling the beautiful, innocent figure of Desdemona' (17 June 1881; in Budden, III, 311). Francesco Degrada, however, has once again caught its actual effect, which 'according to a typical formula of *decadentismo*' juxtaposes rich Roman Catholic iconology 'with the theme of beauty trapped and corroded by death . . . But it is clear that the apotheosis serves only to exalt the macabre pleasure of capturing the extinguishing of that smile in the slash of humiliation and in the pallor of death' ([1976]: 159–60). Iago's contamination of the Homage Chorus with his 'Vigilate', so tellingly set by Verdi (see pp. 150–1 above), is the final, disturbing touch in bringing out this quality.

It is frequently remarked that the opera's Iago is a Mephistophelean character, a familiarly Boitian 'Spirito che nega' (*Mefistofele*, Act I), more explicitly wicked from the beginning than Shakespeare's character – a character, appropriately, born out of the 'ingenious, destructive element of fire' in Act I (Conrad 1977: 57). The reasons adduced are principally three, and all are valid. The first is the presence of the extravagant Act II 'Credo', which does not correspond precisely with any extended passage in the play and which in defining Iago suggests diabolism and a preference of evil for evil's sake. The second is the removal of one of Iago's motives for his hatred, that is, his suspicion about Othello, ' 'twixt my sheets / He's done my office' (I.iii, 369–70; cf. II.i, 276–80). And, finally, Boito's Iago seems to have the full malevolence of his insidious plot firmly in mind from the beginning: there is no development of character, as with Shakespeare's Iago, who is capable of tapping his head and saying, ' 'Tis here, but yet confused' (II.i, 292). Since this much is clear, it may at first seem strange that in the *disposizione scenica* Boito appeared firmly to have contradicted the diabolic conception of Iago: 'The crassest of mistakes, the most vulgar error . . . is to play him as a kind of human demon; to give him a Mephistophelean sneer and make him shoot Satanic glances everywhere' (in Budden, III, 328). The contradiction is only apparent, however, for Boito – surely seconding Verdi, who was explicit on this point in several letters (see pp. 100–4 above) – was merely instructing future performers that the essence of Iago lay in a convincing ability to deceive, to manipulate his own surface appearance. Thus histrionic cape-waving and villainous lurking about in the presence of others would not do – only, as Verdi had put it in early 1880, delightfully receiving Morelli's suggestion, 'Iago with the face of an honest man' (see p. 49 above).

External appearance, however, fails to touch Iago's Satanic core, which is what we are intended to perceive in the 'Credo', with its inventory of *scapigliato* imagery, including atoms, germs, primal mud, worms, graves, and the like. One of the perennial concerns of *Otello* commentators has been to suggest possible hints in Shakespeare's play that might have served as a stimulus for this 'Credo', which no less a Verdian than Julian Budden judged 'a piece of high-flown nonsense' (III, 318). One thinks of a number of phrases that could have been relevant: Iago's purely physical explanation of love as 'merely a lust of the blood and a permission of the will' (I.iii, 326); his 'Hell and night' conclusion to Act I (I.iii, 385–6) along with his 'Divinity of hell!' remarks (II.iii, 317–20); etc. Some have also noted possible sources in some of the misanthropic passages of *Timon of Athens* and *Titus Andronicus* (Toye 1931: 419; Dean 1968: 88). Once again the two pertinent nineteenth-century critics come to our rescue, for it is their interpretations of Iago that seem to be our true sources. To Schlegel, Iago was 'an evil Genius'; 'there was never a more shrewd wicked man (*scellerato*) put on the stage than Iago'; he was 'a consummate master of the art of dissimulation'; 'because he sees everything from the bad side, he destroys harshly the imagination's enchantment in everything that belongs to love'. Even more apposite, François-Victor Hugo's analysis of Iago, which we know Boito to have perused, reads like a groundplan for the 'Credo', once past its 'Divinity of hell!' opening:

Il n'est qu'un critique; *I am nothing if not critical*. But this is a critical faculty that never sees anything but the bad sides [cf. Schlegel]. He is incapable of admiration and enthusiasm. Morally he has the hypocrisy of Tartuffe. Intellectually he has the scepticism of Don Juan. He lacks only supernatural power to be Mephistopheles. Poetically – for Iago sometimes improvises – he never produced nor could have produced anything but epigrams. Lyricism is denied him, as is faith, and for him the sublime is only a neighbour of the ridiculous. Thus, in reality, he regards such a grand passion as Desdemona has conceived for the Moor as perfectly grotesque. Desdemona, a spiritualist and almost a mystic [!] only sees the soul of the Moor and admires it; Iago, a materialist and almost a nihilist, only sees the body of the Moor and laughs.   (1860: 67)

Hugo also helps us to solve the problem of determining the grounds of Iago's motivation in the opera. The following are lines that Boito marked off with a pencil:

But the principal cause . . . of Iago's hatred must be sought in his own nature . . . He admits it somewhere [V.i, 19–20] with cynical frankness: another's *daily beauty makes him ugly* . . . Iago begrudges Othello for being everything that he is not. He begrudges him for being powerful; he begrudges him for being great; he begrudges him for being honest; . . . heroic; . . . victorious; . . . loved by the people; . . . adored by Desdemona. And that is why he wants revenge. At! Othello is genius. Well then, let him be careful! For Iago is envy.
         (1860: 65; the point of Hugo's argument was expanded and
         reiterated in this century by Knight [1930]: 111–18)

Significantly, Boito's *disposizione scenica* description of Iago leads with the line 'Iago is Envy' and proceeds almost immediately to 'Io non sono che un critico', reproduced, as in Hugo, in two languages. 'Iago is the real author of the drama', wrote Boito in that description (Budden, III, 328), and the truth of this exceeds its superficial meaning. *Otello* is the only non-comic opera of Verdi in which the perspective is predominantly ironic, and, as several commentators on the play have remarked, Iago forces us to see things through his eyes. This is one reason why the opera's third and fourth acts can seem so oppressively cruel. The purely good appears both defenceless and totally unbefriended by a complementary, supportive hero or heroine; isolated innocence is held fast, tortured at considerable length, and ultimately murdered. There is a flickering, *fin-de-siècle* sensationalism at work here to prolong the explicit cruelty and injustice. It is distinctively Boitian, and it can be more than a little uncomfortable to witness the more purely Romantic Verdi dabbling in it. In any event (as is pointed out in Adamson 1980: 66–7), the audience, powerless to intervene, must watch these machinations 'from above', alone with Iago knowing what nobody else on stage knows. One reason that the 'Esultate!' strikes us so thrillingly is that as spectators we have not yet been defiled. The world is still pure and strong, and Iago has not yet tapped Roderigo (and us) on the shoulder. Once Iago utters the words 'Su via, fa senno, aspetta / L'opra del tempo' ('Come on, use your head, wait for the working of time'), and the 'secure' E major clouds over with that sinister, confidential C♯-minor string chord (31/3/3) – a master stroke – everything changes. We sink into Iago's world with him, a soulless world of artifice, high polish, cool objectivity, and intellectual manipulation.

It is appropriate that these 'artificial' qualities provide some of the most typical features of the literary-technical structure of Boito's brilliant libretto. Readers familiar with the principles of Italian poetry may recognize in it at once a 'literary' or 'precious' quality unprecedented in Verdian opera librettos. Although many of the lines are direct or nearly direct translations from the play, Boito's rich vocabulary and aestheticist poetic predilections often produce a non-spontaneous language curved in on itself with the connoisseur's relish of learned tricks and 'objective' wordplay. This is particularly evident when one reads the libretto without reference to the more 'direct' music. Mingled with the traditional striving for clear contrasts, strong emotional situations, and the like – things normally associated with librettos – there is an unmistakable craving for the rare, the new, the exquisite, all of which frequently stand coolly above and apart from the more immediate passions of the characters. It is a mannered text very much tied to the special vices of its period. Hence Gabriele Baldini's judgment, for example, that the libretto is 'literarily knowledgeable and mildly pretentious, but of a rapidly outdated taste' (1963: 21; see also the more well-known Baldini [1970]: 71, 95, 123, 127, 246, 276).

A few of Boito's special effects, for instance, suggest ancient Classical metres (the so-called *poesia metrica* or *poesia barbara*) with varying degrees of explicitness and consistency. These were the hallmark, for instance, of the *Odi barbare* of Giosuè Carducci (from 1877 onwards) – very much in the air at the time of the writing of the *Otello* libretto – and Boito had experimented with them in his own radical poetry from the 1860s. Moreover, in the important set of notes appended to his *Mefistofele*, in which the Act IV Classical Sabbath contains examples of Italianized dactylic hexameter and asclepiadic metres – admittedly for very special, dramatically motivated effects – Boito had explicitly defended his use of ancient metres. In *Otello* the most suggestive instance is the eight-line evocation of what seems to be the immense trochaic catalectic tetrameter in the Storm, 'Lampi! tuoni! gorghi! turbi tempestosi e fulmini!' (6/2/1). Significantly, this metre returns for the twelve elemental lines for Otello and Iago at the end of Act II, 'Sì, pel ciel marmoreo giuro! Per le attorte folgori!' (193/3/3; see Lavagetto 1979: 140).

Explicitly trochaic metre also turns up, unusually, in the *senario* (6-syllable) portions of the Homage Chorus. While it is unclear what influence, if any, the experimental tendencies of *poesia barbara* might have had here, Boito certainly felt the need to explain and defend the trochaic accents to Verdi (see p. 38 above). Somewhat more ambiguous are two instances of Boito combining lines of different metres in unusual ways within lyrical stanzas. Even where explicit Classical metres are not followed, such poetry can have a 'pseudo-barbaric', pseudo-antique effect sometimes sought by the poets of the period (Elwert 1973: 202–3). The first, Otello's Act III monologue, 'Dio! mi potevi scagliar tutti i mali / Della miseria, – della vergogna', is built from an unusual juxtaposition of pronounced dactylic *endecasillabi* with *doppi quinari* and, ultimately, *quinari*. Each of its two stanzas thus follows the pattern 11, 5–5, 11, 5–5, 11, 5, 5, 11. All of thus may be – and perhaps should be – scanned without reference to the *poesia barbara*, but, given Boito's fondness for embedded submetrical/supermetrical allusions and double scansions, it may be worth noting that the first line and a half, as far as 'miseria', forms a perfect dactylic hexameter, with caesura after 'scagliar'. Similarly ambiguous are the free, non-patterned combinations of the Willow Song (11s, 7s, 5s, 5 + 5s), which are clearly intended to impress us as something more than the usual 'rhymed-*scena*' verse; moreover its original version, at least, contained a few anomalous *ottonari* (8s; see p. 33 above). One cannot be certain about this point, of course, but any hint of pseudo-classicizing within a poem in which the name 'Barbara' appears twice would have been a thoroughly Boitian conceit.

In short, the libretto brims over with artificial effects. Iago's 'Era la notte – Cassio dormìa – gli stavo accanto / Con interotte – voci tradìa – l'intimo incanto'[9] is in an uncommon triple *quinario* metre (5 + 5 + 5, in some respects a radical accenting and fracturing of *doppio settenario*, 7 + 7), with internal rhymes and, later on, more 'normal' *doppio settenario* interpolations for the direct quotations. (The initial effect is similar to that of a passage in triple *senario* from Boito's earlier *Re Orso*: 'Il refolo buffa – in rabida zuffa – col mare lontan', II.v, 22ff.) Iago's 'Credo' is written in what Boito called a 'metro rotto e non simetrico' ('broken, non-symmetrical metre', see p. 40 above). Like rhymed-*scena* verse elsewhere in *Otello*, it randomly mixes non-strophic rhymed *endecasillabi* (11s), *settenari* (7s), and *quinari* (5s), only here with the clear understanding that the jaggedly asymmetrical procedure is being used to sculpt an incisive, elevated solo piece. The unpredictable mixtures not only guarded against the danger of falling into a symmetrical, parallel-phrased lyricism – something that Verdi clearly did not want at this point (see p. 40 above) – but they also symbolized the moral disorder and decay within Iago. Boito had employed the device before to the same effect, in his 1866 poem 'Case nuove', an attack on the unplanned quality of the new Milanese buildings then emerging; he would use it again in Ford's monologue in *Falstaff*, II.i. Even Boito's rhyming procedure in *Otello* is a study in itself. It ranges from the delicate preciosity, say, of the first four lines of the Willow Song's third stanza (11, 7, 11, 7, but rhymed abba, thus producing a kind of inside-out effect: 'Scendean gli augelli a vol dai rami cupi / Verso quel dolce canto, / E gli occhi suoi piangevan tanto, tanto / Da impietosir le rupi') to the shift in the Act I Love Duet from *rima alternata* (abab) to *rima baciata* ('kissed rhyme' aabb) in the passage leading up to and including the kiss ('Quest'attimo divino / Nell' ignoto avvenir del mio destino', etc.). It cannot be overstressed that the learned aspects of these things were essentially the private games of a literary man. Boito was obliged to be concerned with them, but, from all indications, Verdi was not. This was, after all, the impatient, practical composer who as recently as 28 October 1882, during the *Don Carlos* revision, had flung his typical anti-artifice complaint at Du Locle (via Nuitter), his conviction, that is, that excessively poetic concerns can vitiate the dramatic immediacy of a libretto: 'I believe . . . that for the modern opera it would be necessary to adopt non-rhyming poetry . . . What's more, *the word* (*le mot*), which strikes and sculpts, is sometimes obliterated in a phrase because of the metre (*verso*) or the rhyme' (Günther 1975: 365). For Verdi the primary value of Boito's skilfully wrought eccentricities was as a stimulus for his own creation. It could not have been their literary intricacy or aestheticism that impressed him, but rather their power, as high-relief, incisive words and word-patterns, to give birth to new musical responses and vivid theatrical ideas. Verdi's whole career had been one of demanding the new, the striking, and the strange from his librettists. Doubtless Boito was aware of this while drafting the libretto, as is suggested by his remarks to Giulio Ricordi on 4 September 1879: 'I am applying to this work a particular rhythmic construction throughout (in the lyric part), and I believe that this will greatly interest our *Maestro*' (see p. 28 above).

There can be no doubt that Boito's *recherché* verse did in fact engender much of the composer's musical rhetoric. Still, as Boito had anticipated, Verdi set the text very much on his own terms. He did not hesitate to counterpoint his own musical boundaries against the libretto's poetic boundaries if the theatrical effect could be improved, as is witnessed, for example, by his dramatic overshooting of the poetic structure of 'Dio! mi potevi scagliar' to illustrate Otello's loss of self-control. The aesthetic vision of Verdi's music is more immediate, more direct, more purely 'Romantic' than that of Boito's libretto. The composer was far less concerned with Boito's lifelong dualistic themes and literary pretensions than he was with producing effective music and effective theatre. If in the libretto we sense a cool separation of the writer from the text, the high polish of an aesthetically manipulated poetry, in the music we are confronted with a direct series of body-blows.[10] Verdi's music is always direct, aggressive, tactile. We are continually struck by its sheer physicality and energy, by the way that Verdi can repeatedly take a polished, mannered line (for instance, 'I titanici oricalchi squillano nel ciel', 'The titanic orichalcs [i.e., ancient brass-gold trumpets] ring forth in heaven') and convert it into palpable presence (12/1/1). Boito's vision of Shakespeare's play has aspects of ironic, cool detachment, but Verdi's boils over with scalding immediacy. Even while based – inseparably based – on Boito's text, the music's white heat burns through the residual preciosity of the words. Sheer force of personality overwhelms the text even while honouring it. Verdi's reading of the sense-units is so close, each line so individually underscored and transmuted into the physical, that the danger was of excessive musical faceting and fractionalization, of abandoning the broadly arched, melodic foundation that he so prized as constituting the heart of the Italian tradition. Some of his solutions to these purely musical problems have been suggested in Chapter 7, but it is worth mentioning here the importance of the 'Hugo- or Salvini-like', purer Otello in Acts I and IV (and in 'Ma, o pianto, o duol!', etc. in Act III) and the lyrical Desdemona in counter-balancing what Degrada has called the 'analytical and anticohesive' aspects of the music ([1976]: 163). In any event, we are much closer to understanding *Otello* when we realize that the poetry and the music present us with visions that differ in certain important respects; or, better, that the special quality of the opera is to be found in the interlocking of two powerful, gigantic casts of mind.

A larger, and riskier, issue would be to explore the historical-contextual content of the *Otello* story and Verdi's way of treating it within the Italian musical crisis of the 1870s and 1880s. As has been outlined in Chapters 2 and 3, the crisis was one of identity and individuality: the viability of pure Italian song in an increasingly complex, sceptical, international, and 'realistic' world. Both Italian criticism and Verdi's letters from that period give us a claustrophobic sense of the impending doom of the tradition. The composer's celebrated, if ambiguous, 'Torniamo all'antico; sarà un progresso' ('Let's return to the past: that will be progress'; to Florimo, 4 or 5 January 1871; Ab., III, 355–6) is a *cri de coeur* pleading for the survival of the grand tradition of Italian directness and vocality, ever more abandoned by the young. And, ironically, it was uttered as Verdi was guiding his own music into ever more intricate, subtle paths with the controversial *Aida*. This shipwrecking of the great Italian vocal tradition is one of the profound music-historical events of the later nineteenth century. The formerly pure (because perceived retrospectively as pure), 'naive' Italian practice of glorious, unselfconscious vocality flowing from direct, unmixed emotions was finally, inevitably, being mortally adulterated by contradictory, foreign influences. Verdi had touched and participated in the old world, and whatever he might have gained in his maturity, one also recognizes a deep sense of loss in his letters – and, I think, in his music – at the irrevocable passing of a simpler, cleaner, purely Italian way of feeling. For many composers and critics, it seemed, pure emotional states and the straightforward, standardized procedures that expressed them were no longer artistically viable in the 'modern' world: in a real sense they had lost their aesthetic right to exist, or at least to be ardently embraced in modern composition. But subtlety, it was discovered, was also a contaminator; and, ultimately for Italian opera, it was a poison. One notes that much of the criticism and defence of *Aida*, *Otello* and *Falstaff* in the Italian press revolved directly around this keypoint, the touchstone: the conviction, or lack of it, that this threatened 'melody' still had the upper hand over the increasing orchestral complexity and the disintegration of traditional forms – a somewhat shaky hope that the 'old Verdi' was still present.

It is not difficult to perceive that the *Otello* narrative contains remarkable parallels with the music-historical crisis. It, too, is concerned in its own way with the unstoppable destruction of the innocent, the unmixed, the pure; and with the way that the poison of subtlety, once released, renders the recovery of naiveté impossible. Surely one must not read a crude, heavy-handed symbolism into the opera, for clearly it is not there. Yet we miss something poignant if we fail to notice how the choice of the *Otello* plot echoes some of Verdi's most deeply held artistic concerns. It is significant that the music for the Madonna-like Desdemona, 'not a woman' but 'a type' (p. 96 above), was conceived as a 'melodic line [that] never stops from the first to the last note' (p. 96 above). Since she is explicitly identified with a musical procedure and its way of conceiving reality, we may also recognize within her humiliation and ultimate death the extinguishing of the melodic. The cruel victor in all of this is the subtle, manipulative, and intellectual Iago – and it is significant that in Boito's version he escapes and is not brought to justice. Musically, he is Desdemona's opposite and embodies the annihilation of broad, vocal melody. 'Iago must only declaim and snicker' (p. 96 above). 'In that part it is necessary neither to sing nor to raise one's voice (save in a few exceptions)' (p. 104 above). Initially snubbed by the pure, this materialistic demon is eager to destroy the lyrical symbols of that which he can no longer attain. His vow is explicit: 'Beltà ed amor in dolce inno concordi! / I vostri infrangerò soavi accordi!' ('Let this beauty and love sound harmoniously in the sweet hymn! I shall shatter your gentle sounds!', 151/1/1). Otello, insidiously wrenched from the old world of feeling towards the new, and for much of the opera living divided between them, 'must sing and howl' (p. 96 above). He sings, that is, as an innocent in Act I and then, retrospectively, only in terribly expressive moments of loss and valediction, such as 'Spento è quel sol, quel sorriso, quel raggio / Che mi fa vivo, – Che mi fa lieto!' in Act III (229/3/1ff) and in his final apostrophe to slain innocence in Act IV, 'E tu . . . come sei pallida! e stanca, e muta, e bella', etc. (361/1/1, 'And you . . . how pale! and tired, and mute, and beautiful').[11] And one may discover a similar subtext – poignantly stirring in the context of Verdi's career – within Otello's 'Ora e per sempre addio, sante memorie' (174/1/1).

One might profitably consider the *Otello* style as Verdi's struggle to reconcile two conceptions of art that may ultimately be irreconcilable – a fierce dialectic between the complex, 'modern' techniques and a potent, residual lyrical directness. The whole 'continuous' and 'symphonic-motivic' basis of the opera, stretching the old Italian patterns past their limits, is directly relevant here, and there can be no doubt that *Otello* is suffused with an abstruseness substantially in advance of any of his preceding operas. By its end, as is the case with Desdemona, there is no one left to defend the pure, the simple. This is an important reason why her outburst at the end of the Willow Song is so unbearably moving, 'Ah! Emilia, Emilia, addio, Emilia, addio', (337/1/1). It is also a farewell to a whole way of feeling, a last embrace of the old world, which will never come again. A short, still lyrical prayer follows, 'nell'ora della morte'. And then the light of naiveté is put out forever.

Notes

1. Synopsis

1 This description of *Otello* includes some of the information available only in the 1887 *disposizione scenica* (*DS*), or production book, 'compiled and ordered by Giulio Ricordi according to the [original] staging at the Teatro alla Scala'. This is a set of specific stage directions, read and approved by both Verdi and Boito. (See Chapter 5 below.)

2. Creating the libretto: Verdi and Boito in collaboration

1 Line references and quotations are from the edition of the play in *The New Cambridge Shakespeare*, ed. Norman Sanders (Cambridge, 1984).

2 Most of the significant variants are transcribed in Alessandro Luzio, *Carteggi Verdiani*, 4 vols. (Rome, 1935–47), vol. II, pp. 95–141, although Luzio occasionally conflates two separate readings into one. Some of the variants may also be found in Arrigo Boito, *Tutti gli scritti*, ed. Piero Nardi (Verona, 1942), pp. 1536–41.

3 Julian Budden, in *The Operas of Verdi 3: From Don Carlos to Falstaff* (London, 1981), p. 308, considers the ms. version to be the third version, a response to the famous prescription in Verdi's 15 August letter (see below). Yet this earliest ms. version, although similar in several respects to Verdi's prescription, does not follow it exactly, as Boito claims to have done in his letter of 18 October: 'I transcribed [your idea] without allowing myself to be disturbed by any doubts' (*CVB*, I, 4). Similarly, Frank Walker, in *The Man Verdi* (1962; rpt. Chicago, 1982), p. 478, agrees that in October Boito sent a new version of the finale, 'exactly as envisaged by Verdi'.

4 It remains distinctly possible that this sixth quatrain is a fragment of another version – possibly even the third version, although this seems unlikely: see n. 3 above. In the ms. libretto the fifth quatrain, that of Lodovico, Emilia, the Herald, and the Chorus, is followed by space enough for another quatrain; instead, one finds a large 'X', one of Boito's signs for the end of a section. Still, both Luzio (1935: 111–12) and Nardi (Boito 1942: 1539), after examining the pages of the actual manuscript, joined the sixth quatrain to the fifth without comment. Until a more thorough study of the manuscript is undertaken one is obliged to follow their conclusions in this matter.

190

5 This is the second 'original' reading. An earlier version of the line, also in the ms. libretto, reads 'Ei m'abbandona – la mia memoria'.
6 For a history of the song and its sources, see Peter J. Seng, *The Vocal Songs in the Plays of Shakespeare: A Critical History* (Cambridge, Massachusetts, 1967), pp. 191–9 and the Supplementary notes to *Othello* in *The New Cambridge Shakespeare*, p. 191.

3. The composition of the opera

1 Our knowledge of Verdi's compositional process is lamentably frag-mentary, because of the reluctance of his heirs to release the apparently extensive sketch and draft material reported to exist, and even partially reproduced, in fundamentally important publications in 1941 by Carlo Gatti (e.g., *Verdi nelle immagini* (Milan, 1941), pp. xviii, 64–5, 184, 186–7; and *L'abbozzo del Rigoletto* (Milan, 1941). The few existing materials, as well as the reports of Muzio (pp. 50–1 above) and Ricordi (p. 52) tend to support the hypothesis of the production of isolated sketches, perhaps accumulated over a long period of time, preceding a more continuous draft.
2 Although the original fol. 100ᵛ is completely covered by the new sheet of music paper pasted onto it, its 'hidden' reading (Ex. 6a) is legible after shining a light through the folio.
3 An edition of the 1880–90 years of the extensive Verdi–Ricordi / Ricordi–Verdi correspondence, edited by Franca Cella and Pierluigi Petrobelli, is currently in preparation. Soon to be published by the Istituto di Studi Verdiani, Parma, it promises to be a collection of fundamental importance for Verdi studies.
4 On fol. 242 the first three bars (of four) – Ex. 8, bars 3–5 – are covered with a paste-over replacement. Cf. n. 2 above.
5 Like fol. 100ᵛ and the first three measures of fol. 242, fol. 249ᵛ is an 'original' folio with a paste-over replacement. See nn. 2 and 4 above.
6 In the autograph score these changes – along with a few others – are made in an unusual, violet ink, probably the result of a single correcting session. This was an ink available to Verdi at Casa Ricordi (e.g., it was used by Saladino for the Act IV reduction) and possibly also at the Hotel Milan, where he customarily stayed during visits to that city. The only other known Verdian document in violet ink from late 1886 and early 1887 is a note to Ricordi – still unpublished – datable from its con-tents as 20 January 1887. It remains possible that Verdi might have altered the score during his 24–30 November 1886 trip to Milan, but this seems unlikely: other 'violet' entries in the autograph – for instance, the harmonic changes in the third measure of the Act I Love Duet (his revision, i.e., of the music of Ex. 10) – deal with alterations that did not occur to him until December or, in some instances, later.

4. Compositional afterthoughts and revisions: Milan, Venice and Paris

1 The most current Ricordi scores deviate from the reading in Ex. 12b by

adding a slur, repositioning the 'dolce', and removing the 'ten[uto]'. This is a reading closer to what actually appears in the autograph score, fol. 100^v, bar 1, but since Verdi corrected the vocal-score proofs – and since he surely focussed his attention on this particular bar, as printed, in January 1887 – it is not clear that the multi-layered autograph-score indications in this case ought to be considered the court of last appeal. My preference for a 'definitive' reading is that of Ex. 12b.

2 One might also point out that an ill-advised cut is often made in performance, from the end of B′ directly into the E″ of the reprise. This has the effect not only of ruining the carefully balanced musical architecture but also of removing the very two action-dialogues that Verdi was concerned to emphasize. The cut, that is, renders some aspects of the Act IV plot inexplicable. For Verdi's general views on cuts during this period of his career, see his letters to Ricordi from 7 March 1893 – 'I am an enemy of cuts' – 1 June 1894, and 9 June 1894 (Ab., IV, 499, 544, 545–6).

3 Original Italian text (Ricordi Archives, autograph ms., fols. 7^v–10^v): 'Tuoni un clamor di gloria / Che sperda il nostro duol! / L'astro della vittoria / Splenda su questo suol.' Within this manuscript text 'splenda' (subjunctive) frequently also occurs as 'splende' (indicative). The ms. lacks the stage directions that place Iago in the centre of the stage.

4 Cf. the printed orchestral score in the Paris Opéra library, mentioned in Julian Budden, 'Time Stands Still in "Otello"', *Opera*, 32 (1981), 892. Budden reports that the Paris *partition* contains the revised *concertato* but not the 1894 ballet, thus suggesting that the ensemble changes alone might be definitive. There is doubtless a case that may be made for this conclusion, but it is worth mentioning that the printed score in Milan contains both the new ensemble and the ballet.

5. Of singers and staging: Verdi's ideas on performance

1 A facsimile reprint of the *disposizione scenica* and related *Otello* iconography, with extensive introductions by the present author and Mercedes Viale Ferrero, is currently in preparation and will be published by G. Ricordi & C.

2 The complex issue of the 'Maurel intervention' is discussed in my introduction to the facsimile reprint mentioned in n. 1 above. In brief, the *disposizione scenica* twice calls for Otello to be seated during Act III: during the first part of 'Dio! mi potevi scagliar' (p. 62) and during the Act III *concertato* (pp. 78–82). These appear to be Maurel's suggestions, to which Verdi at one point vehemently objected (see Ab., IV, 365). The precise date of Verdi's written objection, however, cannot at present be ascertained.

6. A brief performance history

1 *Otello* had returned to Covent Garden in the winter season of 1891–92 for two performances with Melba singing Desdemona for the first time,

but with Ferruccio Giannini as Otello and Eugène Dufriche as Iago. Enrico Bevignani conducted.

2 At Covent Garden in 1901 Tamagno also appeared in four performances of *Aida* and two of Isidore de Lara's *Messaline*.

3 As the Otello of the moment, Calleja sang the role at the Teatro Regio in Parma in 1914, but illness prevented his appearing in the first two performances, at which his place was supplied by the relatively unknown Umberto Chiodo.

4 Melchior, in fact, received a single opportunity to sing part of *Otello* at the Metropolitan. The occasion was Gatti-Casazza's farewell concert on 19 March 1935, when the tenor appeared with Elisabeth Rethberg in an abbreviated Act IV.

7. An introduction to the musical organization: the structures of Act II

1 Verdi, of course, did not subdivide the *Otello* autograph score into the traditional separate 'numbers' labelled by genre. The earliest issues of the vocal score and libretto, however, contain an 'indice' that does specify subdivisions, and these are often but not always coextensive with those articulated by dramatic, i.e., libretto, 'scenes'. Generally the subdivisions bear only the name of the relevant singers (e.g., in Act III, 'Otello, Jago', 'Desdemona, Otello', 'Otello', 'Otello, Jago, Cassio', 'Otello, Jago', 'FINALE'), but some are characterized by genre: in Act I, 'URAGANO: Jago, Roderigo, Cassio, Montano, Coro–Otello', CORO: *Fuoco di gioia!*' and 'BRINDISI: Jago, Cassio, Roderigo, Coro'; in Act II, 'CORO: *Dove guardi splendono*, Desdemona'; in Act III the above-mentioned 'FINALE'; in Act IV, 'CANZONE: Desdemona, Emilia' and 'AVE MARIA: Desdemona'. It should be stressed that these primarily editorial subdivisions (perhaps devised by Ricordi) are not infallible guides to the actual internal workings and large-scale structure of the music, although at times they provide interesting information, as in their linking of essentially the final three pieces of Act II under a single title, 'Otello, Jago' (obviously considered together as a single dramatic scene – i.e., with no characters entering or leaving – forming a kind of finale for Act II: see n. 2 below). For some of the problems encountered with these editorial subdivisions, see James A. Hepokoski, 'Verdi's Composition of *Otello*: the Act II Quartet', forthcoming (1987) in *Analyzing Opera: Essays from the 1984 Cornell Verdi–Wagner Symposium*, ed. Carolyn Abbate and Roger Parker.

2 In principle, of course, the last three structural units of Act II could be given separate numbers. I have linked them as Nos. 4a–c, however, partially on the basis of the information provided in the first vocal score's 'indice' (see n. 1 above), but also, more importantly, because Verdi himself seems to have considered the music from this point onwards (or perhaps slightly before this point – Verdi might have been referring to the libretto-scene numbering) to constitute a single 'Finale'. So much may be gleaned from his letter to Ricordi on 4 November 1886:

'In the long scene, Finale, Act II, between Iago and Otello, seven lines before the *Racconto* of the Dream, fix Iago's part like this: "Ardua impresa sa[-rebbe]" ' (unpublished [?]; Ricordi Arch.; omitted from Ab., IV, 298; cf. p. 69 above). When all three units are considered together they provide a provocative, but highly varied, evocation of some of the crucial elements of the standard duet-form (see Robert Anthony Moreen, 'Integration of Text Forms and Musical Forms in Verdi's Early Operas', unpublished dissertation (Princeton University, 1975); Harold S. Powers, ' "La solita forma" and "the Uses of Convention" ', forthcoming (1986) in a *Quaderno* commemorating the 1983 Verdi Conference in Vienna, to be published jointly by the Istituto di Studi Verdiani, Parma, and G. Ricordi & C. Thus the large shape, solo-piece Otello (4a) / solo-piece Iago (4b) / *cabaletta* Otello–Iago (4c), can tempt one to remember the *adagio*'s *proposta* and *risposta* (two often-contrasting lyrical expositions) and the principle of the concluding *cabaletta*, with the whole interspersed throughout with freer, kinetic material.

8. Shakespeare reinterpreted

1 Francesco Berio di Salsa's text for Rossini's opera is quite distant from that of the play; Hilary Gatti finds several of its differences traceable to Jean-François Ducis' French reduction of *Othello* in 1792 (*Shakespeare nei teatri milanesi dell'ottocento* (Bari, 1968), pp. 11–16).

2 For the centrality of Rusconi and a mention of Maffei, see Verdi's letter of 8 May 1886 (*CVB*, I, 103). Carcano's translations of Shakespeare were also some of the main sources for *Falstaff*: see e.g., James A. Hepokoski, *Giuseppe Verdi: Falstaff* (Cambridge, 1983), pp. 23, 30. William Weaver, in 'The Shakespeare Verdi Knew', *Verdi's Macbeth: a Sourcebook*, ed. David Rosen and Andrew Porter (New York, 1984), p. 148, besides suggesting Verdi's acquaintance with several well-known translations of *Macbeth* (including Leoni's), also mentions the presence in Verdi's library of apparently unused François-Victor Hugo French translation and a 'well-thumbed' English edition of Shakespeare – principally for Giuseppina? – brought out by Charles Knight in 1852.

3 Carcano, perhaps less important for Verdi's and Boito's *Otello*, prefaces his *Othello* translation with his own rather brief remarks, quoting, for instance, from François Guizot and especially from the 'freddo critico inglese', Samuel Johnson. From the latter Carcano includes the famous passage from 'The beauties of this play impress themselves . . . ' to the suggestive (for the opera) 'Had the scene opened in *Cyprus*, and the preceding incidents been occasionally related, there had been little wanting to a drama of the most exact and scrupulous regularity.' With regard to Verdi and Schlegel, Francesco Degrada has demonstrated the central role of the latter's thought also in Verdi's creation of *Macbeth* ('Lettura del *Macbeth*' [1977] in *Il palazzo incantato: studi sulla tradizione del melodramma dal Barocco al Romanticismo*, 2 vols. (Fiesole, 1979)). For a convenient English trans-

lation of Schlegel's remarks on *Macbeth*, see Rosen and Porter 1984: 346–8.

4 The point of Emanuel's affinities with the rising school of naturalism seems frequently misunderstood. The clearest discussions of Emanuel's acting style and dramatic aims may be found in Hilary Gatti 1968: 155–67 and Anna Busi, *Otello in Italia 1777–1972* (Bari, 1973), pp. 205–21.

5 William Weaver, in 'Verdi the Playgoer', *Musical Newsletter*, 6 (1976), 24, mentions Salvini's 1902 phonograph recording of a scene from Vittorio Alfieri's *Saul*, 'Il sogno di Saul' ('Saul's Dream'): 'It is an impressive, even eerie, piece of recitation . . . Salvini's style was clearly what we would call today "operatic". He does everything Alfieri wanted: alternating presto and adagio, piano and forte. Obviously, in the past century acting was acting: opera singers (if they were good interpreters) acted very much as Rossi and Salvini and [Adelaide] Ristori acted in the spoken theater. As the recording indicates, it was all acting in the grand style: larger than life . . .'

6 For summaries of influential criticism see Albert Gerard, ' "Egregiously an Ass": the Dark Side of the Moor: A View of Othello's Mind', *Shakespeare Survey*, 10 (1957), 98–106; Helen Gardner, '*Othello*: A Retrospect, 1900–67', *Shakespeare Survey*, 21 (1968), 1–11; John Wain, ed., *Shakespeare: Othello: A Casebook* (London, 1971), pp. 11–33; Robert Hapgood, '*Othello*', *Shakespeare: Select Bibliographical Guides*, ed. Stanley Wells (London 1973).

7 Curiously, on the dramatic stage it was Giovanni Emanuel – of whom Verdi and Boito disapproved – who abandoned Rossi's and Salvini's Turkish costumes in favour of one in the Venetian style (see Busi 1973: 215n).

   One might also note that Victor Maurel criticized Verdi for having favoured a Venetian costume throughout for Otello and argued instead in favour of reinstating an 'oriental costume' for several – but not all – scenes of the opera: Victor Maurel, 'A propos de la mise-en-scène du drame lyrique Otello' [1888], in *Dix ans de carrière* ([Paris, 1897], rpt. New York, 1977), pp. 35–7.

8 In his own 'rival' *mise-en-scène* of *Otello* Victor Maurel ingeniously proposed another way of staging Desdemona's entrance. Upon entering and seeing her husband about to commit an 'act of violence' upon Cassio, Desdemona, as *ange pacificateur*, addresses a 'mute supplication' to him for clemency and pardon, whereupon Otello responds mercifully – with a mere demotion. All of this is to be observed by Iago, who reacts to it with surprise in a theatrical *contre-scène*. Thus Maurel would have us interpret Cassio's fate as the result of a lenient gesture, the result of the first intercession of Desdemona for him – the seed of the remainder of the drama (Maurel 1888: 47–9, 96–8). As Ricordi's own *disposizione scenica* makes clear (p. 31), Verdi and Boito had no such idea in mind.

9 The dashes here are taken from Boito's manuscript libretto. Although they were not carried over into the printed libretto, they both provide assistance in determining Boito's conception of the scansion and reveal how Verdi saw the lines explicitly subdivided as he composed them.

10 Compare, e.g., Blanche Roosevelt's personal impressions in *Verdi: Milan and 'Othello'* (London, 1887) of Boito during the *Otello* rehearsals: '[Unlike everyone else] Boito is as cool as a cucumber. That man has no nerves' (p. 113). According to her general description of him after an interview; 'Boïto has an air *très grand seigneur* . . . From his manner you might take him for a prince of the blood, a statesman, a diplomat, an ambassador, but never for an operatic composer . . . [He] prefers being mistaken for a gentleman rather than a celebrity' (p. 239).

11 Cf. the lines of Othello in the play which, although not literally carried over into the opera, might well serve to summarize the latter's dramatic – and musical – argument: 'Excellent wretch! Perdition catch my soul / But I do love thee; and when I love thee not, / Chaos is come again' (*Oth.*, III.iii, 90–2).

Bibliography

Abbiati, Franco. *Giuseppe Veirdi*, 4 vols. Milan, 1959
Adami, Giuseppe. *Giulio Ricordi e i suoi musicisti*. Milan, 1933
Adamson, Jane. *Othello as Tragedy: Some Problems of Judgment and Feeling*. Cambridge, 1980
Alberti, Annibale, ed. *Verdi intimo: carteggio di Giuseppe Veridi con il conte Opprandino Arrivabene (1861–1886)*. Verona, 1931
Archibald, Bruce. 'Tonality in *Otello*', *The Music Review*, 35 (1974), 23–8
Ashbrook, William. 'Perspectives on an Aria: "Niun mi tema" ', *Opera News*, 49 (2 February 1985), 20–1
Auden, W. H. 'The Joker in the Pack', *The Dyer's Hand*. New York, 1962, pp. 246–72
Aycock, Roy E. 'Shakespeare, Boito, and Verdi', *The Musical Quarterly*, 58 (1972), 588–604
Baldini, Gabriele. 'Nota introduttiva', in William Shakespeare, *Otello, il moro di Venezia*. Trans. G. Baldini. Milan, 1984, pp. 5–22
The Story of Giuseppe Verdi [orig. *Abitare la battaglia*, Milan, 1970]. Trans. Roger Parker. Cambridge, 1980
Basevi, Abramo. *Studio sulle opere di Giuseppe Verdi*. Florence, 1859
Bauer, Roberto. *The New Catalogue of Historical Records: 1898–1908/09*. London, 1947
Beronesi, Patrizia. 'Il prologo storico di Manzoni', *Il teatro del personaggio: Shakespeare sulla scena italiana dell'800*. Ed. Laura Caretti. Rome, 1979, pp. 19–63
Boito, Arrigo. *Opere*. Ed. Mario Lavagetto. Milan, 1979
Tutti gli scritti. Ed. Piero Nardi. Verona, 1942
Bordowitz, Harvey, 'Verdi's Disposizioni Sceniche: The Stage Manuals for Some Verdi Operas'. Unpublished dissertation, Brooklyn College 1976
Bradshaw, Graham, 'A Shakespearean Perspective: Verdi and Boito as Translators' in Heopkoski 1983 [see below], pp. 152–71
Budden, Julian. *The Operas of Verdi: From Oberto to Rigoletto*. London 1973
The Operas of Verdi 2: From Il trovatore to La forza del destino. London, 1978
The Operas of Verdi 3: From Don Carlos to Falstaff. London 1981
'Puccini, Massenet and "Verismo" ', *Opera*, 34 (1983), 477–81
'Time Stands Still in "Otello" ', *Opera*, 32 (1981), 888–93

Busch, Gudrun. 'Die Unwetterszene in der romantischen Oper', *Die 'Couleur locale' in der Oper des 19. Jahrhunderts*, Studien zur Musikgeschichte des 19. Jahrhunderts XLII. Ed. Heinz Becker. Regensburg, 1976, pp. 161–212

Busch, Hans, ed. *Verdi's Otello and Simon Boccanegra in Letters and Documents*. Forthcoming (1987) from Oxford University Press

Busi, Anna. *Otello in Italia (1777–1972)*. Bari, 1973

Busoni, Ferruccio. 'Verdi's *Otello*: eine kritische Studie', *Neue Zeitschrift für Musik*, 54 (1887), 125

Carteggio Verdi–Boito. Ed. Mario Medici and Marcello Conati. 2 vols. Parma, 1978

Cella, Franca, and Petrobelli, Pierluigi, eds. *Giuseppe Verdi–Giulio Ricordi: Corrispondenza e immagini 1881/1890*. Milan, 1982

Cesari, Gaetano, and Luzio, Alessandro. *I copialettere di Giuseppe Verdi*. Milan, 1913

Chusid, Martin. *A Catalog of Verdi's Operas*. Hackensack, 1974

'Verdi's Own Words: His Thoughts on Performance, with Special Reference to *Don Carlos*, *Otello*, and *Falstaff*', *The Verdi Companion*. Ed. William Weaver and Martin Chusid. New York, 1979, pp. 144–92

Coe, Doug. 'The Original Production Book for *Otello*: An Introduction', *19th-Century Music*, 2 (1978–79), 148–58

Conati, Marcello, ed. *Interviews and Encounters with Verdi* [1980]. Trans. Richard Stokes. London, 1984

Cone, Edward T. 'The Old Man's Toys: Verdi's Last Operas', *Perspectives USA*, 6 (1954), 114–33

'On the Road to "Otello": Tonality and Structure in "Simon Boccanegra" ', *Studi verdiani*, 1 (1982), 72–98

Conrad, Peter. *Romantic Opera and Literary Form*. Berkeley, 1977, pp. 57–69

Cooke, Deryck. 'Shakespeare into Music' [1964], *Vindications: Essays on Romantic Music*. Cambridge, 1982, pp. 175–80

Corsi, Mario. *Tamagno: il più grande fenomeno canoro dell'ottocento*. Milan, 1937

Crutchfield, Will. 'Vocal Ornamentation in Verdi: the Phonographic Evidence', *19th-Century Music*, 7 (1983–84), 3–54

Dean, Winton. 'Verdi's "Otello": A Shakespearian Masterpiece', *Shakespeare Survey*, 21 (1968), 87–96

Degrada, Francesco. 'Lettura del *Macbeth* [1977], *Il palazzo incantato* [see below], II, 79–141

'*Otello*: da Boito a Verdi' [1976], *Il palazzo incantato: studi sulla tradizione del melodramma dal Barocco al Romanticismo*. 2 vols. Fiesole, 1979, II, 155–66

De Rensis, Raffaello. *Franco Faccio e Verdi*. Milan, 1934

Eliot, T. S. 'Shakespeare and the Stoicism of Seneca' [1927], *Selected Essays*. London, 1932; new edition, 1950, pp. 107–20

Elwert, W. Th. *Versificazione italiana dalle origini ai giorni nostri* [1968]. Florence, 1973

Filoni, Fabrizio. 'Macbeth, Othello, e The Merry Wives of Windsor nei libretti verdiani'. Unpublished dissertation, Università degli studi di Macerata, 1979–80

Gardner, Helen. *'Othello*: A Retrospect, 1900–67', *Shakespeare Survey*, 21 (1968), 1–11

Gatti, Carlo. *Il Teatro alla Scala nella storia e nell'arte (1778–1963)*. 2 vols. Milan, 1964

Verdi nelle immagini. Milan, 1941

Gatti, Hilary. 'Arrigo Boito discepolo di Shakespeare', *Studi inglesi*, No. 1. Bari, 1974, pp. 317–65

Shakespeare nei teatri milanesi dell'ottocento. Bari, 1968

Gerard, Albert. ' "Egregiously an Ass": the Dark Side of the Moor: A View of Othello's Mind', *Shakespeare Survey*, 10 (1957), 98–106

Gobbi, Tito. *My Life*. New York, 1980, pp. 106–12

Grey, Thomas S. and Kerman, Joseph. 'Verdi's "Groundswell" ', forthcoming (1987) in *Analyzing Opera: Essays from the 1984 Cornell Verdi–Wagner Symposium*. Ed. Carolyn Abbate and Roger Parker

Günther, Ursula. 'Der Briefwechsel Verdi–Nuitter–Du Locle zur Revision des *Don Carlos*', *Analecta musicologica*, 14 (1974), 1–31; and 15 (1975), 334–401

Hanslick, Eduard. 'Verdi's "Otello" ' [1887; orig. rpt. in *Die moderne Oper V: Musikalisches Skizzenbuch. Neue Kritiken und Schilderungen* (Berlin, 1888)], *Vienna's Golden Years of Music: 1850–1900*. Trans. and ed. Henry Pleasants. New York, 1950, pp. 287–302

Hapgood, Robert. *'Othello'*, *Shakespeare: Select Bibliographical Guides*. Ed. Stanley Wells. London, 1973

Hepokoski, James A. *Giuseppe Verdi: Falstaff*. Cambridge, 1983

'An Introduction to the 1881 Score', *Simon Boccanegra: Giuseppe Verdi*; English National Opera Guide, No. 32. Ed. Nicholas John, London, 1985, pp. 13–26

'Under the Eye of the Verdian Bear: Notes on the Rehearsals and Premiere of *Falstaff*', *The Musical Quarterly*, 71 (1985), 135–56

'Verdi's Composition of *Otello*: the Act II Quartet', forthcoming (1987) in *Analyzing Opera: Essays from the 1984 Cornell Verdi–Wagner Symposium*. Ed. Carolyn Abbate and Roger Parker

Hinterhäuser, Hans. 'Präraffaelitische Frauengestalten', *Fin-de-siècle. Gestalten und Mythen*. Munich, 1977, pp. 107–45

Hopkinson, Cecil. *A Bibliography of the Works of Giuseppe Verdi*. 2 vols. New York, 1973, 1978

Hugo, François-Victor, trans. *La tragédie d'Othello, Le More de Venise*, by William Shakespeare. In *Oeuvres complètes de W. Shakespeare*. Paris, 1860, pp. 46–80 (Introduction), 232–384, 393–414 (Notes)

James, Henry. *The Scenic Art: Notes on Acting & The Drama: 1872–1901*. Ed. Allan Wade. New Brunswick, 1948

John, Nicholas, ed. *Otello: Giuseppe Verdi*; English National Opera Guide, No. 7. London, 1981

Jung, Ute. *Die Rezeption der Kunst Richard Wagners in Italien*, Studien zur Musikgeschichte des 19 Jahrhunderts XXXV. Regensburg, 1974

Kerman, Joseph. 'Lyric Form and Flexibility in "Simon Boccanegra" ', *Studi verdiani*, 1 (1982), 47–62

'*Otello*: Traditional Opera and the Image of Shakespeare', *Opera as Drama*. New York, 1956, pp. 129–67

Knight, G. Wilson. 'The *Othello* Music' [1930], *The Wheel of Fire*. 5th edn. New York, 1957, pp. 97–119

Kolodin, Irving. *The Metropolitan Opera: 1883–1966: A Candid History*. New York, 1966

Kunze, Stefan. 'Der Verfall des Helden: Über Verdis "Otello" ', *Giuseppe Verdi: Othello: Texte, Materialien, Kommentare*; Rororo Opernbücher. Ed. Attila Csampai and Dietmar Holland. Reinbek bei Hamburg, 1981, pp. 9–36

Lauri-Volpi, Giacomo. *Voci parallele*. Milan, 1955

Lavagetto, Mario. *Quei più modesti romanzi*. Milan, 1979

'La vita / Profilo storico-critico dell'autore e dell'opera / Guida bibliografica', in [Arrigo Boito] *Opere* [see above], pp. vii–xxxviii

Lawton, David. 'On the "Bacio" Theme in *Otello*', *19th-Century Music*, 1 (1977–78), 211–20

Leavis, F. R. 'Diabolic Intellect and the Noble Hero: or, The Sentimentalist's Othello' [1937; 1952], *The Common Pursuit* (London, 1952), and John Wain, ed., *Shakespeare: Othello* [see below], pp. 123–46

Leiser, Clara. *Jean de Reszke and the Great Days of Opera*. New York, 1934

Luzio, Alessandro. *Carteggi verdiani*. 4 vols. Rome, 1935–47

Maurel, Victor. 'A propos de la mise-en-scène du drame lyrique Otello' [1888], in *Dix ans de carrière* [Paris, 1897]. Rpt. New York, 1977, pp. 1–148

Monaldi, Gino. *Cantanti celebri (1829–1929)*. Rome, 1929

Il melodramma in Italia nella critica del secolo XIX. Campobasso, 1927

Morazzoni, G. and Ciampelli, G. M. *Verdi: lettere inedite: le opere verdiane al Teatro alla Scala (1839–1929)*. Milan, 1929

Moreen, Robert Anthony. 'Integration of Text Forms and Musical Forms in Verdi's Early Operas'. Unpublished dissertation, Princeton University, 1975

Muir, Kenneth, and Edwards, Philip, eds. *Aspects of 'Othello'*. Cambridge, 1977

Nardi, Piero. *Vita di Arrigo Boito*. Verona, 1942

Newman, Ernest. *The Life of Richard Wagner* [1937–46]. 4 vols. Rpt. Cambridge, 1976

Nicolaisen, Jay. 'The First *Mefistofele*', *19th-Century Music*, 1 (1977–78), 221–32

Italian Opera in Transition, 1871–1893. Ann Arbor, 1980

Noske, Frits. 'Otello: Drama through Structure' [1971], *The Signifier and the Signified: Studies in the Operas of Mozart and Verdi*. The Hague, 1977, pp. 133–70

'Verbal to Musical Drama: Adaptation or Creation?', *Themes in Drama 3: Drama, Dance and Music*. Ed. James Redmond. Cambridge, 1981, pp. 143–52

Otello: dramma lirico in quattro atti . . . Giudizi della stampa italiana e straniera [2nd edn]. Supplemento straordinario alla *Gazzetta musicale di Milano*, No. 13. Milan, 1887

Parker, Roger and Brown, Matthew. 'Ancora un bacio: Three Scenes from Verdi's *Otello*', *19th-Century Music*, 9 (1985–86), 50–62

Percy, Thomas, *Reliques of Ancient English Poetry* [1765]. Rpt. New York, 1961, pp. 199–203

Pesci, Ugo. 'Arrigo Boito. – Il libretto', *Verdi e l'Otello*. Numero unico pubblicato dalla *Illustrazione italiana*. Milan, 1887, pp. 35–8

'Rehearsals for *Otello*' [1887; orig. in *Verdi e l'Otello* (see above)], *Interviews and Encounters with Verdi*. Trans. Richard Stokes. Ed. Marcello Conati. London, 1984, pp. 184–7

Pinzauti, Leonardo. 'Verdi's *Macbeth* and the Florentine Critics', *Verdi's Macbeth: A Sourcebook*. Ed. David Rosen and Andrew Porter. New York, 1984, pp. 137–43

Plantinga, Leon. *Romantic Music: A History of Musical Style in Nineteenth-Century Europe*. New York, 1984, pp. 315–23

Porter, Andrew. 'Verdi, Giuseppe (Fortunino Francesco)', *The New Grove Dictionary of Music and Musicians*. Ed. Stanley Sadie. London, 1980. XIX, pp. 635–65. Also available in *The New Grove: Masters of Italian Opera*. New York, 1983, pp. 193–308

Powers, Harold S. 'By Design: The Architecture of *Simon Boccanegra*', *Opera News*, 49 (22 December 1984), 16–21, 42–3

'*Otello* I.2, 3: A Case Study in Multivalent Analysis', forthcoming (1987) in *Analyzing Opera: Essays from the 1984 Cornell Verdi–Wagner Symposium*. Ed. Carolyn Abbate and Roger Parker

' "La solita forma" and "the Uses of Convention" ', forthcoming (1986) in a *Quaderno* commemorating the 1983 Verdi Conference in Vienna, to be published jointly by the Istituto di Studi Verdiani, Parma, and G. Ricordi & C.

Ramous, Mario. *La metrica*. Milan, 1984

Rice, Julian C. 'Desdemona Unpinned: Universal Guilt in *Othello*', *Shakespeare Studies*, 7 (1974), 209–26

Ricordi, Giulio, ed. *Disposizione scenica per l'opera Otello* . . . Milan, 1887

Righini, Pietro. 'Da che male è afflitto il "Diapason"?: i veri aspetti della secolare questione', *Nuova rivista musicale italiana*, 15 (1981), 540–55

Roosevelt, Blanche. *Verdi: Milan and 'Othello'*. London, 1887

Rosen, David, 'The *Libroni*, and Additional Notes on Ricordi Publications of *Macbeth*', *Verdi's Macbeth: A Sourcebook*. Ed. David Rosen and Andrew Porter. New York, 1984, pp. 302–5

Rosenberg, Marvin. *The Masks of Othello: The Search for the Identity of Othello, Iago, and Desdemona by Three Centuries of Actors and Critics*. Berkeley, California, 1961

Rosenthal, Harold D. *Two Centuries of Opera at Covent Garden*. London, 1958

Salmen, Walter. 'Venedig und die Barkarole in Oper und Operette', *Die 'Couleur locale' in der Oper des 19. Jahrhunderts*, Studien zur Musikgeschichte des 19. Jahrhunderts XLII. Ed. Heinz Becker. Regensburg, 1976, pp. 257–68

Schnebel, Dieter. 'Vom tiefen und tragischen Prozess des Lebens in Verdis "Otello" ' [1979], *Giuseppe Verdi: Othello: Texte, Materialien,*

Kommentare; Rororo Opernbücher. Ed. Attila Csampai and Dietmar Holland. Reinbek bei Hamburg, 1981, pp. 257–60

Seltsam, William H. *Metropolitan Opera Annals: A Chronicle of Artists and Performances*. New York, 1947

Seng, Peter J. *The Vocal Songs in the Plays of Shakespeare: A Critical History*. Cambridge, Massachusetts, 1967

Shaw, George Bernard. *London Music in 1888–89 as Heard by Corno di Bassetto . . .* New York, 1937
Music in London 1890–94. 3 vols. London, 1932

Stanislavsky, Constantin. 'Tommaso Salvini the Elder', *My Life in Art* [1924], trans. J. J. Robbins. 1924; rpt. Boston, 1935, pp. 265–76

Thomalla, Ariane. *Die 'femme fragile'. Ein literarischer Frauentypus der Jahrhundertwende*. Düsseldorf, 1972.

Tomlinson, Gary. 'Italian Romanticism and Italian Opera: An Essay in Their Affinities', *19th-Century Music*, 10 (1986–87), 43–60.

Toye, Francis. *Giuseppe Verdi: His Life and Works*. New York, 1931

Turner, J. Rigbie, *et al*. *Four Centuries of Opera: Manuscripts and Printed Editions in the Pierpont Morgan Library*. New York, 1983

Vallebona, G. B. *Il teatro Carlo Felice, cronistoria di un secolo: 1828–1928*. Genoa, 1928

Wain, John, ed. *Shakespeare: Othello: A Casebook*. London, 1971

Walker, Frank. *The Man Verdi*. 1962; rpt. Chicago, 1982

Weaver, William. 'The Shakespeare Verdi Knew', *Verdi's Macbeth: A Sourcebook*. Ed. David Rosen and Andrew Porter. New York, 1984, pp. 144–8
Verdi: A Documentary Study. London, [1977]

'Verdi, Shakespeare, and the Italian Audience', Nicholas John, ed., *Otello: Giuseppe Verdi* [see above], pp. 23–6

'Verdi the Playgoer', *Musical Newsletter*, 6 (1976), 3–8, 24

Discography

MALCOLM WALKER

All recordings in stereo unless otherwise stated.

Symbols

* denotes 78rpm **m** mono recording **e** electronically reprocessed stereo **4** cassette version. Date quoted relates to the year in which the recording was made.

D Desdemona; *E* Emilia; *O* Otello; *I* Iago; *C* Cassio; *L* Lodovico; *M* Montano; *R* Roderigo

Complete

1931 Carbone *D*; Beltracchi *E*; Fusati *O*; Granforte *I*; Girardi *C*; Zambelli *L*; Spada *M*; Pala *R* / La Scala Chorus & Orch. / Sabajno
EMI **e** 3C 153 17076–8

1938 (live performance) Rethberg *D*; Votipka *E*; Martinelli *O*; Tibbett *I*; Massue *C*; Moscona *L*; Cehanovsky *M*; Paltrinieri R / Metropolitan Opera Chorus & Orch. / Panizza
EJS **m** EJS181

1938 (live performance) Caniglia *D*; Votipka *E*; Martinelli *O*; Tibbett *I*; De Paolis *C*; Moscona *L*; Cehanovsky *M*; Paltrinieri *R* / Metropolitan Opera Chorus & Orch. / Panizza
EJS **m** EJS 281

1940 (live performance) Rethberg *D*; Votipka *E*; Martinelli *O*; Tibbett *I*; De Paolis *C*; Moscona *L*; Cehanovsky *M*; Paltrinieri *R* / Metropolitan Opera Chorus & Orch. / Panizza
EJS **m** EJS106

1941 (live performance) Roman *D*; Votipka *E*; Martinelli *O*; Tibbett *I*; De Paolis *C*; Moscona *L*; Cehanovsky *M*; Dudley *R*/ Metropolitan Opera Chorus & Orch. / Panizza
Pearl **m** GEMM267/9

1947 (broadcast performance) Nelli *D*; Merriman *E*; Vinay *O*; Valdengo *I*; Assandri *C*; Moscona *L*; Newman *M*; Chabay *R* / NBC Chorus & SO / Toscanini   RCA (UK) **m** AT303

1948   (live performance) Albanese *D*; Lipton *E*; Vinay *O*; Warren *I*;
       Garris *C*; Moscona *L*; Harvout *M*; Hayward *R* / Metropolitan
       Opera Chorus & Orch. / F. Busch
                        Penzance **m** 18 (A/D)
1951   Lo Pollo *D*; Landi *E*; Sarri *O*; Manca Serra *I*; Cesarini *C*;
       Platania *L*; Stocco *M*; Russo *R* / Rome Opera Chorus & Orch./
       Paoletti   Urania **m** URLP216
1951   (live performance, Salzburg Festival) Martinis *D*; S. Wagner *E*;
       Vinay *O*; Schöffler *I*; Dermota *C*; Greindl *L*; Monthy *M*; Jaresch *R*;
       Vienna State Opera Chorus; VPO / Furtwängler
                        Fonit-Cetra **m** FE28
                        Turnabout **m** THS65120–22
1954   Broggini *D*; Corsi *E*; Guichandut *O*; Taddei *I*; Mercuriali *C*;
       Stefanoni *L*; Albertini *M*; Soley *R* / Turin Radio Chorus & Orch. /
       Capuana   Cetra **e** LPS 3252 **4** MC 145–6
1954   Tebaldi *D*; Ribachi *E*; Del Monaco *O*; Protti *I*; De Palma *C*;
       Corena *L*; Latinucci *M*; Mercuriali *R* / Santa Cecilia Academy
       Chorus & Orch. / Erede   Decca ESC732–34
                        Richmond **m** RS63004
1958   (live performance) De los Angeles *D*; Elias *E*; Del Monaco *O*;
       Warren *I*; Franke *C*; Moscona *L*; Harvout *M*; Anthony *R* /
       Metropolitan Opera Chorus & Orch. / Cleva
                        Gli dei della Musica **m** DMV06/8
1961   Rysanek *D*; Pirazzini *E*; Vickers *O*; Gobbi *I*; Andreolli *C*;
       Mazzoli *L*; Calabrese *M*; Carlin *R* / Rome Opera Chorus & Orch. /
       Serafin   RCA (UK) VLS01969 **4** VKS01969
                        (US) AGL3–1969
1961   Tebaldi *D*; Satre *E*; Del Monaco *O*; Protti *I*; Romanato *C*;
       Corena *L*; Arbace *M*; Cesarini *R* / Vienna State Opera Chorus;
       VPO / Karajan   Decca D55D3 **4** K55K32
                        London 411 618–1LJ3 **4** 411 618–LJ2
1968   G. Jones *D*; Stasio *E*; McCracken *O*; Fischer-Dieskau *I*; De
       Palma *C*; Giacomotti *L*; Monreale *M*; Andreolli *R* / Ambrosian
       Chorus; New Philharmonia Orch. / Barbirolli
                        EMI EX290137–3 **4** EX290137–5
                        Angel SCL3742 **4** 4X3S–3742
1974   Freni *D*; Malagù *E*; Vickers *O*; Glossop *I*; Bottion *V*; van Dam *L*;
       Mach *M*; Sénéchal *R* / Berlin German Opera Chorus; Berlin PO /
       Karajan   EMI SLS975 **4** TC–SLS974
                        Angel SCLX3809
1977   M. Price *D*; Berbié *E*; Cossutta *O*; Bacquier *I*; Dvorský *C*; Moll *L*;
       Dean *M*; Equiluz *R* / Vienna State Opera Chorus; VPO / Solti
                        Decca D102D3 **4** K102K3
                        London OSA13130 **4** OSA–5–13130
1978   Scotto *D*; Kraft *E*; Domingo *O*; Milnes *I*; Little *C*; Plishka *L*;
       King *M*; Crook *R* / Ambrosian Opera Chorus; National PO / Levine
                        RCA (UK) RLO2951
                        (US) CRL3–2951 **4** CRK3–2951
                        CD: RCD2–2951

1985 Ricciarelli *D*; Domingo *O*; Diaz *I*; La Scala Chorus & Orch. /
     Maazel   EMI awaiting release
                     Angel awaiting release

Excerpts

1926 (live performance) Zanatello *O*; Noto *I*; Cilla *C*; Cotreuil *L*;
     Sampieri *M*; Dua *R* / Royal Opera Chorus & Orch. / Bellezza
                     EMI **m** RLS742
1939 Jepson *D*; Martinelli *O*; Tibbett *I*; Massue *C* / Metropolitan Opera
     Chorus & Orch. / Pelletier   RCA (UK) **m** VIC1185
                             (US) **m** VIC1365
1943 (in German) Reining *D*; Waldenau *E*; Rosvaenge *O*; Reinmar *I*;
     Rodin *C*; Husch *L* / Berlin State Opera Chorus & Orch. /
     Elmendorff   Acanta **m** BB21360
1943 (in French) Segala *D*; Sibille *E*; Thill *O*; Beckmanns *I* / Paris Opera
     Orch. / Ruhlmann   EMI **m** 2C 153 16211–14
1950 Steber *D*; Vinay *O*; Valentino *I*; Metropolitan Opera Orch. /
/51   Cleva   Philips (UK) **m** ABL3005
                       CBS (US) **m** ML4499
1950s Moll *D*; Da Costa *O*; Valentino *I* / Hamburg Philharmonia Orch. /
     Walther   Allegro-Royale **m** 1626
1965 (in German) Stratas *D*; Windgassen *O*; Fischer-Dieskau *I*; Lenz *C*;
     Ernest *L* / Bavarian State Opera Chorus & Orch. / Gerdes
                     DG 2537 017

Index